Published in association with *First News* and The Silver Line

First published 2016 by Walker Books Ltd, 87 Vauxhall Walk, London SE11 5HJ

This edition published 2017

2 4 6 8 10 9 7 5 3 1

Anthology © 2016 First News/ Walker Books Ltd
Non-fiction text © 2016 Walker Books Ltd
Jacket and title page illustration © 2016 Andrew Davidson

The stories in this book are as remembered by the contributors. While every effort has been made to check the veracity of the facts contained in the contributors' stories, if any errors have been made, the publisher will be happy to make any necessary corrections in future printings.

The moral rights of the contributors have been asserted. This book has been typeset in Bentham
Printed and bound in China

British Library Cataloguing in Publication Data is available

ISBN 978-1-4063-6598-6
www.walker.co.uk
www.firstnews.co.uk

WALKER BOOKS
AND SUBSIDIARIES

LONDON • BOSTON • SYDNEY • AUCKLAND

VOICES FROM THE
SECOND WORLD WAR

Witnesses share their stories with the children of today

A member of the London Auxiliary Fire Fighting Services taking part in a training exercise in preparation for the war, July 1939

YOUR COURAGE
YOUR CHEERFULNESS
YOUR RESOLUTION

WILL BRING
US VICTORY

A boy looks at a propaganda poster in London, 1939

Foreword by JEREMY VINE

I often wonder why the Second World War seems to get closer as time passes. I was born only twenty years after Hitler shot himself. During my childhood, movies like *A Bridge Too Far* made it all seem like ancient history. I assumed that becoming an adult and getting older would staple the war into a wooden frame like an old photograph – gradually yellowing, looked at less and less, eventually put away.

Time has done the opposite. Now I am 50, I find myself crying at remembrance services. Is it because I understand what sacrifice is, now I have more to lose? When we recorded a special programme about D-Day for Radio 2, a veteran of the landings sang a ballad he'd written about the day itself: an eyewitness account. At the end, every single person in the Royal Albert Hall stood. When the show was over I thanked the audience, and a man near the rafters shouted back at me, "We will remember." And so we do.

For a *First News* report my daughter Martha went to see someone a stone's throw from her grandparents in Tipton St John, Devon. Barbara is an elderly lady, and the story of the encounter is in this book so I won't spoil it by repeating the details here. But I sat and listened as the tales of living during the Second World War poured out. And then it struck me – this was not a pensioner talking to a child, it was two nine-year-olds speaking to each other across the decades. Barbara told Martha about the bombs falling on her home in Manchester as if she had never left her hiding place in the cellar. Barbara will not always be here to tell that story. Yet, by listening, Martha and other young *First News* reporters have framed some precious, startling memories for decades to come. As that lone voice cried in the Royal Albert Hall, we will remember.

TRUE STORIES FROM THE MOST DEVASTATING WAR IN HISTORY

The Second World War changed the course of history. Up to 80 million people died, families were torn apart and whole cities were reduced to rubble. Now, over 70 years after the war, survivors share their stories, passing on their memories so that their experiences are never forgotten. Many of the stories in the book were collected by children who interviewed relatives and family friends. RAF rear gunner Harry Irons recounts his first bombing raid on Germany; Anita Lasker-Wallfisch explains how playing the cello in the orchestra at Auschwitz-Birkenau saved her life; and Takashi Tanemori, who was playing hide-and-seek at school in Hiroshima on 6 August 1945, describes what happened after the atomic bomb fell on his city.

Every person alive today will have elderly relatives or ancestors who lived through the war. Her Royal Highness the Duchess of Cambridge shared her family's story with *First News*. She visited Bletchley Park in Buckinghamshire, the centre of intelligence gathering in Britain during the war, to meet Lady Marion Body, a veteran who had worked

there alongside the duchess's grandmother, Valerie Glassborow. Valerie wasn't a codebreaker but had a crucial job in a small section responsible for managing the collection of enemy signals. The duchess learned that her grandmother had been one of the first to know that the war had ended, as she was working the day shift when a signal from Tokyo was intercepted, announcing that the Japanese were about to surrender.

This unique and moving collection of first-hand accounts of the war is published in association with *First News*, the award-winning children's

Lady Marion Body tells the Duchess of Cambridge about her time working at Bletchley Park during the war

newspaper, and The Silver Line, the confidential helpline for older people established by Dame Esther Rantzen.

SOME OF THE CHILDREN
WHO HEARD THE STORIES

Many of the stories in this book were collected by children,
giving them the chance to learn about the Second World War
from the people who were there.

**"SIR NICHOLAS TAUGHT US MANY THINGS.
HE EXPLAINED THAT WE SHOULD ALWAYS TRY TO
PREVENT OTHER PEOPLE'S SUFFERING AND WALK
AROUND WITH OUR EYES WIDE OPEN."**

*Amélie Mitchell and Daniel McKeever interviewed Sir Nicholas
Winton, who saved the lives of 669 Jewish children by helping to
evacuate them from Czechoslovakia before Germany invaded.*

"I brought Barbara an onion from my grandpa's
garden. She used it to explain to me what it was
like during the Second World War. To show me how
they used to cook it, she boiled it for half an hour.
Then she tipped the saucepan, and the onion thudded
onto the plate like a wet tennis ball. She covered it in
salt and pepper, and spread butter on it. Normally
I don't like onions, but this one was different. The butter made it quite
easy to eat. It made me realize that even though you think people ate
quite disgusting things in the war, they had a way of making them
taste nice. After hearing Barbara's stories about the Blitz the onion
tasted very good indeed."

*Martha Vine, pictured here with her father Jeremy Vine, interviewed Barbara Burgess,
who told her what it was like to live on rations.*

"IT WAS AMAZING TO MEET DR FRANKLAND AND HEAR
HOW HE FELT ABOUT HIS LIFE AND THE THINGS THAT HAD
HAPPENED TO HIM. I FEEL VERY LUCKY AND WOULD REALLY
LIKE TO MEET HIM AGAIN TO HEAR MORE STORIES."

*Lucca Williams interviewed Dr Bill Frankland, who told him
about his experiences as a Japanese prisoner of war.*

"I knew my grandma had been a girl during the war, but I had never
spoken to her about it, so interviewing her gave me the chance to get
to know her even better. I felt special as she was sharing personal
memories with me that would have been lost for ever if I hadn't had
this opportunity to chat to her. I have seen many films and read lots
of books about the war. Hearing my grandma's memories makes
those stories more real to me and helps me relate to them with more
sympathy and understanding."

Eleanor Boardman interviewed her grandmother Mary Boardman about life in Manchester during the Blitz.

"MR PETE IS A GOOD FAMILY FRIEND AND I ENJOYED LEARNING
ABOUT HIS EXPERIENCES IN THE WAR. I FOUND IT SURPRISING THAT
HE WAS MORE AFRAID OF LOSING THE RESPECT OF HIS CREW THAN
OF BEING BOMBED BY THE JAPANESE."

Noelle McDonald interviewed George Bressler (Mr Pete) about his time in the US Navy.

"I enjoyed doing this project with my grandfather as otherwise
I would not have known about his experiences. Grand-père was my
age when France was at war. I can't imagine what it is like worrying
about not having enough food and I can't bear the thought of
eating rabbits! I think I am lucky to live in a country at peace."

*Victor Ghose interviewed his grandfather Dr Francois Conil-Lacoste,
who lived in France during the German occupation.*

"By interviewing my grandfather I learned a lot about him
as well as about the Second World War. I feel that now I
understand what my grandpa and others went through."

*Islay Rose Van Dusen spoke to her grandfather William M. Breed about his
experiences in the US Navy.*

"I was very lucky to be able to talk to Gramps about the war. It means that I understand what it was really like from someone who experienced it first-hand, rather than from a book by historians who weren't there. I think that Gramps and the other Dambusters were extremely brave and I am very proud to be part of his family."

Ellen Gregory interviewed her great-grandfather George "Johnny" Johnson, a bomb aimer who took part in the Dambusters Raid.

"I FOUND IT FASCINATING TO TALK TO SOMEONE WHO HAD ACTUALLY LIVED THROUGH THE SECOND WORLD WAR IN A COUNTRY WHICH WAS OCCUPIED BY THE NAZIS. I AM SO PROUD OF MY DUTCH GREAT-GRANDMOTHER FOR HELPING THE JEWS IN HIDING."

Sasha Devereaux interviewed her grandmother Cornelia Manji, who was a child in the Netherlands during the war.

"I was extremely excited to write to Shirley Hughes. She's been an idol of mine since I was very small and I absolutely adore her books. If I were in the war I'd try very hard to save my sweet rations."

Bill Riley wrote to Shirley Hughes to ask her about life in Liverpool during the Blitz.

"GREAT-GRANDMA WAS A FANTASTIC STORYTELLER AND I REALLY ENJOYED HEARING ABOUT WHAT SHE GOT UP TO IN THE WAR. I'M SO GLAD THAT WE HAVE A VIDEO RECORDING OF IT TOO SO THAT WE CAN WATCH IT AGAIN ONE DAY."

Jamie Brooks interviewed his great-grandmother Monica Miller, who was a sergeant in the British army during the war.

"It was a pleasure interviewing Micheline. She was so happy to talk about her childhood, and she even made some cakes (she is an amazing cook). I particularly enjoyed it because it made her smile."

Lucy Poirrier interviewed Micheline Mura about her experiences as a child in German-occupied France.

"IT WAS A FASCINATING EXPERIENCE AS I LOVE LEARNING ABOUT THE PAST."

Elias Abdo and his classmates at Mile Oak Primary School interviewed Fred Glover about his experiences in the Parachute Regiment.

"Mr Checketts was very nice and interviewing him was really fun. He showed me lots of interesting things that were in a big old trunk, like photos and his navy uniform. I went back to school and told everyone about it. They were all really fascinated. I spent the whole day with Mr Checketts and I enjoyed every moment of it. We went for a walk in the garden together."

Carys Yates interviewed Harold Checketts, a naval meteorologist.

"WE ARE GRATEFUL BECAUSE IF OUR GRANNY HADN'T SURVIVED THE WAR THEN OUR DAD WOULDN'T HAVE BEEN BORN AND NEITHER WOULD WE!"

Wilf, Dora and Chester Clapham interviewed their grandmother, Margaret Clapham, who came to England from Germany on a Kindertransport train.

"I really felt very special hearing Granddad's stories from when he was a little boy. They brought the time vividly to life for me and I was able to understand how difficult it was for him in the war. You can read a book about the war but when Granddad spoke to me about his own experiences, I could almost see what it was like through his child's eyes. I love my granddad even more now."

Aylish Maclean interviewed her grandfather Ken Swain, who was a child living in Portsmouth during the Blitz.

"WE ARE LEARNING ABOUT THE SECOND WORLD WAR AT SCHOOL SO IT WAS REALLY INTERESTING TO FIND OUT ABOUT GREAT-GRANDMA'S EXPERIENCES AND TO BE ABLE TO TALK TO SOMEONE WHO WAS ACTUALLY THERE."

Jonathon Brooks interviewed his great-grandmother Monica Miller, who served in the British army during the war.

"It was very interesting meeting Fred Glover. I learned all about the Second World War and how much life has changed since then. It must have been terrifying! One thing I remember in particular is how he carried on even though his leg was injured. He was a very interesting and brave man and it was a pleasure to hear his unforgettable stories. We should all really start listening to our elders. They have one or two things to tell us!"

Daniella Birchley and her classmates from Mile Oak Primary School interviewed Fred Glover, who took part in the D-Day landings.

"IT WAS A GREAT HONOUR AND EXPERIENCE TO INTERVIEW MR FRED GLOVER AS I HAVE ALWAYS HAD AN INTEREST IN FINDING OUT ABOUT THE WAR AND THE INCREDIBLE STORIES OF THOSE WHO FOUGHT IN IT."

Seb Dutton and his classmates from Mile Oak Primary School interviewed Fred Glover, who took part in the D-Day landings.

"IT WAS AN ABSOLUTE PLEASURE TO INTERVIEW MY GREAT-GRANDMOTHER. IT WAS FASCINATING TO FIND OUT ABOUT HER PLACE OF WORK AND HOW HER INVOLVEMENT IN THE WAR HELPED SHAPE OUR WORLD TODAY."

Chloe Stevens interviewed her great-grandmother Joy Hunter, who worked alongside Winston Churchill at the Offices of the War Cabinet.

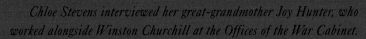

"HEARING ABOUT MY GREAT-GRANDAD'S EXPERIENCES IN THE SECOND WORLD WAR MADE ME REALIZE WHAT DIFFICULT CONDITIONS HE AND ALL THE OTHER SOLDIERS FOUGHT IN. IT ALSO MADE ME FEEL VERY PROUD OF HIM."

Joseph Harrison interviewed his grandmother Gill Harrison. She told him what his great-grandfather, Ivor Robert Phillips, did in Burma during the war.

"I found it really interesting to interview my grandmother. I never really knew exactly what her role was in the Auxiliary Territorial Service, but I realized after interviewing her how proud she felt playing such a central part in the war effort. It is difficult to imagine being so very young, a teenager, and having such a heavy responsibility. There is always the very real possibility that I myself might be faced with a similar task in my life, but I hope that doesn't happen. For her, the war was an opportunity to gain skills and a respectable job. Despite the circumstances, this gave her a sense of belonging and a real purpose which she frequently talks about today."

Millie Devereux interviewed her grandmother Margaret Neat, who worked as a radar operator on anti-aircraft guns.

"WE WANTED TO KNOW MORE ABOUT THE DIFFICULT CONDITIONS OUR GREAT-GRANDFATHER HAD TO ENDURE. WE ARE VERY PROUD OF HIM FOR RISKING HIS OWN LIFE FOR OUR COUNTRY AND EXTREMELY THANKFUL HE SURVIVED."

Samuel and Gemma Preston interviewed their great-grandfather Israel Hyams, who served in the 44th Royal Tank Regiment.

"Interviewing Sir Harold Atcherley was a fantastic experience that opened my eyes to what it was really like to be held as a prisoner of war. I think it is very important for everybody to read about the war so they can see how hard it was for all the brave soldiers who fought."

Seraphina Evans interviewed Sir Harold Atcherley about his time as a prisoner of war.

German troops parade through Warsaw, Poland, shortly after invading the country in September 1939

contents

THE OUTBREAK OF WAR

During the 1930s, dictators rose to power in Italy, Russia and Germany. The most notorious of these was Adolf Hitler, leader of the extreme right-wing Nazi Party, who became chancellor (equivalent to prime minister) of Germany on 30 January 1933 and president and führer for life on 19 August 1934. He blamed Germany's problems on Jews and communists. In 1936, Hitler moved troops into the Rhineland – the region on Germany's borders, which was supposed to be free of military forces – and in 1938 he claimed that the Sudetenland, a German-speaking area of Czechoslovakia, should be part of Germany.

Neville Chamberlain, the British Prime Minister, flew to Munich in Germany on 28 September 1938 for a conference with the German, Italian and French leaders. Czechoslovakia and the Soviet Union were not invited. At the conference, the leaders agreed to allow Germany to take the Sudetenland and signed a peace agreement known as the Munich Agreement, but Hitler had no intention of sticking to it: he was determined to take over Europe. In March 1939 Hitler occupied the rest of Czechoslovakia. Then, on 1 September, Germany invaded Poland and the Second World War began. Fighting between the two opposing forces, the Allies (including Britain, France and the US) and the Axis (including Germany and Japan), lasted until 1945.

Members of the Reichstag, the German parliament, saluting Hitler after his announcement of the "peaceful" acquisition of Austria, March 1938. This set the stage for the occupation of the Sudetenland.

DOUGLAS POOLE

Douglas Poole joined the Territorial Army in 1937, and was one of the first to be called up when war broke out. He has written about his experiences in his memoir, The Time of My Youth.

It was Sunday 6 August 1939. Speculation was mounting about war in Europe; reports of troop movements and pictures of anxious-looking people returning from abroad featured in the press. Against the tide of public opinion, one Sunday paper insisted, on the advice of its astrologer, that there would be no war! On the radio, light music and occasional warlike tunes were played "to keep the spirits up".

Those who had experienced the horrors and suffering of the First World War were understandably more concerned than people like me, who were born later. My mother was very worried by the turn of events, particularly as I had joined the Territorial Army two years previously and I was due to leave for a month's training the following week. My father and I tried to calm my mother's fears by saying that we thought war was unlikely.

My father and I went for a beer before lunch, as we did most Sundays. As we ordered our drinks, my father's friend George hailed him from the other end of the bar.

"My son here is off with the army next week," my dad told him.

"Must have a drink on that," George responded. "What mob are you with?"

Dad told him that I was a non-commissioned officer in the Essex Regiment. The hint of pride in his voice was unmistakable.

As we walked back home, Father said, "We have to humour your mother, you know. It won't be like the last time." He was referring to the year before, when I had been called up for the crisis over the Sudetenland, only to return after five days when the Munich Agreement was signed and war failed to break out.

"I know," I said. "That's why I was so keen to get that shelter dug. But Mother refuses to let me fit her gas mask – she insists it messes her hair."

"I hope Hitler doesn't use gas, for your mother's sake," said my father. We both laughed uneasily.

We were walking through an area where lots of Jewish people lived. I waved at some lads I had been to school with and wondered if they were more worried about the war than we were.

The smell of the Sunday roast greeted us at the front door. "I've made apple pudding for you," my mother said.

"That's more than you'll be getting next week," my father joked.

We both laughed, but my mother turned sharply away.

That evening, I went to church. At the entrance to St Matthew's, a man named Millington handed me a hymn book. "You're not with the choir?" he asked.

"No," I said. "I thought I'd just join the congregation tonight; I'll be going away for a while, you see." I didn't mention the army, for Millington, a fervent pacifist, had voiced disapproval when I enlisted.

"I heard you were, boy," he said.

After the sermon, the vicar said, "These are days of tremendous uncertainties. Some parishioners will be facing unfamiliar or even dangerous ways of life. As you know, a member of our choir leaves in a few days' time for duty with the army. We pray that he may return to us safely and speedily."

Douglas in his army uniform

At the end of the service, some of the congregation came to wish me well. I chuckled to disguise the emotion I felt. "Look, I'll be back in a month," I said. "Probably by Harvest Festival." As I neared the door, Nares, an elderly baritone, called out to me. His son had been killed in the Battle of Loos in 1915, during the First World War, a fact commemorated on a plate at the back of the choir stall. Some folk reckoned that Nares was considerably affected by his loss, which explained his aloofness; I could not recall ever having had a conversation with him.

"You will come back, son, won't you?" He looked at me strangely. "I'll do my best," I said. "In fact, I'll make a point of it."

"God be with you," he said. "Always remember your prayers."

I felt as though he hadn't really been talking to *me*, and I was relieved when members of the choir suddenly appeared. I explained how embarrassed I would be when I returned in a few weeks' time.

Walking home along the cobbled street, amidst deafening traffic, a feeling of sadness overwhelmed me. I was leaving this secure, familiar world of mine; an unknown future beckoned, and nothing would ever be the same. Indeed, it never was.

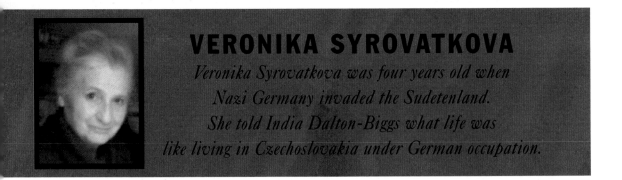

VERONIKA SYROVATKOVA

Veronika Syrovatkova was four years old when Nazi Germany invaded the Sudetenland. She told India Dalton-Biggs what life was like living in Czechoslovakia under German occupation.

In September 1938, when I was four years old, Nazi Germany took over the Sudetenland. It soon became clear that this would lead to the total occupation of Czechoslovakia. The UK and France had agreed to let Germany do this; it was a complete betrayal of our country.

On 17 November 1939, when I was five, the Nazis executed nine Czech students and sent 1,200 students and professors to concentration camps, just because they were protesting against the German occupation of Czechoslovakia. I remember that very clearly, because one of the murdered students was a family friend who I was very fond of. I was very upset.

The war was a terrifying time for us children. Our parents tried to make our childhoods as normal as possible, but we were scared every time there was a knock at the door in the evening. My parents spent a lot of time listening to a radio programme from London, which was forbidden, and they would have been in great danger if the Germans had found out.

Our family had a good Jewish friend named Ruzena Heydukova. Even though she was married to a Christian man, she was taken to a concentration camp in Terezín, also known as Theresienstadt. Ruzena was one of around 140,000 Jews who were taken to Theresienstadt during the war. She survived the camp, but many of her family members did not. My family knew other Jews, too, and we helped them by storing their furniture and keeping their money safe. When they returned after the war, they were happy to have their things back – but their happiness didn't last long. The communists confiscated most people's possessions a few years later.

My family didn't have any German friends, but we did have some distant German relatives. My great-aunt Julia married a German man in the early 1900s, and their two sons joined the Nazi Party. Our relations ended there and then. Once, they visited us in Prague and they brought me a big box of chocolates. I refused to taste even a tiny chocolate – that was my way of showing patriotism. It took a lot of willpower, because chocolate was so rare in those days.

At school we only had to speak German in a couple of lessons – history and maths. Otherwise we spoke Czech. We rebelled against the German occupation by not putting our arms straight up in the air for the Nazi salute during the German national anthem at the start of each school day.

I was around ten years old when the war ended. We all felt a huge sense of relief, happiness and excitement for the future. Unfortunately this feeling only lasted until February 1948, when the communists took over the country. Years of darkness followed.

FRANCISZEK KORNICKI

Franciszek Kornicki joined the Polish Air Force College in 1936 when he was nineteen. He fought for Poland during the war, and after the German invasion he moved first to France and then to Britain, where he fought with the Royal Air Force (RAF).

I graduated as a fighter pilot in June 1939 and was posted to a fighter squadron. The war started on 1 September that year. The Polish Air Force unfortunately had very few aircraft compared to the Germans. Those that we did have were old and slow, whereas German aircraft were by far the most modern in the world at that time. The Germans had

Franciszek (centre) with fellow Polish Air Force College cadet officers

about eight or nine times as many fighter pilots as we did, too. We tried our best, but we didn't stand a chance.

I remember one time I saw a German aircraft and I started firing, but after one or two short bursts my guns jammed. It was impossible to reload. I tried – I unbuckled my harness in order to reach the guns, but I couldn't. So I put my harness back on. I did half a roll to get closer to the enemy but my buckle and harness detached and I fell out of the plane! I managed to open the parachute and I landed safely.

Not long after that, the Polish armed forces withdrew, and on 17 September the Russians, who had signed an agreement with Germany, attacked Poland from the east. Poland never formally surrendered, but that was really the end. All pilots were told to get to Romania and make their way to France. So on 18 September I crossed the Romanian border in a car with three of my squadron friends.

Franciszek and two of his friends posing with their car during the evacuation from Poland

Poland had an agreement with Romania – we would help them, and they would help us. Now we needed their help, but they were under pressure from the Germans to stop us getting out of Romania and to keep us in camps. My friends and I managed to avoid the camps with the help of a young Romanian officer who found us accommodation with a teacher's family and had civilian clothes made for us. We gave him our leather coats and our uniforms in return. He helped us to pass through a checkpoint so we could proceed to Bucharest in southern Romania.

We managed to reach the Polish Embassy in Bucharest, where we were issued with temporary passports and some money, and then we took a train east towards the Black Sea. From there we managed to catch a boat to the French city of Marseille.

We arrived in France in October, and we were supposed to go to a French air force base just outside Lyon, but hundreds of us were held in a huge exhibition hall until February. Poland had a mutual assistance agreement with France and Britain, but some French people believed Poland had started the war because we wouldn't agree to Hitler's demands.

The French had built a line of defences around the country called the Maginot Line, and they thought that would protect them. But when the Germans attacked France, they came through Belgium and bypassed the Maginot Line completely. France had a large army and air force but they were badly led. The morale was poor and they lost the will to defend their country. It was an utter disaster.

I started training to fly French aircraft on 15 May 1940. My first flight in a combat fighter plane ended badly. Shortly after take-off the engine packed up. There was a forest straight ahead of me, so I had to turn back. I just managed to get over the trees near the airfield and landed with the undercarriage pointing upwards. I was not injured but my aircraft was seriously damaged. As I was standing there looking at the wreckage, the commandant of the airfield said, "You owe the French government half a million francs!" I said, "Sir, I can't pay that!"

Franciszek's plane, after it disintegrated during training

Then I realized he was joking. The second French fighter plane I flew performed well. Soon I was strapped in, ready, waiting for orders – but they never came.

When I arrived at the airfield on the morning of the French surrender there were French guards by our aircraft, so we couldn't take them and fly away. All Polish people at the airfield were taken by bus to the railway station. There was no time to collect anything from our quarters. We travelled a few hundred miles and spent the first night at a small airfield. My friends and I didn't want to travel any further by train so we broke into a closed aircraft hangar and found a car, which we filled up with petrol that we'd drained from a few aircraft. The four of us travelled to Perpignan on the French/Spanish border to catch a ship to North Africa, but the naval admiral in Perpignan wouldn't let us – he was already collaborating with the Germans. We had to leave the car there and we travelled by train to Saint-Jean-de-Luz in south-western France to get on a ship to Britain. A French colonel tried to stop us, but we were there with a large group of Polish soldiers, with weapons and ammunition, and we threatened to fight him. So at last, on 24 June 1940, we boarded a British ship, the *Arandora Star*, and sailed to Liverpool in England.

We arrived in Liverpool on 26 June and we were taken by bus to a camp in Cheshire. There were hundreds and hundreds of tents, full of Polish people. I didn't speak a word of English, but I started learning from day one. I found a "teach yourself English" book, and a couple of chaps who spoke English mentored the rest of us. I remember one of them saying, "The most common little word in English is T-H-E, and it's a hell of a job to pronounce it!" We found eight ways to pronounce it, and every single one was wrong.

I was trained to fly Hurricanes (British fighter planes) and did my operational flying from RAF Northolt, which was a home base for three Polish squadrons from 1941 until the invasion of France. I was in 315 Squadron. Our job was mainly to escort bombers who were attacking targets in German-occupied France, Belgium and Holland. We also flew fighter sweeps, looking for German planes all over the sky and attacking ground targets. A lot of blood was spilled – the Germans' and ours.

Franciszek (right) with two of his fellow 315 Squadron pilots at Northolt, ready to fight

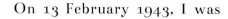

On 13 February 1943, I was appointed squadron commander of 308 Squadron. That lasted thirteen days. During a fighter sweep, at a height of 25,000 feet (7,600 metres), I suddenly got an excruciating pain in my stomach. I managed to land at Northolt and found the squadron doctor. He poked me with a finger, and I yelled. He said, "Your appendix has burst! Don't move!" I was operated on that evening.

Shortly after that I was given command of 317 Squadron and on 1 January 1944, I was taken off flying. Six months later, after the Allies invaded France and forced the Germans to retreat, I went as a staff officer to Holland. The war was going our way. On 7 May 1945, I was flying back to England for a course. When I landed, I was told that the war was over.

People say that we Poles were particularly brave during the war. There's some truth in that, but it's been exaggerated. We had a score to settle – an extra one, because of what the Germans had done to our country.

KEN "PADDY" FRENCH

*Ken French moved to England from
Ireland in August 1939 to start a new life.
One month later, war broke out.*

I remember Sunday 3 September 1939 very well: we were told to listen to our radios at 11 a.m. as there was to be an announcement from the British Prime Minister, Neville Chamberlain. The announcement finished with the words, "This country is at war with Germany." Nobody had any idea what that would mean for us or how long the war would last. Someone remarked to me he thought it would carry on till Christmas at least. Little did we know that we were to spend six Christmases at war. That night we heard our first air raid siren. We didn't know what to expect, so we all got out of bed and sat in the broom cupboard under the stairs. It was a false alarm, and many more were to follow. It was a long time before any bombs were to fall on this country.

In September 1940, the Germans started mass bombing raids on our cities by night to try to destroy our factories and break the morale of the civilian population. The government formed the Home Guard, a sort of citizens' army to support the regular army in the event of an invasion, and I joined up. In those early days,

*Ken with his brother and their friends
in August 1939*

whenever the air raid siren went off at night we would get up and man our posts in case it meant we'd been invaded. This might happen two or three times a night, so we were often left without much sleep, especially as we had to work during the day, but after a while we ignored the sirens and just stayed in bed.

At first the Home Guard was quite laughable – we had no uniforms or guns and how we were supposed to stand up to the might of the German army was anybody's guess. I was armed with a First World War bayonet and an air pistol – that wouldn't have been much good if it came to the crunch. Still, it probably boosted our morale – we felt like we were doing something, at least.

As time went on we became better organized, and we were issued with rifles and uniforms. But one evening on parade, I was called aside by the officer in charge, who told me you had to be British to be a member of the Home Guard. As I was Irish, I wasn't eligible. He said he'd like me to stay on and help them unofficially – I think they needed my bicycle, as I was a sort of dispatch rider (a messenger). I said I would think it over, because it wasn't as simple as it might sound – if there was an invasion, and I was caught, I wouldn't have the rights that an official member of the Home Guard would have had. I told my father about what the officer had said, and he told his friend, a retired British navy admiral. The admiral wrote an angry letter to the British ambassador to Ireland, and in the end the matter was raised in Parliament. A short time later, I was asked to attend a parade on a specific day. The commander for our district told me that due to my father's efforts, the law had been changed and I could become a full member of the Home Guard.

JASMINE BLAKEWAY

Jasmine Blakeway was seventeen when war broke out in September 1939.

When war broke out, I was on holiday in France. During breakfast, the proprietress of the boarding house rushed in and said, "Ils ont bombarde Krakovie!" She expected us to go rigid with fear but we didn't know where Krakovie was. When we realized it was Krakow in Poland, we knew the war had begun. We drove back to England at once, in a tiny Renault – me, my sister, her fiancé, my mother and a man called Phil Rosenthal – so we were very squashed. We dropped Phil off in Avignon to join the Foreign Legion, as he was a German Jew and wanted to fight the Germans. Then we caught a ferry to England. There was a queue of cars waiting to board it. One man was saying, "I've told the Ministry of Transport that they can have my Jaguar, so I must have priority!" Everyone ignored him.

Then in 1940, when I was working in Kent, I went to the train station and helped dish out buns and lemonade to soldiers who had been rescued from Dunkirk. They were euphoric. There were French soldiers, too, and as I spoke French I was able to tell them where they were. The Tommies were thumbs-up and defiant, but the French were very downcast.

After Dunkirk, there was a fear that Britain would be invaded. Hay carts in fields were arranged with their shafts pointed up so that German pilots would think they were anti-aircraft guns; England had only a few of the real thing. People were suspicious of nuns in habits in case they were Germans in disguise. I became a driver with the Auxiliary Territorial Service (ATS) and drove ambulances for the rest of the war.

Almost immediately after the Nazis came to power in 1933, they began to persecute Jewish people. Hitler believed that the Aryan, or Nordic, race was superior to all others, and he thought that Jews, along with black people, Roma (Gypsies) and other minorities, were polluting the Aryan gene pool. Gradually, the Nazis restricted Jewish people's rights, eventually stripping them of their German citizenship. Then, on the night of 9–10 November 1938, the Nazis encouraged people to destroy Jewish homes, businesses, synagogues and schools across the German Reich on what became known as Kristallnacht – the Night of Broken Glass – because of the broken glass that covered the streets the next morning.

That night, almost a hundred Jews were murdered and 30,000 Jewish boys and men were rounded up and sent to concentration camps. Foreign leaders could not ignore what the Nazis were doing to Jewish people. The British Government relaxed immigration laws, and agreed to accept an unlimited number of Jewish children under the age of seventeen, as long as an organization guaranteed that they would be provided with food and accommodation and that they would return to Germany after the war. Between 1938 and 1940, almost 10,000 children came to Britain as part of the Kindertransport (children's transport), a humanitarian mission to help children escape German-occupied territories by train. Thousands more Jews managed to escape before war broke out – but millions never got away.

FLEEING THE NAZIS

Children boarding a Kindertransport train from Vienna to Switzerland

SIR NICHOLAS WINTON

Sir Nicholas Winton told Amélie Mitchell and Daniel McKeever why he set up the Kindertransport programme from Czechoslovakia in 1938.

Just before the Second World War broke out, I spent three weeks in Prague, which was part of Czechoslovakia at that time. I knew that the refugees there, who were mostly Jewish, were under threat from a German invasion, so I started organizing the evacuation of hundreds of children to the UK to try to keep them safe. This was called Kindertransport. It was not an easy task, as I had to get all the official documents sorted out and arrange foster carers for the children once they arrived. That was the most difficult and important part of the whole operation, but at that time, British children were being evacuated from cities too, and the organizations who were dealing with the British evacuees sent me the names and addresses of people who would be willing to take a Jewish child.

The children travelled to the UK by train. Once the children were on the train, they were rescued from the Germans as far as I was concerned. I made certain that the train left the station safely and that the next one was properly looked after. Eight train-loads of children made it to the UK before the Germans invaded Czechoslovakia. I helped to save the lives of 669 children. A few of them were reunited with their families after the war, but most never saw their families again, as they were killed in Nazi concentration camps.

I suppose the best moments for me during the war were seeing the trains that set off from Prague arrive in London. Then you knew you'd achieved something. But I wouldn't say I felt happy during the war. I felt content, because I had pulled it off, but happiness is something rather greater.

I organized the Kindertransport because, politically, I had my eyes wide open at that time. I knew at least as much, if not more, about what was going on as the politicians did. If you've got your eyes open and you see someone crossing the road as a car is coming, you'll very likely try to prevent them getting run over. If you've got your eyes closed, you won't see it.

I'm pleased I saved those children, but it happened so long ago. It's hard to feel proud after all that time – you can't spend your life thinking about one thing. I had to do other things when I came back home, such as earn a living. I feel I've led a fairly normal life.

MARGARET CLAPHAM

Margaret Clapham told her grandchildren, Wilf, Dora and Chester Clapham, what it was like to come to England on the Kindertransport.

I was born in Germany in 1927. My father was Jewish, but my mother was not, and we were brought up Christian. However, in the eyes of the Nazis we were still considered a Jewish family. So in 1938, my parents decided it was safest to send me and my two sisters to England. They didn't really tell us why we were going – they made it seem like an exciting holiday.

You weren't allowed to take a single valuable with you to England, and you were only allowed one shilling to spend on the journey. When my parents came to join us one year later, they were

Margaret (top right) with her sisters in England during the war

only allowed to bring ten shillings. Everything else had to be given to the German Government. But without telling me, my nanny had stitched a diamond necklace that I had been given when I was baptized into the hem of my dress. When I unpacked my suitcase, I was horrified to find the necklace – at border control they went through our cases looking for valuables, and if they had found it I could have been killed. I sold it for £35 in the 1940s, which was a lot of money at the time, and it paid for my university evening classes for two years, which were £15 a year, so I'm very grateful to my nanny.

On the Kindertransport train, children were separated into age groups. That meant that my sister Marion and I would be in one carriage and my youngest sister Ruth, who was only six, would be in another. But Ruth cried so much at the prospect of being separated that we were allowed to stay together.

When we arrived at Harwich station in England, someone took a photograph of Ruth. It was used on a leaflet encouraging the people of England to take in child refugees fleeing Nazi Germany, and thousands of copies were delivered throughout the country. Many people phoned in to ask if they could look after Ruth, but we had relatives to stay with while we waited for our parents to escape Germany too. However, Ruth's picture on the "Caring for the Child Refugees" leaflet encouraged hundreds of families to accept other less fortunate children into their homes.

My immediate family all survived the war. But my family who stayed in Germany weren't so lucky. In 1944, when Germany was losing the war, my two grandmothers were taken to the gas chambers and killed. I don't dwell on that, as it's so horrible.

I have enormous, enormous gratitude and hundreds of "thank yous" for the British Government. I can never be grateful enough. I probably wouldn't be alive now if England hadn't let us in.

This photo of Margaret's sister Ruth was used to encourage British families to take in Jewish refugees

MARY BLACK

Mary Black was born in Austria but moved to England before the war. When war broke out, she was evacuated to Canada.

I was one of the lucky ones. I was evacuated out of England, so I didn't see much of the war. I was fifteen when war broke out, and my boarding school was evacuated to the south coast of England,

Mary (far right) with her two brothers and her cousin Toni

but my parents decided that the smart thing to do would be to send me to Canada. We were Jewish, and my parents were very aware of what might happen if Germany invaded the UK, but my parents stayed in England.

Being sent away was horrible – the worst thing that happened to me in my life. I'd had a very lovely childhood and all of a sudden I had to grow up, so it was very traumatic. I was shipped out to Canada with a family that my parents were friendly with, but I hated them. We sailed in a convoy of about a dozen ships, all full of children being evacuated, but the ships were so far apart that you couldn't tell there were others. I heard that the last ship in the convoy was torpedoed.

I can't remember what I thought of Canada when I first arrived; I was in a daze, and I didn't know who I was or what I was. Luckily I had an uncle who lived in Long Island, in New York in the US. He came up to Montreal and we spent some time together, which was lovely.

For the first month, I stayed with a really lovely family at their country house. Then, after the summer, I met up with about a dozen other girls from my school, and we went to a boarding school in Winnipeg of all horrible places. It is bitterly cold there, and the wind never stops blowing.

I remember going to the movies and seeing the newsreels of the bombings in London. That was pretty hard to take when you knew your family was there. I still have all the letters that my mother wrote to me. She and my father moved out of London to a hotel somewhere to get away from the bombs, but she wasn't well and she died in 1943, so I never saw her again. That was very difficult. I didn't see my father till the war was over, either.

When the school year ended, all of the English students went back to England except me – my parents didn't want me to come. I went to Toronto in the hope of getting a visa to go to the United States, but I had a little problem: I had a British passport, but I was born in Austria, so the American state department considered me to be an "enemy alien". I sat in Toronto waiting for a visa that wasn't coming, and the family I hated from the boat were living there, so I had to see them all the time. I ended up hating them even more.

In the end, my uncle went to the International Student Service and talked to the man who was running it. His name was Joseph Lash, and it turned out he was a good friend of the Roosevelts. He said to my uncle, "I'm just going into another room to make a phone call," and he called Eleanor Roosevelt, wife of President Franklin D. Roosevelt of the United States. Joseph said, "I have a young girl in Toronto who can't get a visa. Can you help me?" She said she would help, because she was a wonderful woman, and a day or two later I was on a train going to New York! It was fabulous. That was in 1941. For a young girl to see New York for the first time, it was really something incredible. The International Student Service got me into a college called Elmira college. I had four wonderful years there and made some dear friends who became my friends for life.

When I arrived, the United States wasn't yet at war. But a couple of months later, on 7 December 1941, Japan attacked Pearl Harbour, a US naval base. Everyone was in shock. After Pearl Harbour, people felt there was no excuse for the US not to be in the war. Some of my friends had boyfriends who went off to fight. My roommate in college married a very nice young man who she'd been in love with for a long time and he was killed just before the end of the war, but that's war.

When I graduated from college, I went to live in a place in New York called International House. Everyone who lived there was an international student. The first Sunday that I was there, I was eating breakfast and a man came over and said, "May I sit with you?" I said "Yes", so we started talking. About ten months later, I married him. His name was Philip. He was an American, quite a bit older than me. I was married to him for 42 years. I couldn't get a job in New York because I was on a student visa, but soon after I married Philip I got pregnant and stayed home with the baby.

My father came out to visit me in New York after the war. I think he wanted to live with us – I had two brothers, but because I was his daughter, he thought I'd take him in immediately. I said no. I had two children by then, and it would have been impossible.

I did go back to the UK after the war, but only to visit my family. I don't know what my life would have been like if I'd stayed in England. I'd have had to do something for the war effort, and I think that would have been good for me, but I never got the chance. It's strange, because I'm not from anywhere. I now live in a retirement community, and everyone talks about their past, but they have no way of relating to my past and I have no way of relating to theirs.

BERND KOSCHLAND

Bernd Koschland came to England on a Kindertransport train in 1939. He told students from New Vic College in London about his experiences.

The strongest memory I have of Nazi persecution before the war is Kristallnacht. That night, 9–10 November 1938, Jewish shops, businesses and synagogues were destroyed. Men and young adults were taken away – my father was taken to Dachau, a concentration camp. I was about seven years old then. My mother probably knew where he'd gone, but I had no idea at the time.

In 1939, when my father was released from Dachau, my parents decided to send me and my sister to England. I will never understand how my parents felt when they made that decision. They promised they would soon join us, which no doubt made us feel better about leaving – but did it make it easier for them?

I travelled to Hamburg with my mother. There I left her, and along with the other children, I boarded the United States liner SS *Manhattan* and sailed for Southampton in England. I was now one of the Kinder of the Kindertransport. Kinder means children in German, and it's a name we still call each other.

We landed in Southampton in March 1939, and from there we were taken to a boys' hostel in Margate. I was the youngest child there, and I didn't speak any English at all, but I went to a local primary school and I slowly settled down into a new way of life. I hoped I'd see my mum and dad again, but once war broke out that became impossible. I could no longer communicate with them because it was too dangerous, and I destroyed their letters on the advice of an older boy.

Bernd as a child

41

In 1941 I was evacuated, along with the rest of the school, because Margate was on the south coast of England, which was vulnerable to invasion. Two of us Jewish lads went to live with a lovely non-Jewish family in Staffordshire who had no children of their own. They cared for us wonderfully but it was difficult to maintain Jewish life there. We did have some Jewish teaching on Shabbat (the Jewish day of rest) in a nearby hall with other Jewish children, but when we stayed away from school on the first day of Rosh Hashanah (the Jewish New Year), our schoolmaster said that if we did not go to school the next day, life would be difficult for us. We went to school, and missed the second day of Rosh Hashanah.

Fortunately, in 1942 I was moved to an orthodox Jewish hostel near High Wycombe. Life was very pleasant for the 25 of us who lived there, and we were freed from attending school on a Shabbat.

My parents never did join us in England. I tried to contact them via the Red Cross (a humanitarian organization) after the war, but they had died in 1942. Did I, do I, miss them? Of course, especially in recent years; I hear other people saying to their parents, "Can we stay with you?" "Will you come over to us?" "Dad, how do I fix this?"

I believe strongly that despite the past, life must carry on, and that you must do something useful with your life. Today, speaking about the Holocaust and the Kindertransport is part of the lives of many who survived. It's so important our memories are passed on to the next generation so that they are never forgotten. Genocide still happens today, and its effects are felt by many. The aftermath of the Holocaust is still with those who survived and for the Kinder who lost their families – the aftermath is still with me. I hope that young people, in whatever way they can, will help to make the world a better place.

RUTH BARNETT

Ruth Barnett was a child living in Germany with her family when Hitler came to power. She was sent to England on the Kindertransport. You can read more about her story in her book, Person of No Nationality.

In September 1935, before I was one year old, the Nazis declared that only proven Aryans could be German citizens. Citizenship was taken away from all the Jews in Germany. My brother Martin and I were only half-Jewish, but that made no difference to the Nazis.

On 21 February 1939, Martin and I left Berlin for England. My mother travelled with us. We got out of the car at Zoo Station and I threw a tantrum because I wanted to go to the zoo, not to England. I remember the seemingly endless train journey; I asked again and again, "Is this England yet?" I was amazed that Germany was so big; it seemed to go on for ever. The next thing I remember is being woken up. We got out of the train in the dark and we walked up a ramp onto the deck of this big boat. I felt very frightened. There were so many people and cases. How could such an enormous boat, with so much in it, possibly float? I was sure it would sink like toy boats at bath time if you put too much in them.

When we arrived in the UK, we caught a train to Merston Rectory, our first home in England. After tea with Reverend Stead and his wife, my mother put us to bed and tucked us up with a story. It all seemed like an adventure – until the morning, when I discovered that my mother was no longer there. I missed her terribly, but

Ruth with her brother Martin and her mother before the war

Mrs Stead was furious when I cried. I desperately wanted to please her, so that she would tell my parents I was being a good girl and they would take me home. Eventually, because my mother never came to get me, I decided she must be dead. It was too unbearable to think that she had chosen to be apart from me.

Life at Merston Rectory was very difficult for us. Reverend Stead was gentle and kind, but Mrs Stead was the exact opposite. They had no children of their own, and I think the reverend took us in as his humanitarian contribution to the war without considering that his wife might find it hard to look after someone else's children.

We had lessons in the schoolroom with Miss Wright, who was Mrs Stead's helper. The first lesson every day was elocution. You had to look in a little hand-mirror and

Martin and Ruth with Reverend Stead

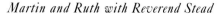

make your mouth into the proper shape to pronounce English words correctly. We were forbidden to speak German, but I thought it was silly that Martin and I weren't allowed to talk German on our own. Martin said it was dangerous to speak German because there were British soldiers around and if they heard us they would shoot us. I don't think I spoke another word of German after that.

Because I was so unhappy, I wet the bed. Mrs Stead tried to cure me by belting me with a leather strap or making me go without food. Martin would sneakily give me some of his food, which meant he often went hungry too. I don't know how long this went on for, but one day Reverend Stead asked us to go for a walk with him and

Martin told him we were both too hungry. The truth came out then, and Reverend Stead insisted we sit down for a feast in the kitchen.

In September 1941 we were sent to a Quaker boarding school. We spent two years there, and I enjoyed every minute of it. Most of the children got very excited at the end of every term when the time came to go home, but Martin and I didn't, because we dreaded going back to Merston Rectory. At the end of one summer term, we were told that we could not go back to the Rectory – the Reverend Stead was very ill and Mrs Stead didn't want us around. The Jewish Refugee Committee was looking for a new foster family for us. In the meantime, we were sent to a children's hostel in Richmond, London. We didn't have a chance to say goodbye to our school friends before we got on the train; life seemed to be full of abrupt endings and no explanations about what was going on.

The hostel was very shabby, dirty and overcrowded. Most of the time there wasn't an adult to be seen, and you never knew when the next meal was going to be. Martin and I used to go for walks to explore the area. Mostly we found our way to the River Thames, and as it was summer when we arrived at the hostel we had fun splashing in the water.

Although we were aware that the river was murky, it didn't occur to us that it might be dangerous. But it must have been from the polluted water that Martin caught hepatitis (a disease which affects the liver). He developed a high fever and was unable to get out of bed, but I couldn't find a grown-up to tell, and the teenagers were too busy to take any notice. Martin became delirious and his skin turned yellow. I was very frightened. He had heard that "an apple a day keeps the doctor away" and he was convinced he needed an apple a day to get better.

Ruth with the doll she sold to buy
apples for her brother

I took Christine, my doll, and sold her to a lady with a baby who I met in the street. I used the few pennies she gave me to buy a big bag of red apples. I don't know how Martin managed to eat an apple a day, but he did, and he gradually recovered.

Not long after that, a lady named Mrs Goodricke came to take Martin and me to a new home in Kent. The Goodrickes' house was enchanting: a real Tudor cottage with higgledy-piggledy black beams with white plaster in-between, and the Goodrickes were a real family with five children, like the pictures of families in storybooks. The Goodricke children called their parents "Mummy" and "Daddy". I very much wanted to be part of the family, so I started calling Mrs Goodricke "Mummy" too. She took me to a quiet corner and explained that I had a mummy and daddy who wouldn't want me to call her "Mummy". I burst into tears and told her my mummy was dead and that I wanted her to be my mummy. But she said my daddy wouldn't like it.

Martin and I were very happy with the Goodrickes, but in 1944 the Germans began sending V-1 flying bombs, also known as doodlebugs, over Kent. Martin knew that the bombs were coming from Germany, and he knew that our mother was there, so he felt as though his mother was trying to kill him. He was so terrified that he had to go to see a psychologist, who recommended that Martin be moved to a place where there were no doodlebugs. The Refugee Committee found a place for him at a grammar school, and he left the Goodrickes and went to live with a family called the Haltings on a farm near his new school. I stayed behind.

On 8 May 1945, the war in Europe ended. All the Goodrickes cheered when they heard the news on the wireless (an old-fashioned radio). I asked Mrs Goodricke, "Can I see my daddy now?" She was very sweet and explained that most railways, ships and planes had been destroyed in the war, so it might be a long time before he could travel from China, where he was living. Then, in the summer of 1945, the Goodrickes told me I would be going to live with Martin on the Haltings' farm. They thought it would be best for me and Martin to live together, but I had convinced myself I was part of the Goodricke family, and it was a great shock to discover that I wasn't.

The Halting family treated me as one of their own, and I gradually settled in to farm life and began to feel very at home. But after what had happened with the Goodrickes, I was very aware that Mr and Mrs Halting were only my foster parents and that they could give me away if they became fed up with me. But by the spring of 1949, Martin and I had been living with the Haltings for four years and I had begun to think I would live there for ever. Mr and Mrs Halting were very fond of me, and I discovered later that they applied to the

Red Cross to trace my parents because they wanted to adopt me. However, in May 1949 we received a letter from my mother out of the blue – the first time we had heard from her in ten years. It turned out she had been in hiding in Germany throughout the war. Soon after that she came to England to take me back to Germany with her. My parents wanted Martin to stay in England as he was studying for a scholarship to Cambridge University.

The Haltings' farmhouse

It is hard for me to describe the huge shock I felt when I was confronted by a strange woman and told she was my mother – I didn't recognize her at all. She wanted to hug me, but I couldn't bear her touching me. To me, it was as though she had suddenly come back from the grave, and I was terrified. She obviously wanted to

Ruth at the Haltings' farm, holding a puppy

mother me and make up for lost time, but it was too late.

The Haltings didn't want me to be unhappy, so they said I could stay with them instead of going back to Germany with my mother, and after a few days and a lot of arguments, my mother went back to Germany on her own. It must have been awful for her to be rejected by her own daughter. My father, who had returned to Germany and was working as a lawyer, served a court order on the Haltings to bring me back. Mrs Halting accompanied me to Germany. She couldn't add me to her passport because I was not her child, nor could I have a passport of my own, as Hitler had taken away my German nationality, and I was not eligible for British nationality because I was under eighteen. The Jewish Refugee Committee gave me a travelling document – a large sheet of paper with *PERSON OF NO NATIONALITY* typed in big letters across the top. At all the checkpoints the officers looked at it suspiciously, and by the time we were allowed through we had missed our train and had to wait for another one. In other words, I went through the Kindertransport experience in reverse. Overnight, I lost my home, foster parents and language, and found myself in a strange world. Only this time I didn't have my big brother to help me make sense of it all.

My parents desperately wanted their sweet little four year old back, the one they had sent off on the Kindertransport, but you can't simply pick up a relationship again after a ten year gap. My mother tried hard to engage me in conversation – I showed no desire to learn German, so she tried to learn English, and she wanted me to teach her. But because I was so angry, I deliberately taught her incorrectly. Once I ran out of the house and didn't come back until the next day. I feel rather ashamed now, because my parents must have been beside themselves with worry. I think that was the moment they realized it wasn't going to work for me in Germany. They said they would let me go back to school in England, on the condition that I came to visit with Martin every school holiday. I readily agreed to that, so I moved back to England to live with the Haltings again.

My repatriation in Germany lasted less than a year. When I arrived back in England, it was not easy to settle down. I didn't feel safe – if the Haltings could pack me off to Germany once, they could do it again – and I had fallen behind at school. When I came to take the School Certificate, I had to put "Germany" as my place of birth on the form. Someone in my class found out I was from Germany, and a small group started calling me a Nazi and made "Heil, Hitler!" salutes at me. I remember screaming that I couldn't be a Nazi because I wasn't even German – I was a Jew!

On 23 January 1953, I turned eighteen and I could become a British citizen at last. As soon as I received the paper saying that I had been "naturalized", I applied for a passport. It was the best birthday present I ever had: a big blue-and-gold British passport. I tore up the loathsome paper with *PERSON OF NO NATIONALITY* written across the top. I wish I had kept that humiliating document; it could have helped tell the story of the Kindertransport and the Holocaust. But I called my book *Person of No Nationality*, so that I could at least commemorate it and tell others of its significance.

THE FALL OF WESTERN EUROPE

On 1 September 1939, Germany launched a series of bombing raids on Warsaw, the capital of Poland, invading the country from both the north and south at the same time. This was a new kind of warfare – blitzkrieg, or lightning war – and the Polish armed forces were not prepared. Then, on 17 September, the Soviet Union, which had signed an agreement with Germany, invaded Poland too. Poland surrendered on 27 September.

Hitler expected France and Britain to make peace with him after his swift defeat of Poland, but they refused. All over Europe, people waited, wondering when the fighting would begin to affect their lives. Children in cities were evacuated to the countryside and British troops went to France, ready for a German invasion. But during the winter of 1939 and the spring of 1940, the war came to a near standstill. The British and Americans called this phase of the war the Phoney War: the Germans called it Sitzkrieg, meaning sitting war. It lasted until April 1940, when Hitler invaded Denmark and Norway, then Belgium, the Netherlands and France, gradually taking control of Europe. Retreating Allied forces were trapped in France, but in an incredible rescue mission, code-named Operation Dynamo, over 800 British boats sailed to Dunkirk in France and evacuated 338,226 men from the beaches. On 22 June, France surrendered to Germany.

Hitler in front of the Eiffel Tower with his architect, Albert Speer, and the sculptor Arno Breker. Hitler had flown to Paris on 28 June 1940 to celebrate the fall of France.

MARGUERITE COLOMBE

Marguerite Colombe was about to turn nineteen when the war started. She told her granddaughter Chloé Tartinville about the fall of France and life under German occupation.

At the start of the war I was living in Lisieux, Normandy, in northern France, where my father worked as a doctor. My family owned a house a few miles away in a village called Prêtreville, and that's where I was on 2 September 1939, the day before war broke out. It was still the summer holidays, and we were playing croquet in the garden. When Daddy arrived that afternoon, everybody realized that the war must be about to start, because he usually only joined us on Sundays. My grandmother, who had lost a son during the First World War, went inside the house with my parents. The rest of us carried on playing – we thought that the Germans would be defeated quickly. But we soon realized the impact that the war would have on our lives: shortly after war broke out, my brother Pierre joined the army, and apart from a brief period of leave in early 1940, he didn't come home until 1945. He was a prisoner of war for five years.

On 10 May 1940, the Germans invaded Belgium and the Netherlands, and soon they invaded northern France too. In June, my dad arranged for three of my sisters and me to go to the South of France with my grandmother; he thought it would be safer there. My grandmother bought a second-hand car for the journey. It used to belong to a baker, and it was full of breadcrumbs! A few miles from our destination, the car broke down on a level crossing. The level crossing gatekeepers let us

stay with them. The next day we found a small hotel. That's where we learned about the armistice: France had surrendered to Germany. I was sad, appalled and ashamed.

After the armistice, we thought it would be safe to go back home. Life went on; the Germans had occupied the second floor of our house, but we almost never saw them. But one day when we were in the garden, a German soldier offered us some chocolate. One of my sisters was about to accept the chocolate, as it was a rare treat, but we stopped her. We often teased her about that later on. From time to time my parents received letters from my brother. They were pre-printed, but there was a bit of space left for him to give us news of the weather and his health.

During the night of the 5–6 June 1944, we were woken by the sound of cannon fire. It seemed unbelievable: the Americans, the English and the other Allies were nearby! At last!

The next day, I had lunch with my other grandma who lived in the town centre. I had no idea that it would be the last time I would kiss her goodbye. That night, the Allies began to bomb France. A big house on the opposite hill was burned to the ground. Our family gathered on the ground floor of our house and prayed.

Early the next morning, my dad came home. He told us about the horrors he had witnessed: the town centre of Lisieux had been reduced to rubble, a lot of people had been killed and even more had been wounded. Later that day, we learned that my grandmother had been killed. One of her daughters (my aunt), who was a nun, had also been killed. It was a terrible moment for all of us, especially for my dad, but he had no time to grieve. He and my sister, Marie, who was a nurse, went back to the hospital, and the rest of us went back to Prêtreville. The town was in ruins, but we arrived safely. It was heartbreaking to go to Grandma's house without her.

We kept going as best we could. Someone in the house started a project to give clothes to refugees, but we soon ran out of supplies. A butcher installed a makeshift abattoir and shop, and toured villages selling meat, which really pleased everyone as we were running out of food. My sisters and I volunteered to work as cashiers in his shop. My dad's hospital was evacuated and his department was moved to Saint-Germain-de-Livet's castle. My dad cycled there every day as there was no petrol left.

The Germans started to retreat, travelling by foot and in horse-drawn carriages. They stayed in people's houses, and one soldier settled in our attic. He was always hiding his bike in the kitchen to make sure his fellow Germans wouldn't steal it. One night, a group of Germans arrived with trolleys full of weapons and ammunition and left them under the apple trees in our courtyard. My dad didn't want us to stay in the house that night in case something happened so we went to sleep in a crowded barn where a lot of refugees had already taken shelter. They were not happy to see us.

We were eagerly awaiting the arrival of the Americans and the Allies, but the wireless informed us that they were still moving through Brittany in north-west France. The fighting came closer and closer, and by August the sound of the machine-guns and the blue light from the tracer bullets at night made us hope that liberation was around the corner. We were finally liberated by the Canadians on 21 August 1944. Everyone welcomed them with open arms – I don't need to tell you how happy we were!

We went back home as soon as we could. Our house was mostly undamaged. It had been hit by a few pieces of shrapnel, one of which had gone through a window, pinning a tablecloth to its table. We had to wait a few more months before my brother came home. He was a lot thinner than he had been, but he was healthy.

FRANCOIS CONIL-LACOSTE

Dr Francois Conil-Lacoste was a child living outside Paris when war was declared. He told his grandson Victor Ghose about his memories.

I was six years old when France entered the war on 3 September 1939. I remember playing in the garden of our house in Massy-Palaiseau, just outside Paris, when I heard the neighbours shouting, "War has been declared!" They had heard the news on the wireless. There was a real commotion and many people started crying. Later on, a town hall official called *le garde-champêtre* beat on a drum to tell people about the war, and posters were put up all over town.

I wouldn't say I was scared, as I had no idea what was ahead of us. I was even a tiny bit excited at the idea of missing school, and I thought that if I had to leave town it would be like a holiday.

My father was a chemical engineer, so his skills were highly in demand for the war effort. We moved to the south-west of France close to Bayonne so he could work in a gunpowder factory there. On our way to Bayonne, we met a peasant whose horse had been requisitioned (taken by the army). The poor man was heartbroken; he started sobbing, and I cried too. Even after all these years I still feel emotional about it.

In October 1939, I started at a new school. I had a tough time because the Basque kids made fun of me for my Parisian accent. But we weren't the only newcomers to the Basque region; lots of refugees gathered there

Francois and his mother

too. Three Polish children joined our class, and I remember Jewish families selling their possessions before trying to board a boat for England or cross the border with Spain.

The German army invaded France in May 1940. On 22 June the armistice was signed, and the fighting provisionally stopped. The first German soldier I saw was an officer with an injured arm. There were metal pieces sticking out of it; that definitely made an impression on me. Soon there were German tanks all over Paris. The Nazi swastika was everywhere, and announcements were made in German. Most of the German soldiers were orderly and well-mannered (at least at the beginning of the occupation). They would give their seats up for ladies or elderly people on the Metro (French train system), which surprised the locals.

The Germans imposed certain restrictions on French people – you had to be at home by 10 p.m., listening to radio broadcasts from Britain was forbidden and it was impossible to get petrol for your car. Until 1942, it was relatively easy to get food, but the years 1942–44 were tough. The Germans took all the good vegetables, and the French were left with things the Germans didn't like, such as Jerusalem artichokes and cauliflowers. If someone was caught breeding a pig, they had to hand it over and pay a fine. By that time we were living near Paris again, and Father was running a factory producing pesticides. We were luckier than most; Father had contacts with local farmers who sold us their products and the caretaker who worked at his factory started breeding rabbits to eat. I ate so many rabbits I got sick of them. We owned a fridge, too, which was a big luxury in those days, and as I am an only child there were only three mouths to feed. Things got worse for my family when the Germans ordered my dad to go and work in Germany. He refused, and had to go into hiding. He stayed with my mother's parents, who owned and ran a small hotel in central Paris. He would rotate between the bedrooms so as not to raise suspicions.

On 4 June 1944, two days before D-Day (the Allied invasion of occupied France), there were terrible bombing raids on France by the British and American air forces. They wanted to destroy things like railways and factories to make it harder for the German army when the Allies invaded. But the civilians had no idea this was going to happen, and many died. The bombing started at about 6 p.m. It was a beautiful day – I vividly remember the bright blue sky – and my mother had sent me to get some milk from a neighbouring farm. Suddenly I saw planes flying overhead. I heard whistling sounds, then explosions. I was terrified. Without thinking, I took shelter under a bridge – one of the most dangerous places of all, because they were targeting bridges. Luckily I wasn't hurt. The bombing lasted about twenty minutes but seventy people in Massy-Palaiseau were killed. The church where I had taken my first communion just two days earlier was reduced to a pile of rubble.

I was at school on VE day. The teachers told us the war had ended and gave each of us a French flag, and we were sent home early. Later in the evening, my parents took me to Paris to celebrate. The whole place was very crowded and people were hysterical with joy.

When we remember the anniversary of the D-Day landings, we rightly pay tribute to all the soldiers who sacrificed their lives. But something like three times as many civilians died in Normandy as members of the armed forces. History books do not often talk about them. We must remember them, too.

MICHÈLE OZANNE

Michèle Ozanne was a child living in France when the Germans invaded. She told Meline Paillard about her experiences.

I was nine years old when the war came to my home in Ardennes, in the east of France. On 10 May 1940, all the families in the area had to evacuate their homes because the Germans had started bombing the region. I was living with my grandparents because my parents lived in Africa, so we left our house and started heading west, where it would be safer. I was sad to leave Ardennes, but the worst thing was leaving Rip, my hunting dog, behind.

We travelled from city to city by car, but we never settled down in one place. The Germans were always bombing nearby cities. After travelling for a few months, we arrived in a region called Deux-Sèvres. The Germans had settled all around the beaches to stop the Allies invading. They built blockhaus shelters, which were little concrete forts to defend the beaches. For some reason, I found the German soldiers cute.

We finally went home five months later, but the Germans were still occupying the city. When we got to my house, I was sad to discover that the Germans had killed Rip. Apparently he hadn't wanted to hunt for them!

Michèle and her brother Claude during the war

MICHELINE MURA

Micheline Mura was nine years old when war broke out. She lived with her parents and little sister in a small town near Paris. She told Lucy Poirrier about her experiences.

When war broke out, my father was called up to fight, and my mother left her job in an embroidery factory to work in a factory that made weapons. She worked at night, so we would stay at our grandparents' house. But one day our grandparents were evacuated because of the German bombing raids. They didn't take us with them – they left me and my sister at the police station instead. My mother never forgave them for that.

After Germany invaded France, my father was taken prisoner. We knew he was in the North of France because he was still able to write us letters. But we were very worried about him.

Eventually, the munitions factory where my mother worked was evacuated. She went to work one day and everyone was told to go home and pack and assemble later in the day at a meeting place. She took us with her – we were all loaded into a lorry and we went on a long journey to the countryside. We could hear bombing all around us; we stopped in cities to eat and sleep, and then continued on our way. When we heard air raid sirens, we went into shelters. Eventually we reached the countryside, and we were safe from the bombing at last.

Every week, my mother travelled by train to get milk and butter for us. The train was always full of Germans and they never once offered her their seat. She had to stand all the way. Our mother couldn't believe how rude they were at first, but she soon got used to it.

We returned home in 1945, when the war ended. When the liberation of France was announced, we took our bed sheet and dyed it red, white and blue to make a French flag. American soldiers paraded past, handing out chocolates, sweets and chewing gum to all the children. My sister and I really wanted to go to Paris to celebrate but my mother wouldn't let us. She thought it would be too dangerous, and she was right – a lot of people were killed that day by German soldiers who refused to surrender.

Everything went back to normal after that, but my father still hadn't come home. But one day I was at my grandparents' house when my grandfather called me and my sister into the garden. Our father was walking towards us, across the field opposite our house. I can't explain what I felt – the feeling was so strong. He was ill when he came home, but he got better in no time.

I was glad the war was over. I was tired of being afraid.

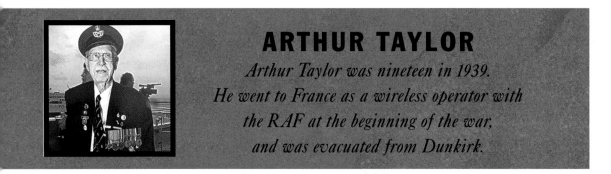

ARTHUR TAYLOR

Arthur Taylor was nineteen in 1939.
He went to France as a wireless operator with
the RAF at the beginning of the war,
and was evacuated from Dunkirk.

In January 1940, I joined 13 Lysander Squadron as a wireless operator and went to France. I was the forward ground controller, working with both the artillery and the Lysander aircraft. Our guns would fire a shot, the crew of the Lysander would tell me where it had hit, and I would pass the information back to the gunners so they could fire again until they finally hit their target.

When Germany invaded France, we moved right up to the River Dyle in Belgium. The Germans were on the other side of the river, firing at us, and we were trying to hit them. We lost the Lysander – whether it was shot down or whether the pilot had had enough and escaped back to England I don't know – but I was left on my own.

After that I was attached to the Royal Signals as a radio operator and I made my way back to Dunkirk with them. I was operating in a 15 cwt (hundredweight) small lorry with a radio aerial on top, which I sat in and listened to the radio. We got to a bridge over a canal at Bergues and the military police wouldn't let us go any further. The vehicle had to be driven into the canal with all my kit, and my kit was all lost. The lieutenant who was with me told me to cover up my RAF uniform and to put on a black mac, gumboots and a steel helmet because the British army were beating up the RAF personnel. The Germans were dive-bombing our men all day, every day, and the army thought the air force weren't supporting them. Afterwards they found out they were wrong.

We got orders to evacuate to Dunkirk, so we set off on foot. By the time we got there we hadn't eaten or drunk for days, so we pulled into a restaurant. We went to the bar and asked the woman working there to fill our bottles with water. She said, "I'm sorry, but the Germans have blown up Dunkirk's water supplies – there is no water at all. But if you give me your bottle I'll fill it with red wine for you."

On the beach we were bombed day in and day out, even at night. When we got there, we had the option of going left and getting in a queue a couple of miles long,

Arthur in his RAF uniform

or going the other way and getting rescued in the water by the little ships. We decided to go left. It took us 21 hours to get to a little pier called the Mole. We shuffled along and dropped down onto this fishing boat, the *Lord Grey* – 163 of us on one little boat. We lay down and went to sleep, and slept all the way to Dover.

From Dover, we caught a train to London. Ladies were dishing up tea and feeding people through the carriage windows. It was the first food and drink we'd had for four days – the 21 hours we were on the beach, and three days before that. When we arrived back in London, we were invited into the restaurants and had a beer or two. We didn't even know that Winston Churchill was the British Prime Minister at that point.

I'm president of the Bournemouth Dunkirk veterans. Every September we go to Kingston and get on the little ships. We sail down the river to a place called Weybridge Mariners Club and have a party. Two years ago I went to the Southampton Yacht Club lunch. The president said a few words so I decided I should say a few words too. I thanked them for having us, and said that in case they didn't know, we were the Dunkirk veterans. Everyone stood up and clapped. It was so embarrassing – being clapped like that just for being a Dunkirk veteran. It's like that at every event we go to.

British prisoners at Dunkirk, France, May 1940

EVACUEES

The Nazis discouraged evacuation at the start of the war, as they thought it was a sign of defeat. But in the expectation of bombing raids, the British Government arranged for children and other vulnerable people to move to the countryside as soon as war broke out. Around 1.5 million people, mostly children, left their homes and went to live with host families, but many returned home soon afterwards when bombing raids failed to take place immediately.

Many child evacuees had no idea where they were going or how long they would be away from their families for. Often, children had happy experiences – they were treated as part of the family and enjoyed learning about life in the country – but some were very homesick. Occasionally, children were treated cruelly by their hosts.

For all evacuees, readjusting to life at home after the war was difficult. Some had spent as many as six years away from their families – most of their lives, in many cases – and had grown used to a different way of life.

A truck-load of evacuees leaving the East End of London for the country

PETER BARNES

Peter Barnes was eight years old when he was evacuated. He told his grandson Andrew Barnes-Rider about life as an evacuee.

I was evacuated during the Phoney War, to a place called Birch in Essex. My mum took me to the station; it felt a bit like going off to Cub camp. I didn't really know what was going on, so it was a big shock when we got there. We sat in lines and adults came along to choose the children they wanted to take home. A lady picked me and took me to live on her farm, along with a boy I didn't know. I had to share a bed with him.

Peter as a boy

On the farm I had to bring the cows in and give water to the shire horses that pulled the ploughs. The other boy and I ate our meals in the room where the farmer stored his guns, and we were only allowed to eat with him and his wife at weekends. Eventually I moved to a cottage to live with another family, as the farmer's wife had a bad arm and couldn't look after both of us properly.

I used to play in the haystacks with the other village children. We often got told off for scrumping, which is when you steal fruit from trees that don't belong to you.

I was in Birch for less than nine months. I was so homesick that my parents let me come back to London.

KEN EDWARDS

Ken Edwards was just two years old in 1939. His family lived in London and he was evacuated three times to get away from the Blitz. He told his granddaughter Aimee Edwards and the children of Tigers Class, Laleham Primary School all about it.

The first time I was evacuated, I went to a farm in Norfolk with my mother and my brother Ron. Sometimes, when the farmer was in a good mood, he would let us ride on the hay cart, which was great fun. After we left Norfolk, the three of us went to live in Aberfan in Wales, where we stayed with a miner and his family. I quite liked living in Wales; everyone was very nice, and the village blacksmith made spinning tops for me and Ron. The only downside was that I got a bit of a Welsh accent, and when I returned to London the children at my school laughed at me because of it.

Shortly after returning to London, we were evacuated one final time. This time we went to a village called Burbidge in Leicestershire. We stayed with a lovely family who had a dog, and

on the day we arrived the dog jumped up and bit me on the lip. I still have the scar to prove it! Despite the aggressive dog, what I remember best about Burbidge is that the school had a swimming pool. We didn't have any swimming costumes, so my mum had to knit us some. Unfortunately knitted swimming costumes get very heavy when they become wet, and mine fell off in the swimming pool once. I found it very embarrassing because my friends were there with me!

Ken with his brother Ron

*Evacuees from London,
carrying their gas masks, in
the Devonshire countryside*

DOROTHY WEST

Dorothy West was seven years old when war broke out. Her family lived in London, so she was evacuated to the countryside. She told Alicia McKenzie what happened.

During the war I was sent to Devon, in the countryside. It was very scary being separated from my mother and father – it didn't feel right to be away from them – but after a while I got used to it. I wrote my parents and uncles lots of letters and they wrote back.

Staying with a new family was very strange at first but they were very patient and welcoming. I still remember the first meal I ate with them. I didn't eat much, because I was so scared and upset, but the next night we had a meat pie with home-grown roast potatoes and vegetables, and I thought it was the best dinner I'd ever had.

The family had a baby girl, and I shared a room with another evacuee, Bethany, who was a year older than me. We soon felt like a proper family and I didn't feel so alone or scared any more. They even threw a party for my birthday to make me feel better. I became great friends with the other evacuees in the village, too, but I still missed my parents and my real home.

I was happy to go home after the war, but I was also sad to leave my new family and friends and the countryside, which I had grown to love. I had learned so many new things, like how to ride a bicycle, how to milk a cow and how to grow real vegetables. I kept in touch with all of my friends and with the family who looked after me.

BLITZED BRITAIN

By the summer of 1940, Germany controlled most of Europe. Then Hitler turned his attention to the last country in Western Europe to hold out against him: Britain. Germany invaded the British Channel Islands at the end of June, and on 10 July the Luftwaffe (the German air force) began fighting the RAF in the skies above England. This became known as the Battle of Britain. Then, in September, Germany launched a devastating series of bombing raids on Britain. British newspapers called these attacks the Blitz – the German word for lightning. Between September 1940 and May 1941, cities across the country were bombed almost every night. Millions of homes were destroyed and tens of thousands of people were killed. But Britain remained undefeated, and by the autumn of 1941, Hitler was forced to give up his plans for invasion.

Children in the East End of London, sitting outside the wreckage of their home, September 1940

MARGARET CONNOR

Margaret Connor was fourteen years old when war broke out in 1939. She lived in Jersey in the Channel Islands, and her life changed dramatically on 30 June 1940, when the German army occupied the islands. She told Kaisha Page about her experiences.

When the war started, everything changed. German soldiers were billeted (lodged) in buildings in the neighbourhood, so you could be living next door to them. The Germans introduced a curfew, which meant that we were not allowed out at certain times of day. I was working as a cleaner in a hotel, and I often started work early in the morning or finished late at night, so I had special permission to travel after curfew, but I was only allowed to go to certain places.

No one was allowed to listen to the wireless. If you were caught with a radio you went to prison, so people hid their radios under floorboards and in closets, listening to the news from the BBC whenever they could and sharing what they heard with their family and friends. You could still go to the cinema, but the newsreels said that Germany was winning the war, which wasn't true.

The identity card Margaret had to carry during the German occupation of Jersey

Food got scarcer and it had to be rationed. Even fishing was banned, and I remember eating boiled seaweed. We did eventually receive food parcels from the Red Cross, which were greatly appreciated. Coal was hard to come by, and clothes were limited too. We had to "make do and mend" or wear hand-me-downs.

The war was extremely hard for people in Jersey – we were often hungry, we didn't want to live under German rule and we desperately wanted things to go back to normal. When the war ended on 9 May 1945, we hugged each other and cried with relief. We still celebrate the anniversary of Liberation Day every year.

ARTHUR TAYLOR

Arthur Taylor worked as a wireless operator throughout the war. After being evacuated from Dunkirk he served at RAF Hawkinge during the Battle of Britain.

RAF Hawkinge was just outside Dover. We had no aircraft there but during the Battle of Britain planes used to come in from other camps early in the morning, because our camp was nearer to France and they had a better chance of attacking the German planes from there. When the Spitfire and Hurricane planes landed, my job was to service the radios and wind up the Pip-Squeaks, which were little clock-type instruments that gave out signals when the planes were airborne, telling the people on the ground where the planes were.

You could see the aircraft going up and firing at the Germans, coming down, refuelling, getting more ammunition and going up again. I was lucky not to be a pilot, but we suffered on the ground too. We could also see the German planes, taking off, bombing us and going back, and we were bombed and shelled all day. One day, in the middle of August 1940, we had a very severe bombing. After our shift, we walked back to base to find that one of the hangar doors had been blown off. The door had hit a corporal right across his back and killed him. We went back to our billet, but it wasn't there. It had been completely destroyed. I'd lost all my kit again – it was the second time I'd lost everything.

After the Battle of Britain, I was posted to 116 Lysander Squadron. One night I was driving through the docks in Bootle, Liverpool, in this little radio van we had, and a chap stopped us – his warehouse was on fire and he needed help. We managed to put the flames out with some sacks, but then

Arthur and his wife on their
wedding day

the Germans dropped a high explosive on us. We fell through the floor and I was pinned by a piece of wood about ten inches (25 centimetres) square, right across my back. I couldn't move and I was in danger of being burned alive, as the explosive had started another fire, but luckily someone lifted me out. My back has caused me pain ever since – I'm still suffering today.

Not long afterwards, I came down to Christchurch in Dorset, and in the summer of 1941 I met my wife. I married her in October and in November I sailed for South Africa to instruct pilots in Morse code. It was three and a half years before I saw my wife again. We kept in touch by writing – you wrote on an A4 piece of paper which was photographed and reduced down before it was sent. I've been married 75 years this year. We've had a lovely life.

WOLFGANG SUSCHITSKY

Wolfgang Suschitsky is an award-winning photographer and cinematographer whose films include Get Carter *and* Theatre of Blood. *He lived in London during the Blitz and took photographs of the bomb-damaged city.*

I was born in Vienna. For a long time it was a very socially democratic town, but then the fascists took over. My father owned the first socialist bookshop in Vienna and it became impossible for us to stay there, so we came to London in 1934. I'm lucky – I wouldn't be alive if we hadn't. But it was too late for my father. He was heartbroken about the loss of his business and he killed himself. We got my mother out later though and she lived until she was 102.

Shortly after I arrived in London, I married a Dutch woman and moved to Amsterdam. She left me a year later, which was another bit of luck – I'm sure I wouldn't still be here if I'd stayed in Amsterdam after the Germans invaded.

I was already a photographer when I moved to England. My father had bought me my first camera and I had studied photography in Vienna. When war broke out I worked with Paul Rotha as a cameraman, making films for the Ministry of Information – mostly newsreels which were shown in the cinema before the feature films. I remember we made one about how women had taken over from men, working in factories making munitions. They had been told the job would be too difficult for them and they proved everyone wrong. We made films about the new planes that had been invented and how to build a barrage balloon, that sort of thing.

Our office was in Soho Square and we had to be on the roof

overnight with a bucket of water in case a firebomb landed. I lost a flat through a firebomb – my wife, our baby and I went to a shelter in my sister's basement one night and when we came up in the morning, we found that our flat had been damaged. The most unfortunate thing was that I lost one or two albums of negatives.

I took a lot of photographs of London during the war. I took some of London Zoo; I remember it was difficult for them to feed the animals because of rationing and they had to kill the poisonous snakes in case they escaped during a bombing raid. There were air raid shelters built in the tunnels that led from one part of the zoo to another. They used camels to transport sandbags to protect the entrances to the tunnels.

I took photos of London after the bombing raids, too. It wasn't dangerous to enter the city after the raids – they mainly took place during the night. I wanted to record the destruction. I never staged photographs; I always observed things and took photographs of what I saw. I took one from the top of St Paul's Cathedral, over the empty city up to Tower Bridge. I thought I had to record what had happened for my children and for other children. And the grown-ups have forgotten what the destruction was like, too. But I still remember some things vividly, like the sound of glass being swept from the houses after bombing raids.

On VE day I went to Piccadilly Circus and took at least one photo before everyone got drunk.

After the war I travelled around the world making films and taking photographs. I photographed many famous people – Alexander Fleming, Vincent Price, Aldous Huxley and many others. I still take photographs – just snapshots, though. Nothing serious because I can't print them any more. I have no darkroom.

The photo Wolf took from St Paul's Cathedral
the day after a bombing raid

SALLY BURR

*Sally Burr was nine years old when war broke out.
She lived with her family in Wimbledon, London.
She told her great-grandson Jack Connell what life
was like for children in London during the war.*

Everyone must have been worried about what would happen when war broke out, but they didn't talk about it in front of children. My parents arranged for us to go to North Wales to stay with our family there, but after six months they missed us, so we came back in time for the Blitz.

Life became harder after war was declared. We couldn't just go to the shop and buy sweets – we were given coupons for food and clothing and you could only have a certain amount of everything. We had to carry gas masks in a box on a string with us everywhere and we had to go into the shelters when the air raid sirens sounded.

If an air raid happened while we were at school, we picked up our gas masks and went to the air raid shelters that had been dug under the grass of a nearby park. We each had a little Oxo gravy tin with some food in it in case we had to stay in the shelters for a long time, and we sat on a bench and waited for the All Clear signal.

If an air raid happened while we were at home, we went to the Anderson shelter my father had built in the garden. Our neighbours used to come through a hole in the fence and join us. In the shelter, my sister and I slept on a little bed, my baby sister had a cot, and my parents and big sister slept on the floor. My father read Psalm 91 from the Bible every night. It starts: "He who dwells in the shelter of the Most

*Sally (right) and her sister
Fay in front of their house*

High will rest in the shadow of the Almighty. I will say of the Lord, 'He is my refuge and my fortress, my God, in whom I trust.'"

Several bombs did fall near our house. During the night, anti-aircraft gunners would travel along the railway track firing at the enemy planes. It was very noisy. One day I was playing in the garden with my sister when a German plane flew over, so low that we could see the pilot. We were very frightened, but before we could run inside we saw that the pilot was waving to us. We waved back and the plane flew off. The pilot offloaded his bombs on Wimbledon Common so that no one was hurt.

My father was too old to fight, so he became an air raid warden. He helped people who had been bombed and made sure everyone had drawn their blackout curtains at night so enemy planes couldn't see any of our lights. My eldest brother Tip was in a protected occupation, which meant his job was necessary for the war effort. He worked during the day and was in the Home Guard at night, manning the anti-aircraft guns on Wimbledon Common. My other brothers were in the armed forces – Harry was in the navy, sweeping for mines, Billy was in the RAF and then the army, and Bobby was a gunner in the navy, protecting the merchant ships. Everyone in my family survived the war except for Bobby. He died when his ship was bombed in Italy in December 1943. He was only twenty.

When the war ended, we went crazy. We had a street party and danced in the street – I danced with the lady across the road. But not everyone celebrated; many people were still waiting for loved ones to come home. My husband's father, John Burr, was still serving as a stretcher-bearer in Burma in south-east Asia on VE day. The war with Japan didn't end until August 1945, when the Americans dropped atomic bombs (nuclear weapons) on Japan.

Sally (far right) with her neighbour Hughie and sister Fay

BARBARA BURGESS

Barbara Burgess was three months away from her sixteenth birthday when war broke out. She told Martha Vine what it was like to live in Manchester during the Blitz.

During the war, we ate boiled onions as a treat. My friend, who was also called Barbara, used to ring up and say, "What would you like for your supper?", because they had a special oven next to their fire. I'd often say a baked potato, but her father was very fond of boiled onions, so sometimes I would ask for those instead. To cook the dish, you boiled it for half an hour. Then you covered it in salt and pepper and spread butter on it.

The war was hard for me and my family. I was evacuated with two close friends just before the fighting started – the government wanted to move all the children out of Manchester because of bombing. Nobody would take three girls, but I was the eldest by one month, so I had to be brave and say I would go to a family on my own. I wore a yellow evacuee tag to show me which train to catch. Sadly my father's printing business went bust so I had to return home after only a few weeks. My father couldn't get another job because printing was his profession. He had broken his leg when he was young and it hadn't set right – it was crooked – so he was disabled. I had to get a job to bring the money in. That meant I was in the house when German bombers struck the city.

We had a dugout (bomb shelter) under the kitchen floor. You couldn't sleep with all the noise. We could hear

Barbara's evacuee tag

MANCHESTER (1) School Ev/No. **Mcr.** 402.

(2) WHALLEY RANGE HIGH School, Manchester

(3) NAME JACKSON BARBARA
(Surname first, in block letters)

(4) Address 12. Woodside Road
Whalley Range   M/c 16

(5) Age 15   F 4

Barbara during the war

the noise of the incendiary bombs (firebombs). They would whistle down, making a horrible noise – sssssshhhhheeuuw – like fireworks. We were very frightened because we thought the house might fall on top of us or an incendiary might go through the roof. Luckily our house wasn't hit, but it was horrible walking around Manchester afterwards. Everywhere was bricks and broken glass.

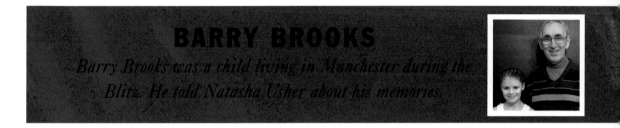

BARRY BROOKS

Barry Brooks was a child living in Manchester during the Blitz. He told Natasha Usher about his memories.

During the Blitz, my mother took my brother and me to sleep in air raid shelters every night. I was four and my brother had just been born. My dad had gone to London to work for the fire brigade, because they needed all the help they could get – the bombing was even worse down there – so my mum was alone with us, and she was terrified. We could hear the bombers flying over the Heartshead Pike hill to bomb Oldham and Manchester; they wanted to destroy the factories which made Lancaster bombers and ammunition. As soon as the All Clear signal sounded, all the older boys and girls would rush out of the air raid shelters looking for shrapnel.

We still had to go to school, but the teachers looked after us all very well. We had to practise what to do when the air raid warnings sounded. The teachers were very strict when we were practising, but they made us feel important, like little soldiers.

JOAN WHITAKER

Joan Whitaker was a child living in Tottenham, North London, during the Blitz. She told her granddaughter, Jemma Beauchamp, about what happened to her.

One day I was at my cousins' house, eating winkles (a kind of seafood), when a bomb dropped very close by. My cousins and I quickly got under the big table for protection. Then sirens started going off and there was a terrible drumming sound on the table. We were terrified – we thought we were being shot at by machine-guns – but it turned out the vibrations of the rockets had sent the winkles flying, and that's what was making the drumming noise.

Another time, my mum and I were supposed to go to my aunt's house for dinner, but I was ill. My mum told me I would have to stay in bed, but I pleaded with her to let me go. She gave in and we went to my aunt's house together. When we got back, we found our neighbours standing around in shock: a bomb had dropped on our house. All the stairs were broken, and a policeman tried to stop my mum going inside because it was dangerous, but she went in anyway. She walked up the broken stairs and before she even got to the top she could see that my bedroom ceiling had caved in, and was all over the bed and the floor. I'd have died if I'd stayed behind.

A church near our house got bombed, too. A lot of children played in it, which was very dangerous. Once, a mean little boy picked up a broken brick from the church and threw it as far as he could. It hit me and I fell to the

Joan during the war

ground, bleeding. My mother thought I would heal quite easily, so she didn't take me to hospital. Besides, it was the middle of the war, so there were a lot of people with more serious problems. My cut did heal but I've had a scar there ever since.

KEN SWAIN

Ken Swain was living in Portsmouth with his family when war broke out. He told his granddaughter, Aylish Maclean, about life during the Blitz.

When the Second World War began, I was four years old. Being a child during the war wasn't nice at all. Because Portsmouth was a dockyard for all of the British naval ships, it was a main target for the Germans. I remember looking out of the window one day and seeing two aircraft, a British Spitfire and a German Messerschmitt, having a dogfight (close-combat fight) directly above our house. I went and told my mum that one of the planes had smoke coming from the back, and we went to hide under the stairs in case it fell on our house, because we didn't have an air raid shelter.

The gun raids made our house shake, which was quite scary. Barrage balloons were put up to try and stop the German planes from flying too low, but the balloons in the school playground were shot down by the Germans.

When it was no longer safe for us to stay in the city, we moved to a village called Clanfield in the countryside. Clanfield was safer than Portsmouth, but once when I was playing in the garden I saw a plane being shot down. It was so high up when it was shot that it had

turned to ashes by the time it reached the ground.

There were a lot of searchlight crews located around the village, shining huge lights up at the sky to show the anti-aircraft guns where the German planes were. I once looked out of the front window of our house and saw a plane with three searchlights on it!

The Germans would drop aluminium foil called "chaff" from their planes to confuse the British radars – the radars couldn't tell the difference between the foil and a German plane. When we woke up in the morning after they'd dropped the chaff it was like Christmas – all the trees were covered in foil, and my friends and I would go and collect it.

The Germans threw out flares on silk parachutes, too – the flares would light up the ground and show them where to drop their bombs. The silk from the parachutes was very valuable, so in the morning after the flares had been dropped women would go out and collect the remains of the parachutes. They made clothes out of them.

One night, my friend (who lived next door) and I were planning to camp in the garden. As we were getting ready, we heard a V-1 going over the house. Suddenly we couldn't hear the engine any more. The V-1 dropped to the ground and there was a huge explosion. We had to sleep in the shelter that night, and as we lay there among the straw and hay with the sound of V-1s going over us, we kept praying that their engines wouldn't stop. Thinking back, that was one of the scariest moments of the war for me.

Although we'd moved to Clanfield, my dad was still working in the Portsmouth dockyard, which was a very dangerous place to work. He was there one day when the dockyard was struck during an air raid. He and his fellow workers rushed into an underground shelter but 25 men died. My dad was one of only three who survived. After the raid he went to work in Worthing, and as there were no cars he had to cycle all the way to Clanfield every time he wanted to see us. The journey was made even more complicated because all the road signs had been taken down so that if the Germans invaded, they wouldn't know where they were!

JOYCE FERRARI

Nick Ferrari's mother Joyce was born in Barrow-in-Furness in 1920 but moved to Kent during the war. Here he tells her story.

My mum, Joyce Ferrari, moved to live by the River Thames in 1941, which enraged her parents, as the Luftwaffe were flying bombing raids there every night and sometimes during the day too.

One afternoon, as she was hanging out the washing, the skies turned dark. She thought a storm was on the way, but when she looked up she realized the sky was full of German bombers. They were flying so low that she could almost see into the eyes of the pilots. But she didn't panic – she just took in the washing. That prompted her to join Kent Police as a Junior WPC to "do her bit".

One night, the guns on the Thames brought a bomber down. One of the crew tried to parachute to safety but a member of the Home Guard found him hanging from the branches of a tree, dead. Joyce strode up and took the Nazi armband from the dead navigator. It's now a grisly but prized family possession.

The Nazi armband that Joyce took from the navigator

Life for ordinary people changed dramatically when war broke out. Many countries introduced rationing, to limit the amount of food and other goods people could buy, as it was much harder to import things. Blackouts were introduced too, so that enemy planes would find it harder to bomb their targets: people were expected to hang thick curtains so that no light could escape into the street, and there were no streetlights or traffic lights at all. Almost everyone was expected to "do their bit". Men and women were called up to the army, navy and air force; women were recruited to work in jobs which had previously been reserved for men; and those who couldn't fight volunteered as air raid wardens or firefighters. Even children were expected to help out, growing vegetables, knitting socks or hats for soldiers, learning first aid or raising money for the war effort.

A member of the Observer Corps (a volunteer aircraft spotter) in London

THE HOME
FRONT

PHYLLIS ROWNEY

*Phyllis Rowney worked as a land-girl during
the war. She remembers what life was like for
people in the British countryside.*

I worked on a farm during the war, so rationing wasn't as bad for me as it was for some people. People supplemented their rations by buying and selling food on the black market (run by illegal backstreet traders). The Food Agency said you were only supposed to kill one pig at a time, but my boss killed two and sold a side of bacon to a lady who worked at the White Lion pub, so that she could make food for her customers. She rang up the next morning and said, "I've got the Food Agency people coming to inspect me! Where do I hide the bacon?" My boss went down to the pub after the Food Agency people had left. He said, "What did you do with the bacon in the end?" She said, "I hid it inside the piano!"

Every Tuesday, the farmer's wife and I used to go to the cattle market, and afterwards we'd have a meal out. Once, we sat down in this café, and we were served whale meat. I didn't know what it was till halfway through, but it was horrible. I took one of the toothpicks and I scratched into the table, "Unconditional surrender!"

Everyone tried to do their bit for the war effort. Lots of people knitted things like socks and balaclavas for the soldiers. There was a concert in the village hall to raise money for it, and I went along. A man

Phyllis and her sister in their land-girl uniforms

stood up to sing a song called "The Laughing Policeman", and as he was singing the "Ho, ho, ho" bit, his teeth shot out!

It wasn't all fun, though, by any means. I remember the bombing of Coventry. All those planes. We could hear them droning as they passed overhead and my boss said to me, "Those are Germans, you know. They're going for Coventry." We could see the glow of the burning buildings after the raid.

SHIRLEY HUGHES

Shirley Hughes is the author and illustrator of over 70 books for children, including Dogger, *the* Alfie *series and two novels set during the Second World War:* Hero on a Bicycle *and* Whistling in the Dark. *She told Bill Riley about life as a child in the Liverpool area during the war.*

I was twelve when the Second World War was declared in 1939. We lived in Cheshire, quite near Liverpool, and in the winter of 1940–1 the city was relentlessly blitzed by Hitler's Nazi air force, the Luftwaffe. They were targeting the docks, because at that time we were totally dependent on the ships of our merchant navy to bring us food and weapons from the US, which had not yet entered the war. The crews of those ships were heroic; the Atlantic Crossing was very dangerous because the German U-boats were out there, relentlessly torpedoing our ships.

Wartime for children and teenagers, when it was not frightening, was extremely boring. The seaside was covered with barbed wire and gun emplacements, travel was discouraged unless absolutely necessary, petrol was rationed and private cars were put out of use except for emergencies. We spent endless time queueing for food. The rationing system was very fair: there was enough to keep everyone healthy, but luxuries like sweets were a rarity. You had a monthly ration of them and you could either scoff the lot in the first few days and go without for the rest of the month, or try to eke them out a little at a time. Many unselfish parents gave their sweet ration to the rest of the family. We were all growing up with good teeth but that seemed like poor consolation at the time. The worst thing, especially for girls, was that nice clothes and nylon stockings were almost impossible to get hold of. Except of course on the black market, which no patriotic person would have stooped to using, though quite a few were tempted!

I was not evacuated; I stayed at home with my mum and went to the local high school, carrying my gas mask (which I never used, thank goodness). A school from Liverpool was evacuated to us, so we doubled up in the classrooms. When the air raid sirens went, we all had to go into shelters until the All Clear signal sounded, but most of the bombing over Liverpool took place at night.

All children were expected to do war work, such as collecting salvage (things like tin cans and old newspapers that could be recycled and used in the war effort) or serving in a youth organization. I joined the Women's Junior Air Corps. We wore uniform, marched up and down and learned to spot enemy aircraft. What we were supposed to do if we actually saw one remained unclear.

My latest novel, *Whistling in the Dark*, is set near Liverpool during the Blitz, so as you can imagine, it's quite autobiographical!

Shirley as a child in Liverpool before the war

SYLVIA SIMMONS

Sylvia Simmons was a child when war broke out.
She lived in Hungerford, Berkshire, with her family.

Even in our rural setting, we were not safe from the effects of the war. Almost from the beginning, our house seemed to be full of people; cousins and aunts from Portsmouth and Southampton came to stay with us, as our two uncles were in the navy. In 1940, when the Blitz started, I had to travel to school by train each day, which was quite frightening as everyone knew the German bombers were targeting railways. Once we were on our way home when an air raid took place, and the train was shunted under a bridge for safety. The next day the air was still full of brick dust, and we found out that a school

Sylvia (left) and her family before the war

and a church near the station had been hit in the raid. Luckily most people had already gone home.

Most of the local young men were in the forces, and some of the women were too, but quite a lot of women worked in munitions or became land-girls. When friends and neighbours lost sons, my mother cried, and I cried with her; these things were not talked about much, but we felt the losses deeply.

We were issued with clothing coupons, which did not go far, so bed sheets were made into all sorts of things. The sewing machine was very important in our home, because lots of our clothes were home-made. My sister and I each had a dress made from left-over, pre-war curtain material, which was dark red with green cord trimmings. I was very proud of that dress – it was certainly different. And of course we knitted socks, gloves, scarves, hats and even slippers with cardboard soles. Mine were pink with a drawstring with tassels on the ends. I wore them till they fell to bits. We unpicked and re-knitted anything and everything.

I was a member of the Girl Guides, and we did all sorts of things to help the war effort: we practised semaphore and Morse code in case we were needed as messengers and did jobs such as gardening and cleaning the church brasses. We went around the town collecting jam jars and aluminium saucepans, which were melted down and used to make weapons. The metal railings around churches and public buildings were collected and melted down, too.

When the Americans arrived in the town, it was like a breath of fresh air – or a whirlwind, even. It was quite exciting. They looked so smart; their uniforms were made of a smooth material and they wore beautiful soft leather boots. They were very friendly, calling the lads "pal" or "buddy" and the girls "honeybunch", "tweetie pie", etc. We all laughed and lapped it up. Our Saturday night "hops" (dancers) were really livened up. Some of the local girls became good at doing the jitterbug (a fast American dance), which entertained the rest of us. Swing music came to Britain with the Americans. Our family got to know some of the Americans personally, and we carried on writing to them and their families after the war. But in early June 1944, all the troops were moved out overnight. The town was unnaturally quiet after that, and there was a sense of sadness and foreboding. We knew times like that would never come again.

When VE day came, there was great rejoicing. Church bells rang, street parties were organized and beacons were lit right across the country. There was such a sense of relief, wonder and elation. Some of the wartime restrictions were still in place, and food rationing lasted until 1954, but we felt safe.

Sylvia as a girl

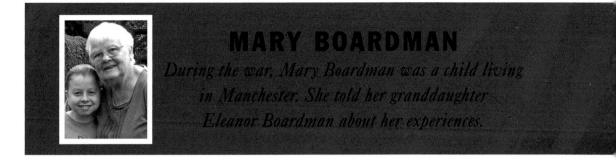

MARY BOARDMAN

During the war, Mary Boardman was a child living in Manchester. She told her granddaughter Eleanor Boardman about her experiences.

My earliest memory of the war is being in the hospital having an operation on my eyes. All the windows were shut, partly because we weren't allowed to have any lights showing at all, but also to protect the glass from being shattered by an explosion.

At the time, I was at junior school in Manchester. I carried a gas mask instead of a school bag and I remember feeling very proud of the case because it was bright blue and I thought it was wonderful. I had a halfpenny every day to get a baking apple from the corner shop. As this was the only fruit we got, it was a real treat.

We didn't go hungry during the war – we made good meals out of next to nothing. Everyone ate lots of potatoes, cabbages and other vegetables that were in season and grown locally. Because we were only allowed one egg a week, Dad made omelettes out of dried egg – they were more like pancakes. We had big pans of cockles and mussels, as we lived close to Fleetwood, on the coast. My mother used to make bread and prove it (make it rise) on the hearth, although it was difficult to get flour. We used to make cakes with liquid paraffin, as butter was rationed. Every Saturday morning, my sister Ivy would queue up at the bakery for ages for half a dozen cakes to eat on Sunday.

The shelves in the sweet shops were almost empty and there was very little sugar of any kind. In the winter, we used to have the smallest glass of warm ginger ale to stop us getting cold on the walk to school. We suffered a bit with scurvy and patches of very dry

skin, but other than that we were very fit and healthy.

Because clothes were rationed, we didn't have shoes – we had to wear clogs. They had rubber horseshoe-shaped things on the soles. I wanted metal ones so that I could make sparks on the concrete, like horses do.

The war affected my dad a lot. He was a coal miner working underground in deep mineshafts and we were always afraid for him; if a bomb had hit the shaft it would have collapsed and he would have been trapped. My mother worked in the munitions factory, making bullets, and the powder from the bullets made her poorly. My older sister Alice didn't have to work because she had a newborn baby. She had a very special gas mask kit for the baby, which was a bit like a cot. Fortunately, she never had to use it.

We were never allowed to have the lights on, and there were no streetlights either. Imagine all those years in blackness – only the moon and the stars for light at night. My dad told us to eat lots of

carrots so that we would be able to see in the dark. I remember seeing streetlights, traffic lights and lights in shop windows after the war. I was amazed – to me, it was like the Blackpool illuminations.

My Uncle Tom was killed on D-Day; he was unloading bombs from a lorry when one of them exploded. On VE day, when everybody else was celebrating the end of the war, I wasn't allowed to join in because we were in mourning. I had to play in the backyard on my own and I wasn't allowed to go to the party.

Mary as a bridesmaid just after the war

JOHN SIMMONS

John Simmons was at school in Hungerford during the war. He told the children of Abbymeads Community Primary School about his experiences.

John as a boy

During the war, we grew vegetables on the school playing fields and kept chickens for eggs, too. Sometimes you could see the fires burning in London flickering on the horizon at night, even though we were 65 miles away.

One night, at about two in the morning, an ammunition lorry caught fire near the green where I lived, and bullets flew everywhere. Our parents woke us up to watch. I could see the fireman trying to extinguish the fire, and I was very glad I didn't have that job. The burned-out lorry stayed on the green for the rest of the war.

My family befriended two American soldiers. One of them had two sons and my friend and I became his surrogate children, because he missed his kids. We would go up to the American camp and watch them training, and at lunchtime we'd line up and eat with them.

John with his two sisters outside their house

One day at Christmas time in 1943, the Americans drove into Hungerford with empty army lorries and collected up every child they could see. I was in the garden, messing around, and this American lorry came along. Lots of my mates were already in the back, and my mum said I could go with them, so the soldiers heaved me up into the lorry and took us off to their camp for a slap-up tea.

HEATHER GARDEN

Heather Garden was ten years old in 1939. She told
her granddaughters Amy and Jennifer Thomas
about her experiences.

We still went to school during the war, but certain things were different. There was an air raid shelter in the school grounds. It was deep, dark, wet and smelly, so we dreaded hearing the siren. The gas masks were horrible. I will never forget the smell of the rubber and the choking feeling of wearing it. And woe betide you if you lost or forgot your mask – you had to have it with you at all times.

One morning, in the middle of a history lesson, the ground suddenly moved to the right and then back again, taking the school with it. We all looked at each other, terrified. We later found out that an underground storage depot full of weapons had exploded eight miles away. It was the largest non-nuclear explosion ever to happen on British soil. If you visit Hanbury in Staffordshire today, you can still see the crater. It's three-quarters of a mile wide!

I had four brothers and sisters, so it was always a struggle to make sure no one went hungry. Like most families, we tried to help ourselves by growing vegetables and fruit and by keeping chickens. Certain foods were not available during wartime – I didn't eat a banana for six years. Having a cake on your birthday was a really special treat, as you had to save up several weeks worth of rations to get the ingredients. One day, my mother asked me to warm the cold butter over the fire to make it easier to spread. But my hand slipped, and the butter all slid into the fire! It was a disaster. Everyone looked at me in shocked silence. I felt so guilty. We had dry bread for tea for the rest of the week.

FRED HEMENWAY

Fred Hemenway was still at school when war broke out but he volunteered as an Air Raid Protections (ARP) messenger in his spare time.

Dad joined the ARP very early on in the war and I followed him soon after. He was a warden and I was a messenger (the only one in our ward, or area, at the time). If the telephone system broke down, I would have to deliver messages to ARP headquarters at the Guildhall in York. I also delivered the time sheets from eight posts and our ward headquarters to the head warden's house every Sunday evening, whatever the weather. I did it in deep snow sometimes.

We had no air raid shelters at school, so we had to go in on a Thursday to collect homework for the rest of the week. It wasn't quiet enough for me to do my work at home – there was an electricity generator next door on one side, a laundry on the other, and an engineering factory opposite – so I used to go to the ARP post and do it there. It was very quiet at the post, so after I'd finished my studies I played cards and darts with the warden. I had plenty of darts practice so I got a bit good, and our post usually won the ward darts competition.

I was a fire watcher, too. Watching is about all we could do – we only had a hand-operated pump and two buckets, which wouldn't have been much use in the event of a fire.

Fred (back row, fifth from left), his father (middle row, fourth from left) and their colleagues in the ARP

THE
RESISTANCE

Across Europe, people were forced to adjust to life under foreign occupation. They were faced with difficult choices: should they keep their heads down and accept the occupation? Or should they fight against the occupying forces in any way they could?

People who actively helped the occupying forces were known as collaborators. After the war, many collaborators were punished or shunned for helping the enemy. Fighting against occupation was known as resistance. Resistance work ranged from distributing leaflets and providing the Allies with information to guerilla warfare and blowing up roads and bridges. Allied organizations were set up to help the resistance: the British Special Operations Executive and the American Office of Strategic Services parachuted agents behind enemy lines and provided resistance fighters with weapons and other supplies. Being a member of the resistance was extremely dangerous. Those who were discovered were often tortured, sent to concentration camps or executed.

Resistance fighter Paola Del Din (centre) just before parachuting into Fruili, Italy, with the British Special Operations Executive

JAN PIEŃKOWSKI

Artist Jan Pieńkowski is a two-time winner of the Kate Greenaway Medal and is the co-creator of the Meg and Mog series. He was born in Warsaw in 1936 and his book The Glass Mountain *brings to life the Polish folk tales he loved as a child. During the war his family were involved in the Polish resistance movement.*

At the beginning of the war, I was living with my mother and father on my father's estate near the River Bug. My mother's family lived in Warsaw, the capital of Poland; she had two sisters, and her younger sister, Zosia, was married to a very bright young man who went to England to train as a spy. Because her husband wasn't in Poland, Zosia and her little daughter, Magdalena, moved in with her

Jan with a fox cub

mother – my grandmother – who was a highly thought-of doctor. My grandmother had a big practice in a nice street in Warsaw, overlooking a park. Dr Zand, my grandmother's pre-war colleague, lived there too. Dr Zand happened to be Jewish, and Jews were being exterminated, so she didn't get out very much – she didn't want to draw attention to herself.

At that time, the English were parachuting spies into Poland. One of these chaps contracted a serious disease. He was looked after by people in the Polish resistance – the AK, as it was called – and they passed him from one house to another. He was getting worse, and everyone worried that he might die, so

Jan with his mother, 1941

they approached my grandmother; she had room to shelter him, and because she was a surgeon, she would know how to cut up and dispose of his body if he died. So my grandmother took him in. She had to keep working, so Zosia looked after him day and night. When he got better, he should have left, but he didn't – I'm not sure if he and Zosia had a romance, but he was certainly very taken with her. Unfortunately, he drew attention to himself – he had English friends who came and visited, and because his room was on a first floor with a big balcony opposite the park, they were spotted. One day, the Gestapo (the German secret police) arrived and nabbed them all. Poor Dr Zand was carted away and never seen again, and my grandmother and Zosia were taken to Auschwitz-Birkenau, which wasn't yet an extermination camp. They both died of malnutrition. The English chap was sent to a prisoner of war camp. I met him in Cambridge after the war – he had tears in his eyes as he spoke to me about it.

The Gestapo stayed in the house for a week after they'd carted everyone off, just in case anyone else turned up. My Uncle Stefan did visit the house, but he was a clever chap – he pretended to be shocked that they had been housing this Englishman, and said, "I always suspected they were up to something." He managed to get away with it, and he said that he would be happy to work for the Germans, but he didn't really want to – he went into hiding and changed his name.

When my mother found out what had happened, she was terrifically upset; she had been very close to Zosia. She wore black mourning clothes for a long time.

My father's house was completely destroyed in the conflict between the Germans and the Russians, so we moved to the west of Poland, which had become a part of Germany. My father got the

job of running an estate, which had been taken over by a very nice German man named Neumann. We lived in a little house next to the blacksmith for about three or four years. The house had an enormous garden where we could grow our own vegetables, and we had eggs and meat. I had other children to play with, and it felt like peacetime.

We were on quite good terms with Mr Neumann. He was a perfectly decent man. Both of his sons died in the war, but before they were killed, one of them came on leave to his father's house. I was in the park and I happened to see this young man sitting on the steps, in uniform. I went up to him and he fished out a piece of fruit from his rucksack and gave it to me. I'd never seen this kind of fruit before. It was very large, and it was orange, a very bright colour. I rushed home to my mum and showed it to her. She turned pale as a ghost and said, "Where did you get that?" When I told her, she said, "You shouldn't have accepted it." She didn't think I should have taken a gift from a German soldier. Would you, if your sister had been killed? That was my first realization that something was wrong.

My father was in the AK. When things started to get bad round our neck of the woods, and men started to vanish, he went to Warsaw and changed his name. He had to get permission from Mr Neumann to leave, so he made up some disease and said he had to go to hospital. Mr Neumann must have known perfectly well why my father wanted to leave, but he gave him permission anyway, which shows you what a decent man Mr Neumann was.

I remember the day my father left for Warsaw; he went in a horse-drawn carriage. When the driver came back with the horses and the carriage, but without my father, I was very upset.

The driver gave me a paper bag with an orange in it. I burst into tears and said, "I don't want an orange, I want my dad." After a few months we joined him in Warsaw under a new name. The nice thing was that my mother could be with her elder sister.

I'd never been to school before, as they had all been closed, but in Warsaw I went to an underground school. It was on the second floor of a house on Marszalkowska (Marshal Street), one of the main streets in Warsaw. When we were bored, we looked out of the window. I remember seeing little crosses marking the places where people had been shot. Sometimes the Gestapo lined up young men at random and shot them – it was too much hassle for them to work out who was in the resistance and who wasn't. People put the marks on the walls to commemorate them.

Towards the end of the war, when the Germans were losing and the Russians were advancing towards Warsaw, the AK decided they weren't going to wait for the Germans to leave – they'd *make* them leave. And they did. But then the German bombers came back and bombed Warsaw out of existence as punishment. There was nowhere to live, so we went to Vienna, because my father had an aunt who'd married an Austrian officer. We stayed in her flat and my father got a job on a big estate in the country – he could speak German, because he'd been to a German university. Then we moved to Bavaria, and he worked on another estate. Living in Bavaria was like living in *The Sound of Music* – it was everyone's dream of a German village, with mountains in the background. There were no men at all, apart from my father – they were all dead. There were just women and children. The women did everything.

Then the Americans came. I remember asking my mother for a day off from lessons. She asked why, and I said, "Because the war is over."

PER LINDEBLAD

Per Lindeblad was a freedom fighter in the Danish resistance movement. He told Nikoline Eriksen about his experiences.

I remember the day that Denmark was occupied very clearly. It was 9 April 1940. I was fourteen years old, living in Bredgade, a street in the centre of Copenhagen, and I had a view over St Ann's Square. Suddenly hundreds of planes appeared, dropping thousands of flyers from the sky. They were so loud, and it scared me a bit. I looked up the planes in our encyclopaedia and found out that they were German planes. So I called my head teacher and told him that the Germans had occupied Denmark. I think I called a national newspaper, *Politiken*, to confirm it. The head teacher said, "What nonsense." I said, "Do I still have to come into school today?" And he said, "Of course, silly boy." He didn't believe me. I biked through the city to school, but the Germans were blocking all of the roads with bin lorries so I had to ride my bike through the park. I was an hour late for school, because I'd had to do such a big detour. The first lesson of the day was German.

I first got involved in the resistance movement a very short time after Denmark was occupied. I was part of a nationalist group of boys, and we went around the city taking down road signs that the Germans had put up, so that it would be difficult for them to find their way around Copenhagen. But that was just boys being boys, I guess. I became part of the Conservative Party's youth group. I became group manager there. Through that, I came into contact with a group called BOPA – Borgerlige Partisaner, or Civil Partisans. That's when it really started. We took part in different operations – downright sabotage operations. We took orders from London – everything we did was on their orders.

For example, there was a property near where I lived which a bunch of German women were supposed to move in to. The house had been completely done up for them. A few of the guys from BOPA managed to tie up the German officers standing guard, and we went into all of the dormitories and poured petrol on all of the mattresses. Then we switched on the gas taps and put firebombs in the stairwell and ran off. I left my bike behind by accident, and when I went to get it two weeks later it was still there. The building was completely ruined, so no one could live in it.

Once I walked past Hotel Phoenix, where the Germans were staying, with firebombs in the basket of my bike. I was so naïve. And I had my own private bike shed at home with a padlock on it, where I stored stuff for BOPA operations – firebombs or grenades or whatever we were using at the time. I would have been shot straight away if the Germans had found out!

I took part in seven or eight operations throughout the city. We destroyed workshops, factories and a big garage on Falkoner Allé – we went out there one morning at 5 a.m. and I think we blew up around sixteen German lorries.

I was also involved in the illegal underground press, *Studenternes Efterretningstjeneste* – The Students' Secret Service. We would cycle to this coffee shop in the centre of the city and pick up the illegal magazines. Then we would cycle around town and deliver them to people. I still can't believe that it was all taking place in the centre of Copenhagen.

The Germans never found out about *Studenternes Efterretningstjeneste*. BOPA's meeting place was an art gallery and we held secret meetings there for quite a few years, but somehow someone found out and a few people were arrested.

There was a strange sense of comradeship in the community. Strange because we didn't actually know each other – we only knew each other's codenames. Only the group leaders knew who we were and where we lived. That meant we couldn't tell the Germans anything if we were ever caught. I never saw any of them again after the war ended, not even in the Veteran Association. But I know that some of them went to America after the war.

All of the operations took place at night and we would cycle everywhere. I was lucky enough to have a room with a separate entrance to the rest of the house, so I could come and go as I pleased. Quite often I would get home at 6 a.m. and my mum would come and wake me at 7 a.m., because I obviously still had to go to school. My parents had no idea what I was up to, because I would be in my bed "sleeping" when they came into my room in the morning. They didn't find out I was in the resistance until I was arrested by the Germans, because I was arrested at home. My mum was at the communal bathhouse at the time, and my dad was at work. I was arrested in 1945, when I was eighteen years old.

I was arrested because a snitch had been to a meeting I had held in my house. He had seen that I had a Sten gun (a submachine-gun), which I was supposed to take to someone later in the day. I believe the men who came to my house were from the Schalburg group – Danish people who were working for the Germans. They came to my door and rang the bell and unfortunately I was at home, because I had fallen off my bike the day before and hurt my knee. They left again, but ten minutes later they came back. And then I got really frightened. They searched the whole house and broke into all of the cabinets and closets. They stole all of my parents' cigarettes and an old sabre (curved sword). It was an antique sabre, and they later beat me with it. They beat me to a pulp. There was blood everywhere and I found out later that when my mum got home she was incredibly distraught.

I couldn't tell the men much because I didn't know anything! I knew about the operations of course, but I obviously didn't tell them about those. They dragged me up the stairs to the third floor, and then one of the men cocked a big gun and told me that it would be a lot better if they just pushed me out of the window or shot me then and there. After that they dragged me back down the stairs, and a man said – I remember it so clearly – "Go and wash your ugly mug." I went to the bathroom and washed my face, but when I came back into the room they started beating me again. They hit me in the face and I got black eyes – it was awful. Then they took me outside and the German police came to pick me up. I think they were from the SS (the Schutzstaffel, a Nazi military organization). Outside, people were lining up to catch a glimpse of me. There was a women's hat shop where the royal family used to go, and all of the ladies there were standing outside feeling sorry for me. They had known me since I was a little boy.

Being arrested wasn't the most horrible thing I experienced. The beating I got at the police station was. But the arrest was very awful, it really was. I was driven straight to the police station where I was put in a corner. I had to wait there for several hours, and every time a German walked past, he smashed my head into the wall. I was facing the wall and I couldn't do anything to protect myself.

They kept me at the police station for a month and interrogated me repeatedly. They knocked my two front teeth loose during the first interrogation. When I was taken back to my cell that night I discovered that one of my fellow prisoners was a dentist, but he couldn't do anything except move my teeth back into place.

My front teeth turned blue so I had to have them capped later on.

After a month, they took me to Vestre Fængsel, Copenhagen's main prison, and that was really horrible as well. We all got head lice there. We were four men in each tiny cell. All of my fellow prisoners were resistance people too – doctors and an opera singer, very famous people, a lot of them. We just sat there and stared at the walls. When we were allowed outside in the small triangular courtyard, the opera singer, whose name was Henry Skjær, would sing a song called "Flyv Fugl Flyv over Furesøens Vove" ("Fly, Bird, Fly Across the Billows of the Lake"). That was a bit tragicomic. But I guess it kept our spirits up a bit.

I was there for a month as well. Then we were put in lorries in the middle of the night and driven to the train station. On the way there we could see the smoke from the ruins of the Shellhus, which was being used as Gestapo headquarters. A couple of days previously we had heard planes, and we thought that the Brits were coming to free us by knocking the wall of the prison down, but instead they accidentally dropped bombs on the building and it was still burning two days later. A hundred and twenty-five civilians were killed. The SS put us all in cattle trucks, 50 prisoners in each. The Mayor of Helsingør was one of my fellow prisoners – King Peter, we called him. Half of us already had body lice when we were put in the cattle trucks, and by the time we arrived at Frøslevlejren, a prisoner of war camp near the German border, everyone was crawling with lice. The journey took three days. When we needed the loo, we all had to go at the same time on the side of the train tracks, and the Germans would form a ring around us pointing their machine-guns at us so we wouldn't escape.

On the way to the camp, the only food we got was a quarter of a loaf of rye bread and a horrible sausage each. But on the second day, when we reached Fredericia, the Red Cross was waiting for us and they gave us some decent packed lunches to take with us.

Someone had broken a piece of wood off the back of the cattle truck to make a hole so that he could look out and keep track of where we were. A German officer discovered this. He shouted that if the piece of wood wasn't replaced immediately, he would pull someone out of the truck at random and shoot them. We very quickly managed to close up the hole.

We arrived at the camp at night. It was 29 March 1945. It was so grey and scary. The Germans patrolled the grounds with mean dogs. It was raining as well, it felt very dramatic. Because we were all completely crawling with lice, we had to hand over our clothes to be disinfected. We were all standing there naked, and a guy with a big broom – he happened to be one of my old friends from BOPA – would dip the broom in a very strong-smelling liquid and wash us down with it, front and back.

It's hard to say at what point in all of this I was most scared. I think it was when one of my friends came back to our cell in Vestre Fængsel after he had been interrogated. He had been beaten so badly – they had even beaten the soles of his feet – that he had to be carried back to the cell. And the next night, a German came to the cell and gave him a pen and paper and told him to write to his wife and daughter. He was being taken to the fields outside the Shellhus to be executed. He is buried out there I think. That made us all think. We were all afraid that we were going to be next.

When they were taking someone away to be executed, we would all stand up, and some of the very tough guys, who almost looked like bikers, would sing the song "Altid Frejdig Når du Går", which is a psalm about fighting and living for what you hold dear. It was a strange sight. But that's how it was.

It is important for people to know that we strived for freedom. No matter how weird it sounds, idealism and nationalism were the main driving forces for most of us. I grew up in a bit of a strange environment where it was all about God, king and country, so that probably affected me. But generally speaking we fought for Denmark's freedom. That was all our heads were full of. To me, there is nothing positive to say about the war. Definitely not. It was so brutal. I don't see that anything positive came from the war.

In Vestre Fængsel there was this German prison guard. He used to be a ship owner. He had lost everything – his family and his home in Hamburg. We pitied him, we really did. He was really kind. He also smuggled out a few letters from some of the prisoners, I recall. He didn't believe what Hitler was doing was right. But overall they were very rough, the Germans. There was also one in Frøslevlejren who was nice, though, so of course they were all different.

We only found out on the morning of 5 May 1945 that the war had ended. It happened on the evening of 4 May, but we weren't told then. We were all lined up for roll call when suddenly someone brought out a big flagpole with the Danish flag on it and then we all knew what had happened. It was a very moving moment.

I don't really remember how we celebrated the end of the war. We didn't really have anything to celebrate with. Except for our joy of course. Most people wanted to go straight home, but I stayed for another two weeks as a volunteer to keep hold of the Nazis and the Germans who hadn't fled. Now it was their turn to be arrested and go through all the hardships they had put us through. After that I went home to my parents in Copenhagen. I had sent a telegram saying that I was coming home, but I got the day wrong, so they were very surprised to see me a day earlier than expected.

My parents didn't really know anything about what I had been through, because I wasn't allowed to have contact with anyone while I was in prison. I only received care packages from the Red Cross. That's when I started smoking, because there were always cigarettes in the packages. I've smoked ever since.

My parents knew I was alive through the Red Cross. That was their only connection to me. And then, 57 years later, the German government gave me 60,000 Danish Krone (around £6,000) in compensation because I had been tortured. I thought it was a strange thing to do, partly because 57 years had passed. It was the biggest compensation sum you could get, because I had been beaten so severely in all possible ways. Luckily I don't have any permanent injuries from the beatings. We didn't have psychologists and stuff back then either. I don't know how I would have turned out if it hadn't happened; I'll never have a chance to find out.

I have two children, three grandchildren and three great-grandchildren. Yes, those five years happened, but otherwise I have had a very happy life, and those five years have just turned into a little black dot. But it's good to be reminded of them once in a while. Strangely enough, last year I was invited to the synagogue with my daughter. I had never been there before, and it was because I helped the Danish Jews to escape to Sweden during the

war. They had saved my address for 70 years! I was so surprised when they invited me. People gave speeches and there was a singer. It was to say thank you to everyone who had helped them during the war. It was a wonderful experience.

I went into the resistance because I was idealistic and starry-eyed. But I have never regretted it. Definitely not. You have to stand up for what you believe in.

Per, two years after the war, when he served in the army

CORNELIA MANJI

Cornelia Manji was born in the Netherlands in 1942, two years after Germany invaded the country. She told her granddaughter Sasha Devereux how her family helped Jewish people during the war.

I was born on a tulip farm in Holland, in a little village called Avenhorn, 22 miles from Amsterdam. When the Second World War started, my father stopped growing tulips and started to grow vegetables instead. He bought some pigs and dairy cows, too, so there was always food available during the war.

Every Wednesday, two Jewish people would cycle from Amsterdam to our house overnight with empty saddlebags on the back of their bikes. They had come to collect food to give to the Jewish people in hiding in Amsterdam. If you were Jewish and in hiding, you were not given any food coupons because the authorities didn't know you existed – and if they did know, you'd be sent to a concentration camp.

When the two Jewish people arrived in the morning, my mother would give them a good breakfast and lunch, and when it was dark again they would set off for Amsterdam, their saddlebags full of food.

Two Dutch Jews living in a tiny cellar during the Second World War. The room is too small for them to stand upright and the only person who knows they are there is the porter hiding them.

PAOLA DEL DIN

Paola Del Din was a student during the war.
After the Nazi occupation of northern Italy,
she joined the Italian resistance.

Paola, 1942

I was born in 1923 in the Dolomites, a mountain range in Italy. My peaceful life ended in 1934 when the army was sent to the nearby border to stop the Nazis invading Italy. The situation worsened day by day and eventually war broke out. That changed everything: my sister Maria moved to Sicily with her husband, who was in the army, and my brother Renato, a young officer in the Alpine Regiment of the army, was sent to the tough Yugoslavian frontier.

In July 1943 Benito Mussolini, the Italian Prime Minister, was dismissed. The king put Marshal Badoglio in charge of the government – all the fascists seemed to have disappeared. Ordinary people celebrated; everyone expected the war to end. We didn't realize what lay ahead.

At 7.30 p.m. on 8 September 1943, my mother and I were listening to the wireless when Badoglio announced that he had requested an armistice from the Allied forces. The Allies had occupied southern Italy, but the Germans controlled northern Italy. The country was divided in two. We lived in the German-controlled North, but my sister was in the South. Now our family was divided as well. I asked Mother, "What now?"

Mother answered, "We shall see what the Germans will do."

Soon after Badoglio's announcement, the Germans began to stop young men in the streets, ask for their personal documents, and take them away. They captured Italian soldiers too, and sent them to prisoner of war camps. On 12 September 1943 my brother came home. He told us that he would keep the oath he had sworn at military school and fight to protect his country. My mother and I wanted to join him in fighting for the freedom of our fatherland and our people.

Renato and his fellow soldiers didn't have personal documents, just military ones, which meant they would have been shot on the spot if they'd been stopped in the street by Germans, so I went to the university and asked one of the professors to register the young soldiers as students so that they could have university papers. Then Renato contacted a group of soldiers from his regiment who were also faithful to the Italian Royal Government, and they started planning for the resistance. We managed to contact a lot of people – military, civilians, parish priests, men and women of all ages – who were willing to join in the struggle for freedom.

There were two branches to the resistance in the very north of Italy: the Garibaldi, who were communists, and the Osoppo, who wanted freedom and Western democracy. We were in the Osoppo. There were three leaders of the Osoppo, who we used to call by their codenames: Verdi, who had been a teacher of the arts, Mario, an accountant, and Aurelio, a priest. Renato was made the leader of a battalion of Osoppo resistance fighters in Pielungo. Mother and I watched from a window of our flat as he left on his bike for the mountains. Mother was very worried about what would happen to him, but I was young and optimistic.

My job in the Osoppo was to find out information. I used to listen to gossip in shop queues and I often visited some German-speaking people I knew, pretending I wanted to practise my German. One of them, who was an interpreter and possibly a German spy, once told me the names of three old retired Italian officers who were going to be arrested. I went to visit the one I knew, who lived close by, but he didn't believe me. I couldn't get in touch with the other two, who lived out of town. Soon afterwards, all three were forced out of the country and none of them came back. I felt guilty that I couldn't find a way to save them.

Renato kept in touch quite regularly but all of a sudden we stopped hearing from him completely. No one seemed to know where he was, so I went to see Verdi. He told me what had happened to my brother: Renato had bravely gone to attack a fascist and German camp in the mountains. He had been wounded in the stomach, but he stood up again, still firing and shouting, "W l'Italia libera!" ("Free Italy!") Then he was wounded in his head, and killed. Against police orders, a crowd of around 2,000 people held a solemn funeral for him, and even collected money to buy the land for his burial. One young woman was forced out of the country and several others went to prison for their involvement, too.

When I came home from Verdi's house, I didn't have the courage to tell my mother that Renato had been killed. Instead, I said that he hadn't come back from a mission in Slovenia.

In July 1944, the Osoppo leaders gave me an important mission. They sent me to meet Beckett, an English major who had parachuted into Italy one month earlier; he was a member of the Special Operations Executive, a British organization involved in spying and carrying out sabotage behind enemy lines. Beckett told me that the British were planning to land in northern Italy to bring the war to an end as soon as possible, and they needed someone to carry some information to them in Florence and wait there for it to be passed over the fighting lines. They said I should only hand over the papers to the commanding officer of the SOE unit in Puglia. I said I would do it.

The papers I had to carry were ready the next day. They were typed on very thin paper. I didn't want to know more about their content – that way, if I was captured after delivering them, I could do no harm, as I would have no idea what the papers said.

Before I left for Florence, I told my mother about Renato. She didn't cry; she said, "You must carry out your mission. Otherwise Renato's death will have been in vain."

My mother helped me hide the papers under my clothes and I packed a suitcase with a few personal items, my ID, a German grammar book and a book of linguistics, because I still needed to study for my final university exams. Then I set off on my long journey. I told my mother that I'd be home in November – that either the war would be over, or I would parachute in, like the SOE officer had.

I couldn't simply hitch a ride to Florence – the city was still in German hands and was out of bounds for people from northern Italy. I made it to Bologna and I went to German Command to ask for a permit to enter Florence. I said that my mother had fallen sick there and I had to go and find her. The old German lady in charge of the office said no one could enter the city any more and that I was a silly, stubborn Italian for insisting, but when she left the office the two younger people working there said, "You poor child, don't worry. Go to the two towers at 2 p.m. That's the time the military cars pass through Bologna. Someone going to Florence will pick you up and take you with them."

I arrived at the towers at 2 p.m. sharp. I approached an ambulance driven by two German soldiers and told them my story. They were very sympathetic, as the war had been rather hard on both of them. They took me as far as a small village, and from there I hitched a ride on a lorry carrying ammunition. The lorry driver left me at the crossing into Florence, and two young SS guards started questioning me. I got them on my side by offering them some fresh fruit, and they let me get into a car going to the city itself.

As soon as I arrived, I turned a corner and found myself in front of a group of German soldiers. I knew they'd chase me if I ran away, so I decided to go and talk to them. I said I had just arrived in Florence and that I hadn't slept for two nights, and they said I could sleep in the garden they were camping in. I told them I was looking for my mother, and they even agreed to look after my luggage while I went to find her.

I left the soldiers and went to Via Gioberti to visit the parents of Renato's friend Giorgio, who was already active in the resistance. They would have let me stay with them, but they were both quite old, so Giorgio's father arranged for me to stay at a school run by a generous and brave nun. I went to collect my luggage from the German soldiers; I told them I had found my mother, and they said they were pleased for me. I felt bad for lying to them, but that's war.

I hoped that I would only have to stay at the school for a few days, but one morning I opened the door of the classroom where I was sleeping and saw German soldiers in full battledress entering the nuns' cells. The nuns were terrified – some of them had been in the convent for more than 70 years. Everybody was told to leave the building, so lots of us slept in the gardens around the church. We had hardly any food, but luckily over the years the nuns

had saved scraps of bread and a few dried peas.
The bread often had cobwebs on it and the peas often
contained parasites, but at least we could give
some food to parents who had nothing else to
give their children.

On 15 August 1944, a resistance uprising freed
the city centre. At last I could get to the office of the advanced
SOE unit. I met an officer named Captain Gubbins who read the
note Beckett had given me, and checked my password, which was
"I want to talk to the fair major". He said a car would pick me up
the next day and take me to Rome, and from there I would go to
SOE headquarters in Puglia to hand over my papers.

When I arrived at the SOE office in Rome, the young officer in
charge asked me to give him the papers. I told him that my orders
were to give them directly to the commanding officer of the unit
in Puglia. He said that the commanding officer was in Florence,
but Captain Gubbins had said he was in Puglia, and I insisted on
sticking to the orders I had been given. The next day, the young
officer said that if I didn't hand over the papers he'd have to shut
me up. I refused again, but that night I told the woman I was staying
with what had happened, and she advised me to give him the papers.
So the next day, I had to hand them over.

After that, I was flown to Monopoli in Puglia where a villa in
the countryside had been taken over by Allied Command. Over the
next few days, several officials came to question me. I gave them all
of the information I had been able to collect during my trip.
One of the officers, Lance Corporal Willetts, said, "You must give
us the papers you were given. At Command, they suspect you
might be a spy." I felt insulted and angry. I told him that I had
been obliged to leave the papers with the rude young man in Rome.

Lance Corporal Willets investigated, and it turned out the rude young man had put the papers in a safe and forgotten about them.

Before I had left for Florence, my mother had suggested that I ask the British to bring my father home from the prisoner of war camp in India where he was being held. I asked one of the lieutenants in Monopoli, Gerard Thistlethwaite, whether he could do anything. He was very sympathetic, but he said that was dealt with by a different department. Shortly after that I was sent to parachute school, and I thought I would hear no more about my request. But then Gerard got in touch to tell me that my father was coming home after all. Gerard went to the airport to pick up Father himself. When I went to meet my father in an SOE apartment, the first thing he asked was how my mother and Renato were.

I had to tell him the terrible news. It was heartbreaking; my father had survived prisoner of war camp by focusing on our family, and now Renato, the apple of his eye, was dead. Father had always seemed like a giant to us children, but now he was a poor, weak man. After two days in the apartment, he wanted to go out to look for a church where a Mass could be celebrated for "his boy". He was at a loss walking through the streets, as he wasn't used to lorries and cars and people and movement. How many people from all over the world must have experienced

Paola with her father in Rome, 1945

the same thing when they came home?

Soon after that my father went to Sicily to stay with my sister, and it was time for me to fly north. I was very pleased that I would keep my promise to my mother that I would be home by November. I was going to parachute into Friuli. I had only had four days' training at the parachute school. At first they probably thought I wouldn't be any good at it, because I was a girl, but they soon realized that I was as smart as anybody else. I was even awarded a chocolate bar because I was so quick to jump out of the plane. We had to abandon several attempts to fly north because of bad weather, so when the time finally came to jump, on 9 April 1945, I jumped so quickly that I forgot to take off the gloves I had been given to keep my hands warm during the flight. That meant the pull cord was slippery, and I hit the ground hard.

At last I could go home and tell Mother the good news about my father's return. When I got there, she told me that she had been arrested and imprisoned for 40 days – the German police had arrived, looking for Renato and me, and they had imprisoned our mother as a hostage instead. She willed herself to survive as she thought I must be dead, and she was determined to preserve the memory of her family.

Shortly after my return to Friuli, I went to visit Verdi, Aurelio and the other Osoppo commanders. They had just survived quite an adventure – they had been captured by German police, but they escaped using fake exit permits, as the police didn't know who they were. They were pleased I was safe, and they still remembered my dear, brave brother. They gave me two messages to take to Buja, which wasn't too far from Friuli. As I travelled there, the rain poured day and night. I watched the German army retreating towards the Alps, marching silently and looking as miserable as the weather. Just as I had arrived to deliver my first message, fighting started between the resistance and the German army. I asked for a gun, but a man told me it wasn't my job. Two resistance fighters died, but after the fighting Buja and the countryside around it was liberated.

On 1 May 1945, I was able to come back to Udine. The Italian flag was already high up on the castle flagpole by the time I arrived – we were free. I watched the Allied column arriving from the Venezia Road. My father was with them. He went home quickly to my mother, and then he rushed to City Hall to witness the political developments. Officers from the newly reformed country of Yugoslavia wanted to rule Friuli – they had already succeeded in taking over the nearby towns of Trieste and Gorizia. But luckily an English officer said that he was the representative of the Allies, and that they were taking over. The leaders of both Osoppo and Garibaldi agreed that this should happen.

Gerard came to Udine to visit us before he went back to England, I went to Mr Willetts' home to be introduced to his wife and daughters, and Beckett sent me a thank you note. We have never forgotten our British friends, and at every event commemorating the war we have a wreath with British colours to remind us of the values of freedom and democracy.

Paola greeting Italian paratroopers in 1947

FRANCESCO GNECCHI-RUSCONE

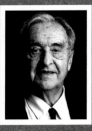

Before the war, Francesco Gnecchi-Ruscone was a schoolboy in northern Italy. But his life changed when Italy entered the war on the side of Germany in 1940. This story was first told in his book, When Being Italian Was Difficult.

I grew up in fascist Italy, but my family did not support that regime. This meant we were torn between our values and our loyalty to our country. As soon as Italy entered the war in 1940, we knew we were fighting on the wrong side.

In 1943, Italy signed an armistice with the Allies and the country was occupied by the Germans. My family got involved in the resistance. At first, we helped Allied prisoners of war who had managed to break out of concentration camps and were trying to reach neutral Switzerland, some 40 miles from our country house. We hid them and fed them during the day, and at night we guided them down country lanes to their next hiding place. My task was to cycle ahead to make sure the road was clear and then hand the prisoners of war over to the guide for the next leg of the journey.

After the armistice, the Germans set up a puppet government in Italy (a government that was supposedly independent but was actually controlled by the Germans) and tried to recruit young Italian men into the army. To avoid having to fight, I went into hiding for a period. After that, I formed a small resistance group with some university friends. We were all deserters, and we would have been shot without trial if we'd been caught. We soon became attached to the general headquarters of the resistance movement, which had just been set up, and we were provided with false papers which said we were excused from fighting in the army.

Our group's main task was organizing aerial drops of supplies to the newly formed partisan units. We were young and inexperienced and we were just learning as we went along. I usually had to set up and command roadblocks to defend the drop zone (the place where the supplies would be delivered). I was often in charge of older, more experienced men who trusted me. I worried that my inexperience might endanger their lives but I soon realized that if I showed any insecurity they would lose confidence in me and that might compromise the whole action. Luckily all the drops I was involved in went smoothly. It was tough, but doing this work helped me grow from a boy to a man.

In the summer of 1944, my resistance group became attached to an Italian intelligence unit called Missione Nemo which had landed in the occupied North of Italy. I was studying architecture, so I was supposed to be able to draw, and my new job was to survey a new defence line that the Germans had started to build at the foot of the Alps, from Lake Garda to the Adriatic Sea. Until then, my base had been my family home, just north of Milan; now these duties called me further afield. I wrote a loving letter to my parents, pinned it to my bed and pedalled off on my bike.

My first stop was Milan, where Missione Nemo supplied me with a set of false German papers, full of eagles, swastikas, seals and signatures. They were a masterpiece! I began cycling to hidden lookouts where I would draw and make notes about the defences that the Germans were building. I made my notes on maps which were delivered to me every week by a courier. The next week the courier would deliver new maps and collect the ones I'd drawn on. At night I sheltered in farms. My hosts never denied me a bed of straw, even though most of them must have suspected I was involved in partisan activity. Perhaps this is why they let me stay.

I soon learned that cattle barns were warm and haystacks were cold.

My false papers enabled me to mix with German soldiers and often I saved myself long hours of pedalling by catching lifts on German lorries; all I had to do was sing "Lili Marlene" with the boys. I pretended not to understand German, and their chatter sometimes supplied me with useful information about their units, their destination and so on. Once, however, I was with some German soldiers when we were attacked by three American planes. I lay flat as a leaf in a wet field, expecting to get stitched to it for good by American bullets, as the pilots dived at us again and again. Eventually they decided to go home for supper, leaving lorries burning, many Germans dead and many wounded and screaming. Luckily I was unhurt so I pedalled away, thinking it was hard to see friendly fire as friendly when you were at the wrong end of it.

One of my other jobs was gathering information about how the Germans were crossing the larger rivers. By then, the Allies had full control of the northern Italian skies, and all the main bridges had been bombed. To transport troops and supplies to the front, the Wehrmacht (the German armed forces) had to form nightly convoys and cross rivers using pontoon (floating) bridges that they set up at sunset and camouflaged along the riverbank during the day. I had to spot them and communicate their position so that the Allied air force could take them out. One morning on the bank of the River Po, I was looking for pontoon bridges when I was stopped by a German lieutenant. He was quickly satisfied by my false papers and he stopped for a chat. He asked what I had been doing before the war, and I told him I had been studying architecture. It turned out that he was an architecture student too, and that we were both in our first year. We chatted for a while about our courses and teachers. Then he told me he was in charge of a mobile bridge, and that he had just hidden it. "It's there," he said, "under those poplars." He was a nice unsuspecting lad. I knew that in a few days I would have him bombed and I felt like a traitor and a murderer.

All went well until January 1945: I had drawn around 100 kilometres of the defence lines, and I had passed on some useful information. But then I was arrested by the fascist police for the supposed theft of a ration card. Ironically the ration card was my only legitimate document – I had cut off the top, which showed my name and address, so that it wouldn't contradict my other forged papers! I was taken to the police station, but luckily I was left alone for a moment in a room on the first floor so I dropped out of the window, ran back to my bike and set off to my base in the city of Padua as the snow started to fall. The police had confiscated my papers and without them I could not pass the roadblocks around the city. The only way around it was to wait until dark and swim across the river with my bike. It was cold!

Then I made a mistake. I spent a day warming up and drying my clothes, and instead of waiting for the courier who brought me the maps to help me, I sought out a Frenchman from Alsace who was working in a German office. He had previously given me news on Wehrmacht transport, so I thought I could trust him. I asked him to pinch a blank Ausweis (pass) for me. He said he would, and we arranged to meet at a cinema the following evening. But as soon as I arrived, the Feldgendarmerie (military police) appeared from every direction. There was no easy getaway this time.

The next morning the Feldgendarmerie handed me over to the Sicherheitsdienst (SD), the military branch of the Gestapo. "They'll know how to make you talk," they told me. The SD took me to their headquarters, tied my hands and ankles and locked me into a small, dark cubicle. There wasn't enough room for me to stand or stretch, just to curl up, and I developed cramps in my shoulders and stomach. Luckily my mind remained sharp and incredibly clear, so I was able to prepare for the coming interrogation.

At last, I was collected and taken to an office. There was a calendar that told me I had been in my black hole for four days and four nights. A Sturmführer (SS lieutenant) was in charge of my interrogation, and there were two SS men with rubber-coated clubs and two more with a dynamo machine to give me electric shocks. For a whole day, I was questioned, hit, kicked, shocked and questioned again, on and on. The interrogation continued into the next morning but they never got any information out of me. Why did I not talk? Obviously I didn't want to let down the side or betray my friends but at the bottom of it was stubborn, bloody-minded pride: I, Francesco Gnecchi-Ruscone, was not going to give in to a Sturmführer and his thugs. After my interrogation I was told that I had been found guilty of distributing anti-German leaflets, a crime of which I was totally innocent. I was sentenced to death by hanging.

I was taken back to the basement, but this time I was put in a proper cell with a bed, blanket and bucket. I was kept there for three weeks, nursing a fractured knee, a broken nose and assorted bruises as best I could. I was fed once a day (though it barely counts as being fed) with a rotten potato boiled in saltless water. Then the Gestapo transferred me and some other prisoners to Padua's main prison, as they needed our cells to question new prisoners. That was a welcome change. We went from isolation to overcrowding: there were 52 of us in a cell meant for 14 people. At night we slept on the floor, which was covered with straw mattresses, often dampened by a flooding lavatory.

But then my luck changed: Missione Nemo intercepted a message from the Gestapo in Padua to their headquarters in Milan, delivering a transcript of my interrogation. Now my friends knew where I was – and they also knew that I had not spilled the beans and betrayed them. They got in touch with an SS colonel who agreed to transfer me to Milan and release me there, in return for money; with the looming prospect of a German defeat many SS officers, anxious to escape war crime trials, were taking bribes to gather cash.

After I was released, I had a short stay in hospital where I was patched up properly. Then I rejoined our original resistance group, which had swollen to around 70 men. We took part in the uprising that liberated Milan, some three days before the Allies got there. We had the pleasure of securing the surrender of a Kommandantur (military headquarters) with two generals, and of a couple of lesser units. When the first Allied jeep arrived at our quarters, carrying a Major Wilcox, we toasted him with a bottle of Campari liqueur that we found in what we pretentiously called our mess. We knew that the liberation would not have been possible without the Allied offensive across the Po valley, but we felt we could invite him as a guest – we too had fought for Italy's freedom rather than just waiting for the Allies to liberate our country.

Francesco, 1945

But the war was not over yet. Missione Nemo sent my friend Guido and me to a castle in Alto Adige in the very north of Italy, which was still occupied by the Germans, to retrieve some 40 crates of documents that had been taken from the Italian State Archives at the time of the armistice. We drove there, overtaking the advancing American troops and, eventually, the retreating German troops, and we reached our castle at dawn. We decided to bluff our way, claiming to be "Allied Intelligence officers", and, waving a dubious pass in front of their eyes, we demanded that they give us the stolen crates. There the commanding SS captain caught us off guard by saying he could only give us the crates after we had accepted the surrender of the soldiers who were stationed at the castle. That was flattering but embarrassing – the two of us did not want to get stuck guarding and feeding a whole company of SS until the Allies arrived. "Why don't you just go home?" we suggested, but they wanted to surrender to cosy American captivity and avoid being captured by the notoriously cruel Soviet Red Army advancing from Vienna. Luckily the first Allied unit soon appeared on the main road. God bless them, they were Italian Bersaglieri (an elite infantry corps) from Divisione Legnano, a division that had been fighting with the British Eighth Army since 1944. Oh boy – you cannot imagine what it meant to Guido and me to see 100 SS men put their weapons down at the feet not of Britons or Americans but of *our* Bersaglieri!

The war in Europe ended eight days later, but my war wasn't over quite yet. In the final few days of the war, the Yugoslav army had occupied the Italian city of Trieste, intending to incorporate it into Yugoslavia. In early June a New Zealand battalion of the British Eighth Army entered Trieste and liberated the city for Italy. As part of an agreement between the British and Italian Intelligence, I had been appointed liaison officer with the New Zealand battalion, so I spent the summer of 1945 monitoring that situation and witnessing the Iron Curtain being born.

That autumn, I was demobilized – I became a civilian again. I had just turned 21. I returned home to resume my architectural studies – but that is another story.

Francesco as liaison officer with the
New Zealand battalion that liberated Trieste

WOMEN AT WAR

Before the Second World War, very few women worked outside the home. Women could enter professions such as law, medicine or academia, but only a small minority did so – most working women had traditionally "female" jobs such as making or washing clothes, caring for children and acting as maids for the rich. When war broke out and men were called up to fight, there was a huge demand for women to fill the jobs they had left behind. Hitler didn't believe women should work outside the home, so most German women didn't work, but in Allied countries, particularly Britain, America and the Soviet Union, millions of women went to work in farms and factories. Many were also called up to work on the front line, as nurses, radio operators and auxiliaries (support staff) in the armed forces. Some women fought, too – because of the huge casualties suffered by the Soviet air force, by the end of the war almost one in ten Soviet pilots were women. Women had proved they were just as capable as men, and many were reluctant to return to their traditional roles after the war.

Princess Elizabeth changing the tyre of a vehicle as she trains as an Auxiliary Territorial Services officer at the ATS training centre in England, 18 April 1945

JEAN BARKER,
BARONESS TRUMPINGTON

Jean Barker, Baroness Trumpington, is a Conservative member of the House of Lords. She told Gemma Carolan about her experiences working in naval intelligence at Bletchley Park, the central site for Britain's codebreakers during the Second World War.

When the war broke out, my life changed very quickly: for one thing, I had no home, as my house was taken over by the army. As the Lloyd George family were great friends of my mother and grandmother, I was sent to their farm in Surrey. Surrey was very peaceful – a bit too peaceful when you're nearly seventeen. I was terribly lonely in a way, so eventually I left there and I went to London. I took a secretarial course, and that eventually saw me to Bletchley. From then on, that was my war.

When I arrived at Bletchley, there were approximately 400 people. When I left, though, there were around 6,000. It was very dirty and scruffy, nothing was pruned or looked after. It was a horrible place, but it was doing very important work. My job involved typing German submarine signals, which then had to be translated. That was where Alan Turing came in.

Turing's machine called Colossus interpreted the signals. Extraordinary! Turing was the grandfather of computers. His birthday, 23 June, is celebrated all over the world. It is very sad that what would now be perfectly OK – his homosexuality – wasn't then, and so he killed himself. I imagine he suffered a great deal.

There were about eight of us in the same room.

Baroness Trumpington during the war

We had terrible shift systems that changed every week, so you never got into a sleep pattern. You either worked 9 a.m. to 6 p.m., 4 p.m. to midnight, or midnight to 9 a.m. But we had a lot of fun because we were all friends. We used to go up to London and dance all night, and also get up to naughty things in the room. I mean, if you're typing away for eight hours you do get awfully bored. You start to lose sense of the importance of what you're doing because it's very monotonous. One of the things we did to keep ourselves happy was learn the "Horst-Wessel-Lied", which was the marching tune of Hitler's army. We used to sing this loudly and we got into great, great trouble. We were all separated from being on the same shift, and it took three weeks to get back together again.

One night I went to a thing called the Queen's Charlotte Ball, and from there a young man tried to take me to the Café de Paris (a London nightclub) – but it had been bombed. The entire band was killed, and everyone on the dance floor. It was a terrible, terrible thing. The Blitz was pretty damn scary.

None of us could talk about Bletchley. If chaps asked us anything, we told them that we were the girls who chose the medals that the boys should get. It was quite untrue of course, but we thought it was terribly funny. As you can imagine, we were very popular with the boys. We all knew each other terribly well, but we never spoke outside Bletchley and my parents never knew what I did, nobody did. I never told anybody and neither did the others. But once a year my friend Sally Astor used to give a lunch party in her flat and all eight of us who worked together used to go. We never stopped talking, because we could, at last. It was extraordinary. That was the only time we spoke about it; afterwards we went back to being silent again. Nowadays I still can't talk about it. It's funny, isn't it?

EVE BRANSON

Eve Branson was just fifteen when the war started, but she joined up as soon as she was old enough. She told Livvy and Poppy Le Butt about life as a WREN.

I was fifteen years old when the war started. I was too young to be too horrified and I thought it would all be over in a month. I remember there being nothing to eat, not much to wear and no petrol. We were denied so much. We grew our own vegetables. We were all on rations – no meat, no milk, and just one egg a week – so we were all very thin.

I wanted to do something for the war but I was too young – I couldn't join up till I was nineteen. But I wanted to help, so I dressed up as a boy so that I could have glider lessons and teach the younger boys to glide. This was good training for when they became pilots.

Eve in her WREN uniform

It was hard to join up as a woman, as there were fewer jobs for us to do. When I turned nineteen, I decided to become a WREN (Women's Royal Navy Service) because I rather liked their bell-bottom trousers and their saucy hats. I had no qualifications at all – I had always been hopeless at school, and I became a ballet dancer as soon as I left – but I found out where the WREN headquarters in London were, made friends with the doorkeeper and persuaded him to tell me when they were recruiting. I told white lies when they asked me if I could speak any other languages and whether I had nurses' training. I waited for a week, and then I got a letter saying that I could become a WREN. I was so excited. I was sent straight to a ship, HMS *Warrington* in Lancashire, where most of the training took place.

Eve with her fellow WRENs and a naval officer

We were taught how to signal Morse code to the ships using ten-inch lamps. I still remember the code – A is *dash, dash, dot.* I can't spell, so it was quite hard sometimes!

During the war, I fell in love with a naval officer. I was flashing to him on his boat, and I looked through my telescope and saw a very handsome man. He didn't understand my flashing, so I asked him to come to my pier in the middle of the night. I gave him cocoa and said that I liked his white jersey. The next day a parcel came, marked, "For the WREN who was on duty last night." It was the white jersey. I married that officer when the war was over.

I was so proud to be a WREN. I'm still friends with one of my fellow WRENs – we still see each other, and I'm godmother to her child.

Eve with her son, Richard Branson

MOLLY ROSE

Molly Rose flew for the Air Transport Auxiliary (ATA) during the war, delivering and collecting aircraft. She told her granddaughter Minna Rose about her experiences.

I started learning to fly before I went off to school in Paris, and when I came home in the Easter holiday in 1937 I gained my flying licence at the age of seventeen. I was invited to join ATA in 1942.

My colleagues were all from different backgrounds. Most were flying instructors, but one was a grandmother, another was a pilot who did tricks in the circus and another was a commercial pilot. We were doing "a man's job", and there was great trouble convincing the Air Ministry and the RAF that it was worth having girls doing the work. Initially the plan was that we would just fly important people around in non-military aircraft, but eventually we were allowed to fly every kind of aircraft, including bombers.

The biggest aircraft I flew was a Lockheed Hudson, which needed an engineer purely to operate the landing gear. The largest aircraft that I flew solo was a Vickers Wellington, which was usually crewed by six men. My favourite aircraft to fly was the Supermarine Spitfire Mark XI. This was a reconnaissance model (it was used for gathering information rather than fighting) so it had no weapons, which meant it was very fast and manoeuvrable.

My scariest moment was when the engine cut out in a Fairey Swordfish I was flying over the Wrekin, a famous hill in Shropshire.

Molly Rose, 1942

After I had switched everything off and on again, and pushed and pulled everything I could, I selected a suitable-looking field to crash-land in. Unfortunately, as it was on a hill, I ended up going through a hedge and turning the plane over, leaving me hanging upside down.

Meanwhile my husband was a tank commander in North Africa and Italy, and then was part of the D-Day landings at Arromanches in France. After that, he was captured by the Germans and taken to a prisoner of war camp, where he remained until VE day. Even though we were both rather different people when he returned, we still enjoyed 57 happy years together.

Molly Rose (front left), 1943

The war affected my life completely. There was a wonderful atmosphere – everyone knew that we had our backs to the wall and everyone was doing their very best for the country. But it's difficult to talk about how you felt, because so many of our friends were in the services and were killed. You could hardly enjoy what you were doing, but we were lucky enough to have jobs that were extremely interesting and involving. It was a tremendous relief when the war ended, and it was wonderful to get my husband home again.

GLADYS LAMBERT

Gladys Lambert joined the Women's Land Army at the age of twenty and worked in a market garden, growing fruit and vegetables.

I joined the Women's Land Army in 1940, the year that women were going to be conscripted. A lady in my village was in contact with the Land Army department of the war office, so she put me in touch with them, and they sent me a letter telling me to come to the office in Nottinghamshire for an interview. I was a shop girl at the time, so I had to wait for my half-day holiday. I cycled up there, and I told them that I was very fond of gardening and that I had my own little greenhouse. They said, "We'll write and let you know." I cycled home, wondering if I'd get the job.

About a week later, I got another letter, asking me to call at the Land Army office again. I waited for my next half-day holiday and I cycled back, full of hope. Low and behold, they accepted me. They said, "As a matter of fact, we have someone who's looking for a land-girl at the moment." His name was Mr Glazebrook.

I went to see Mr Glazebrook that very evening. He was a very quiet man – he didn't ask me a lot of questions – but he showed me around his garden. He took me into his big greenhouse, full of tomato plants, and he said, "I'd like you to weed this tomato bed, please." He wanted me to prove that I knew what I was doing.

Of course, I agreed to do it. I didn't have any gardening gloves, but he gave me an apron to kneel on. I went along the rows of plants, removing any dead leaves and any side shoots. It took me about an hour and a half. Mr Glazebrook didn't watch me, but he came back when I'd finished, and he said, "I can see you've done that job before." I said, "Well, I learned all my gardening skills from my family. My granddad was a gardener at Chatsworth for the Duke of Devonshire." I always put that bit in, because it helped! That was the end of the interview. I got the job, and Mr Glazebrook asked me to start that Monday. I said, "That suits me fine."

On my next half-day holiday, I went to the Land Army office. They gave me a great coat, a green jumper and a pair of shoes. I cycled home, singing all the way, with my great coat on. I was a land-girl!

Mr Glazebrook had a market garden – he was a florist. Because of the war, he cut down his flower growing and planted more vegetables, so I was planting Brussels sprouts and cabbages and onions, and picking rhubarb and apples. At Christmas time, when we couldn't do any gardening, we made holly wreaths. I worked there for two or three years.

I got married during the war. My husband was in the army. He was in the Royal Engineers and he went over to France nine days after D-Day. He was a parachutist, and when it was windy and raining outside, I thought, "How awful to be jumping out of planes in this weather." But he thought it was wonderful. My husband was wounded by a mortar bomb. He got a medal for valour from the queen, but when I asked to see the citation, he just tore it up. He didn't want it broadcast that he'd been a hero – he was a soldier and he was doing his job. As soon as he came home on wounded leave, I became pregnant, so I had to leave Mr Glazebrook's garden.

I much preferred being a land-girl to being a shop girl. The garden has always been my love. I live in a care home now, but I still garden – I've got tulips and crocuses and bluebells coming out, in big pots.

Gladys on her wedding day

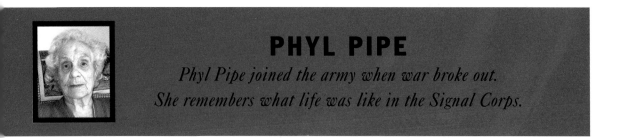
Before the war I was an accountant. When war broke out I joined
the army, and I ended up in the Pay Corps, which was all accounts,
because that's what came naturally to me. Then I passed the course
to get into the Signal Corps. I thought, "Oh good, let's get out of
here," because being in the Pay Corps was so boring. But I'd jumped
right out of the frying pan and into the fire.

Phyl (bottom right) in the Signal Corps, 1941

Phyl with her friends, 1942

We were sent to the Isle of Man, off the coast of Scotland, where we spent a year learning how to take down Morse code extremely quickly. Then we went on duty to a wireless station outside Harrogate in Yorkshire, at the edge of a moor. We'd be given the frequency of a German Morse code operator. He would be sending messages to his control, and we would cut in and intercept the messages, writing them down at his speed, which was quite fast – the German operators were very good.

It was very stressful. We had no social life whatsoever; we didn't see a single man. We just ate, slept, got on the convoy, went up the moors, got on the convoy and came back. We took over from each other every four hours. We had five hours off on the fifth day. That's when we washed. It went on like that for three years. At the end of the war, I thought about joining up for another ten years, but I didn't – I wanted a private life.

I didn't see my family once in all that time. We had ten days off in three years. We didn't know when it was Sunday, or Christmas, or anything. My mother told me that my father was upset with me because I didn't send him a birthday card. Well, I didn't know what day it was, and anyway, there was nowhere to buy one!

Phyl (right) on the Yorkshire Moors, September 1945

MARGARET NEAT

Margaret Neat joined the Auxiliary Territorial Service, known as the ATS, when she was just seventeen and a half years old – the youngest age you could join the forces. She told her granddaugter Millie Devereux about her experiences.

During the war, I was a radar operator on anti-aircraft gun sites at different places around Britain, part of a team that monitored the radar equipment for the British forces. We had to look into special screens to check the sky for incoming enemy aircraft. We recorded the position of the planes in the sky and this information went to the gunners so they could shoot in the right direction.

My first posting after my initial training in the ATS was to a gun site in London. It was my first experience of London air raids. All of the guns in the surrounding area would open fire and the noise was deafening. It was terrifying. Even today the noise of bombs and gunshots scares me.

Once I was staying at a gun site at Barking Park in East London when a V-1 flying bomb hit a local school. Our dormitories were destroyed, so we had to sleep in the gun pits operated by the Home Guard afterwards – there was nowhere else to go. Sleeping in a live gun pit might sound a bit frightening, but we didn't really think about it like that. We just thought it was fun.

I felt very special being a woman working for the forces. I knew I was valued; my job was secret and important – absolutely nobody could know what we were doing. The war gave women like me opportunities that we would not have had otherwise, and it was very exciting.

Margaret in her ATS uniform

MILDRED SCHUTZ

Mildred Schutz worked at the Special Operations Executive, a secret British organization that helped resistance movements in German-occupied countries to fight the Nazis.

At the start of the war, I did part-time nursing at evenings and weekends. When there were air raids, St Thomas's Hospital in London used to evacuate patients out to Chertsey in Surrey. I would go out there and help. We saw some horrible things – it was very distressing, particularly because we weren't very old ourselves. When you're seventeen and you're shoved into a hospital, you grow up very quickly. Once, after a bad air raid on the town where I lived, I went into the operating theatre and realized the girl being prepared for the operation was someone I knew very well. That was horrible. A bomb had dropped on her house and her parents were killed. I think it was a direct hit.

When I was nineteen, I was called up. They asked whether I wanted to do more nursing, work in a factory, or work for the "Inter-Services Research Bureau". That was a cover for the Special Operations Executive. I said, "I'd like to do that." I had three interviews in private houses, and then I went to Baker Street in London, which was the headquarters for SOE. There, they initiated you into what they were really doing. Everyone was really sworn to secrecy. That was impressed on us – when you started working there, you were on trial all the time. They kept an eye on what you did and who you spoke to and what you were like as a person. They tested you too. There were no names on any of the doors. They'd say, "Take this file to Colonel So-and-So, he's third door on the left." Next time they'd just say,

"Take this to Colonel So-and-So," and you'd have to remember where he was. A little group of us decided to go out for dinner one evening and we were horrified when we got back because they'd recorded our conversations.

After two months, they asked if I wanted to go in the field (behind enemy lines in a German-occupied country). I said yes, I would. They said, "You'll have to do parachute jumping," and I thought that would be lovely. I was very young and silly.

To go into the field, you had to qualify to be a FANY (a member of the First Aid Nursing Yeomanry). There were 200 of us who were given our initial training together. Then one day, another girl and I were called in and given our commission. We weren't allowed to go back and say goodbye to our friends – ten of us were just put in the back of a lorry. Our kit had all been packed, and we were sent to catch a train to London

The night we left, bombs dropped close to the train we were travelling on and the windows were all damaged. Bombs dropped near the farm where I lived, too, and I didn't know for weeks whether my family were OK or not. That was horrible.

In London, we were fitted out with our uniforms and then we were taken up to Liverpool and put on a troop ship. We sailed in a convoy for ten days. The German U-boats (submarines) managed to sink one ship on our convoy. If the ship was hit, you were supposed to put on a life jacket and hope you got onto a lifeboat, but there were hundreds and hundreds of men on the troop ship – I don't think many would have survived.

Eventually we got to Italy, but I had been seasick on the journey, and apparently when you use a parachute you swing back and forth, which makes you feel seasick too. Because of that, they

Mildred in the field, Florence, Italy, 1944

wouldn't let me train to use a parachute, but they said they'd find something useful for me to do. A couple of us were transferred to Monopoli, the headquarters of the SOE in Italy. Our job was organizing partisans – the Allies would take a town, and then the locals would say they were partisans and that they wanted weapons. But you couldn't just give weapons to anyone, in case they were on the side of the Germans – we had to check who they all were.

We knew there was a certain amount of danger. If you went out in the evening, you had to have a male escort, and we didn't go into the main town unless we were in a military vehicle. The biggest danger was from Germans who had deserted the army. They were living rough and they'd attack our kitchen to get food.

Our commanding officer wouldn't let us have weapons. He said, "A woman with a gun is more trouble than she's worth." The Yugoslav girls strutted around the town with guns on their belts – we didn't think it was fair.

On VE day, the town went absolutely mad. Another girl and I were going home in a jeep, and the people got us out of the jeep and put us on their shoulders and carried us around town. It was a relief to be going home – we knew the Germans had been sending flying bombs over to Britain, and we didn't have any information about whether our families were OK. A couple of girls knew their families had been bombed, and we were all worried.

As soon as the war ended, SOE abandoned us. We were told we'd be taken to Naples in Italy and shipped home. If the people you had worked for before the war were willing to give you a permanent job, you could leave and go back to that. Jobs were very scarce as so many people were coming back home. I was offered my job back, so I did that.

JOY HUNTER

Joy Hunter worked in the Offices of the War Cabinet during the war. She told her great-granddaughter Chloe Stevens what it was like to work with Prime Minister Winston Churchill.

During the Second World War, I was part of the secretarial team in the Cabinet War Rooms, which were underground in Whitehall, in central London. To begin with, working at the Offices of the War Cabinet was pretty difficult because I didn't know anyone and the others were all much older than me. I did have all the appropriate skills, though, because I had studied at a renowned secretarial college, so I soon became more confident.

Joy in the Girls' Training Corps, 1942

The War Rooms were the hub of decision making and planning and our work was immediate and urgent. We had to sign the Official Secrets Act. We received hourly reports from army, navy and air force all over the world, giving us the exact locations of bombs and the number of casualties after air raids. I typed many important documents including the orders for D-Day. We saw Winston Churchill often, usually dressed in his self-designed siren suit (a suit that you put on over your nightclothes in case of an air raid during the night). He was always very pleasant, occasionally inviting us to join him to watch a film late in the evening when we'd finished work. Even when we didn't see the Prime Minister we knew he was there because of the smell of his favourite cigars.

The entrance to the War Rooms was guarded by marines,

so we had to buzz to get in and out. We worked long hours and rules and timekeeping were very strict. We were allowed short breaks for meals and to go upstairs to the washrooms, but everything was timed, and if we were a minute or so late we were closely questioned. Every third day we started at 3 p.m. and worked through until 4 p.m. the next day, sleeping on wooden bunks in airless rooms. The air con in the War Rooms was very primitive and lots of people smoked. When working a late shift, I would sometimes eat my lunch sandwiches in nearby St James's Park with the V-1 bombs flying overhead. They were OK while you could hear them, but when the engine cut out you knew they were coming down and you had to dive for cover.

I was chosen to attend the Potsdam Conference in 1945, when Soviet leader Joseph Stalin, British Prime Minister Winston Churchill (replaced halfway through by the new Prime Minister, Clement Attlee) and US President Harry S. Truman met in Germany to negotiate terms for the end of the war. Just six of us were chosen to form the secretariat (administrative department) for the Potsdam Conference. It was very exciting. None of us had flown before, or even been abroad. Our days were a mixture of frantic work, hastily arranged dances put on by the soldiers each evening, trips in army vehicles to wherever the driver was going and receptions given by Service Chiefs of Staff. At one event I shook hands with Stalin and Truman as well as Churchill.

I felt a big sense of responsibility working in the War Rooms because many people depended on my work, but everything had to be checked so if we did make mistakes, they could be corrected. It was a long time ago now but I guess my job played a small part in helping to win the war.

Joy working in London during the war

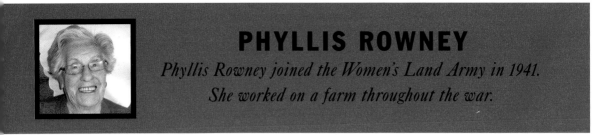
When I was first called up to the Women's Land Army, the government sent us to a Farm Institute in Staffordshire, England. We were there for a month and we were supposed to be fully trained when we left. I was trained to work on a dairy farm – I remember the farm manager coming with fake cows' udders, made of rubber. He filled them with warm water and told me to milk them! We were taught how to clean the cows out and look after the calves, too, and then we were sent to a farm in the Redditch area, in the Midlands.

I was a bit nervous of the cows when I first arrived on the farm, because of their horns, but in the end I could milk anything, any time. I did all the dairy work and the tractor work on the farm. I used to look after the calves when they were taken off their mothers. I had to get them used to drinking out of a bucket, so I would put my thumb in warm milk and get them to suck it. I had a wonderful time. I was even interviewed by a Sunday paper. They took a photo of me and the farmer, looking over the top of a half-door. I wasn't as tall as the farmer, so I had to stand on a bucket.

Being a land-girl was hard work, especially driving a tractor early in the morning. They didn't start on their own – you had to swing a handle to get them started, and it nearly broke your wrist. We had to get up at 7 a.m. and if we were harvesting we worked till midnight. I remember being so tired

The photo of Phyllis and the farmer
that appeared in the newspaper

that I woke up in the morning lying on the top of the bed with my boots and my britches (knee-length trousers) on! We didn't get much time off. I went home for a week every five weeks.

We had prisoners of war working on the farm. One of them was German, and he used to tell me the Luftwaffe would come and bomb me. The prisoners were brought to the farm by prison officers, and taken back at night – they came to cut the hedges and things like that. Once, there were two prisoners of war doing some work on the farm and I was on the tractor at the top of this hill. I was bursting to go to the loo, and I didn't know what to do. I thought, "They're so far away, they won't notice." So I went behind a bush. And then a loud voice came and said, "Now wash your hands!" Another time, when I was helping out on another farm, two prisoners of war had a fight, and one of them cut the top off the other one's head!

I had a boyfriend in the RAF who was serving in Rhodesia, Africa. He had sent me an engagement ring, but we didn't see each other for four years – and then he wrote me a letter to say he'd found someone else. So I stayed on the farm, and the cowman there said to me, "There's a young man I know at the local pub, and he'd like to take you out – he's been watching you." I said yes to the date, and I ended up marrying him. I didn't know him at all when we got married, but we were married about 56 years. After the war, we lived on a smallholding. I loved farming.

At the end of the war, I had to give all my gear back – even my gumboots. I remember going to a march in Worcester to celebrate the end of the war. My sister was in the Land Army in Staffordshire, and she came too. We were all dolled up and we had to march through the town. As we started marching, a brass band started playing the George Formby song "You'd Be Far Better Off In a Home".

MONICA MILLER

*Monica Miller told her great-grandsons
Jonathan and Jamie Brooks about life for a
woman in the army during the war.*

I joined the Territorial Army when I was 21. I'd been trained as a shorthand typist, so when the war broke out I did a lot of administrative work. I joined the army as a sergeant, and by the end of the war I was a major. We had to wear khaki shirts, skirts and ties, and a khaki jacket with brass buttons.

My job involved organizing things for my boss. He was fantastic. He expected hard work and he got it because we admired him so much. I worked very long hours – I got to work at 8 a.m., having walked an hour to get there, and I would leave at about 7 p.m. – but it was worth it. In those days, there weren't any emails or anything like that. All records were on paper. Somebody would bring me letters that my boss had to deal with, and I would put them in the correct file and refer him to any other letters in the file that would help him to answer it.

Sergeant Miller, 1938

During my two weeks leave a year, I used to go and stay with my mother in London. She was a voluntary nurse in a suburb outside the city. At the beginning of the war, I was at a camp outside London, and from where I was, I could see the flames of London burning. I knew my mother was there, and it was very frightening. It was easy for the German bombers to find their way to London because of the River Thames. You couldn't black that out.

After the war, Germany was divided into zones. The Russians

occupied Berlin and the East, and the French, the British and the Americans had a zone each. At one time, the Russians weren't getting what they wanted, so they put a big wall around Berlin and they closed the roads into Berlin so nobody could go in. They closed the railway stations too. The East German people relied a lot on the West for food and other essentials. The West supplied East Germany by air, so a lot more airfields had to be built. I was responsible for getting the stone from the quarries to make the airfields. One day when my boss was out, the phone rang. I answered it, and it was the general in charge of all of the British troops in Germany. He said, "I need to speak urgently to the officer responsible for supplying stone for the Royal Air Force airfields." I said, "That's me." He didn't think a woman could have that job. Then he started asking me questions, and it just so happened that the previous day I'd been to several quarries in person, so I could answer all of them.

Monica with her mother Winifred Tait, before the war

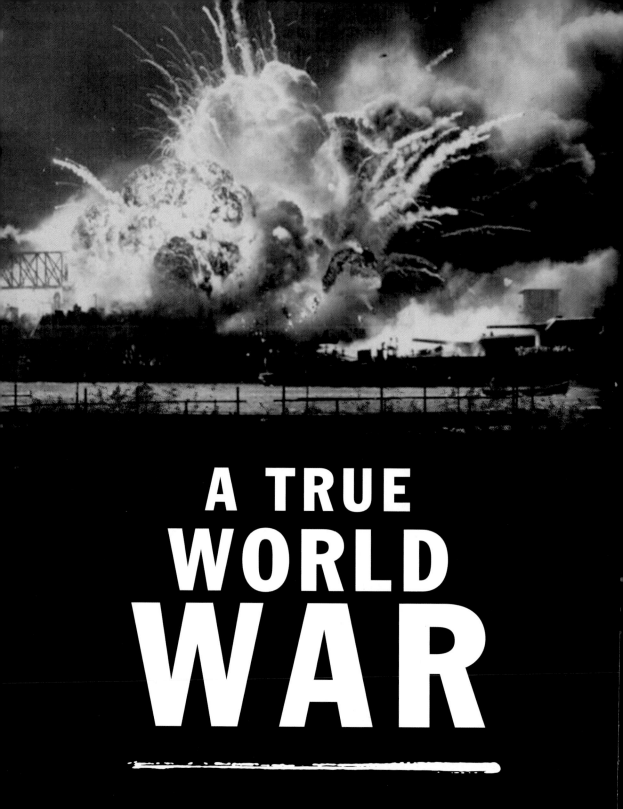

A TRUE
WORLD
WAR

What started as a European war soon spread. Many European countries had territories in Africa, and in September 1940 Italy attacked British forces in Egypt. Britain responded by attacking Italy's colonies: Ethiopia, Libya and Italian East Africa. Africans were forced to fight against their will for both sides, suffering huge losses. The British then fought the German Afrika Korps along the coast of North Africa, winning the first major Allied victory of the war in the battle of El Alamein, which began on 23 October 1942. Winston Churchill called this battle "the end of the beginning" of the war.

The Germans were fighting a fierce war on the Eastern Front too – three million German troops had invaded the Soviet Union on 22 June 1941, breaking the neutrality pact between Hitler and Stalin. Germany hoped to conquer the Soviet Union in four months, but the Russians fought on against the odds, finally defeating Germany four years later. 27 million people in the USSR lost their lives in the war – more than any other country.

The war in the Pacific also began in 1941, when Japan, who had entered the war on the side of Germany, launched a surprise attack on an American naval base at Pearl Harbour in Hawaii on 7 December. This changed the course of the war: America declared war on Japan and gave Britain, France and the Soviet Union a powerful new ally. Every continent on Earth was now caught up in the fighting.

USS Shaw *exploding during the Japanese raid on Pearl Harbour, 7 December 1941*

LEN BURRITT

Len Burritt joined the army aged eighteen in 1936 and became the first of the famous Desert Rats – members of the 7th Armoured Division who fought in North Africa and Italy during the Second World War.

I joined the Royal Corps of Signals at Catterick, North Yorkshire, in August 1936, and trained as a wireless operator. I was posted to Egypt at the end of 1937, and was stationed at the headquarters of the British troops in Egypt.

In September 1938, Germany invaded the Sudetenland, part of Czechoslovakia, and it seemed as though war was about to break out. Major General Percy Hobart was sent from England to Africa to form an armoured division, equipped with tanks and all-terrain vehicles (ATVs). At the time it was called the Mobile Desert Division, Egypt, but it became the 7th Armoured Division. I was in charge of the command centre, where I worked with the officer commanding the division.

One day in 1940, not long after the war in Egypt started, I was sitting outside my command vehicle in Egypt with Major General Sir Michael O'Moore Creagh. A boy came along to sell us eggs, and he had a jerboa (desert rat) in his pocket. The general asked me to gather some stones, and he arranged these in the sand in the shape of a desert rat. He wanted to call our division the Jerboa Division, and I suggested to him – you can't tell a commanding officer anything, you have to suggest – that we should be called the Desert Rats. The general's design was sent back to Cairo, and nurses stitched six badges and sent them back. The general gave me the first one and said, "You are now the first Desert Rat." That name has stuck for 75 years, and it's still going.

While we were in the desert, we worked and slept in lorries, tanks or ATVs. At the beginning of the war we just used Morse code, but then we developed radio telephony, which meant people could speak to each other through a microphone – a bit like an early mobile phone. The general sat next to me in the ATV, and if a message came through for him I would hand him his mic. We had a four-foot square battlefield map in our ATV too. As we advanced or retreated, new maps would appear, and we used chinagraph (wax) pencils to put in the names of each regiment and brigade and their positions. I knew, having spent four years doing the job, exactly what was happening on the board. Sometimes the brigade officers used to come in for briefings and before they saw the general they would come and ask me to put them in the picture.

I was personal wireless officer for the first five generals. In some battles the general had an armoured car. He would stand behind me, directing tank fire and artillery fire and so on. Bullets used to ricochet off the armoured car, and two of the generals were injured and had to be sent back to England.

I think my worst battle was at Sidi Rezegh in Libya, on 23 November 1941. It lasted for seven days, and being in the signals, we had to keep our wireless set open 24 hours a day. When the fighting had finished, the tank crews and gunners were able to relax a bit and eat a meal, but I was still on duty because I was the only wireless operator in that ATV. I only had forty winks in four days. The 7th Armoured Division was heavily defeated by the German Afrika Korps in that battle. We started out with 150 tanks, but by the time we withdrew there were only four left.

The longest battle we had was at El Alamein in Egypt, which began on 23 October 1942. When it started, about 1,000 big guns opened up – it looked as though night had been turned to day. The barrage kept up for about five hours, and eventually our troops moved forward, but we never got very far. The battle went on until 5 November, when we finally broke through. It was the first real victory for the Allies in the war.

After El Alamein, the Desert Rats pursued the enemy. We travelled almost 2,000 miles (3,200 kilometres) in about 180 days, from El Alamein through to the Libyan frontier and up to Tunis, the capital of Tunisia. When we'd driven the Germans out of Africa, we invaded Italy. Then, in December 1943, we were sent back to England. We spent Christmas at sea and when we landed we travelled to Norfolk and spent five months training for the D-Day landings.

By the time we got back to Britain, I hadn't seen my family for seven years – I'd grown up in the meantime. I was given a weekend's leave to see them. I got married while I was back in Britain, too. My wife Connie was in the Auxiliary Territorial Service. She was a predictor on the heavy ack-ack (anti-aircraft) guns guarding Glasgow docks – she told the guns where to fire so that they could shoot down enemy planes. I'd known her since she was fourteen, and we decided to get married before I left for D-Day. Our wedding day was 1 April 1944. I was in uniform, and my wife wore a dress made from a piece of material I'd bought in Italy. We had one night of honeymoon in the Ship Hotel in Grimsby. One week later the hotel was bombed, so that was a piece of luck.

Then, on D-Day, I sailed from Tilbury Docks in Essex to Juno Beach in Normandy, France, as part of the advance party. We set up a settlement so that when the tanks landed we could form up again into the 7th Armoured Division. After that we travelled on through France, Belgium and Holland to the German border, but then orders came that anyone who had served over five years without a break should go home. I was at over 100 battles in fifteen countries during my time at war.

I had to change my ways when I came home. I had been living on lorries for five years. When you're among men in action, a lot of swearing goes on, so I had to stop that.

For two generations, the war was never spoken about. The first generation lived through it, and the second generation didn't want to tell their children about it. It's only just now I'm being asked by my great-grandchildren about the war. You never talk about the gruesomeness of war. You skip all that – I try to, anyway. If I could give the younger generation a message, it would be that you gain nothing by war in the end. The way I see it as a 96 year old, Angela Merkel, the German Chancellor, has won the peace without a shot being fired – the European Union is very important in uniting our countries and keeping the peace. Today's war is very different, of course. In Afghanistan, where we used to lose 1,000 men a day, the British sometimes lost one a week. We didn't have the technology that they have today. Plastic hadn't been invented, so we didn't even have biros. The only technology we had was pencil and paper – and my wireless set.

Len in his uniform. You can see the Desert Rat badge on his shoulder.

When I first went to sea, I joined HMS *Trinidad*, a colony class cruiser, as a midshipman. I was the lowest of the low. The midshipman's main job was manning the air defence position, so I was in charge of the lookouts. We worked in shifts – four hours on and four hours off. The main excitement was a nice cup of cocoa.

Our first job was patrolling between the Faroe Islands and Iceland. The sea was very rough. We had a Supermarine Walrus seaplane on board, which we fired off by a catapult, and it flew around trying to spot submarines. It would land on the sea and we had a crane to hoist it back on board. After that we escorted convoys carrying aircraft and tanks from the United States to Russia. We picked them up in Iceland and delivered them to Murmansk, one of the only two ice-free ports in Russia.

In March 1942, we were attacked by German destroyers on the way to Murmansk. We torpedoed one destroyer, but we were then hit ourselves. Part of the torpedo which had hit us was found in the ship and we realized it was one of our own – our torpedo mechanism was faulty and the torpedo we had fired at the enemy had come back and hit us. Thirty-two men died. Subsequently, *Trinidad* was known as "the ship who torpedoed herself". We managed to reach Murmansk and we had to stay in the port for two months while our ship was repaired.

We left Murmansk again in May. It was now daylight all the time, so it was not surprising that on the way down, off the coast of Norway, we came under fire from German Junkers Ju 88 bombers. One bomb struck part of *Trinidad* that had been damaged in the torpedo attack and the ship burst into flame. Sixty-three men died. We couldn't put the fire out so it was decided that everyone on board would disembark on to our destroyers and that we would sink our own ship. My mother was a WREN working in the cipher office in Portsmouth at the time and she was actually deciphering the reports from *Trinidad* and the escort ships, so it was a very worrying time for her when we sank.

I then joined HMS *Bermuda*. We escorted convoys for Operation Torch, the Allied invasion of French North Africa.

In the lead up to D-Day I joined HMS *Volage*, a V class destroyer. We went to the Far East just as the Japanese war was ending and took part in an operation targeting a Japanese convoy near the Andaman Islands, which were occupied by the Japanese. Our ship was hit during the operation. We were not seriously damaged but one man was killed and a couple were wounded.

After that, we were sent down to South Africa for repairs. I was the navigator, so I had the fun of getting the ship all the way down to Durban. I spent two months ashore and we had a lovely time. One of the doctors in Durban was very keen on giving people chest x-rays, so I was x-rayed and they found a shadow on my lung – it was tuberculosis (TB). My father had died of TB after the First World War. I was sent to a demobilization camp – there was no treatment available for TB at that time, just rest.

When war ended I was sent home to the UK, and after two days in the naval hospital I was allowed to join the signal officers' school at Petersfield, Hampshire, to continue my naval career.

Early in 2014, all those involved in escorting the Russian convoys were presented with medals to thank us for what we had done during the war. Britain awarded us the Arctic Star and Russia awarded us the Ushakov medal. Better late than never!

DOUGLAS PHILLIPS

Douglas Phillips graduated from the New York State Merchant Marine Academy in 1937. His first US Navy assignment was aboard USS Castor *and he later reported to the USS* Ramsay *in Pearl Harbour on 6 December 1941, the day before the Japanese attack.*

I remember very well what I was doing on the morning of 7 December 1941. It was a beautiful sunny day, and my first aboard the USS *Ramsay*. I was the first to arrive at breakfast, and then I went up on deck to admire the scenery. I was pretty happy.

About three minutes later I saw planes coming over. At first I assumed they were American planes, but then it dawned on me that they were Japanese. They came very, very close to the *Ramsay* and then they lined up to torpedo the USS *Utah*, which was one of their designated targets. A spy had sent a map to Tokyo showing the location of the ships in Pearl Harbour, so they knew exactly where the carriers and battleships they wanted to take out were.

Douglas during his time in the navy

When the attack started, the officer of the deck sounded general quarters (battle stations). The captain came up on deck and said, "Who sounded general quarters? I'm the only one that gives the order to general quarters." The officer of the deck said, "Yes, sir. But those are Japanese planes. And sir, I have to go to my battle station."

The captain hadn't even realized there was an attack – there was a lot of confusion.

The planes managed to get several torpedoes into the *Utah*. We watched dumbfounded, just a short distance away, as the battleship rolled over, a matter of minutes after the first attack. As it rolled, the crew couldn't stand up, and men fell off the ship – they didn't have time to close the watertight doors. Sixty-four men died on the *Utah*. That was the start of the whole thing.

In the meantime, a Japanese midget submarine had managed to sneak into Pearl Harbour – several of them had been brought to the harbour entrance waters without the US realizing. The one that got inside Pearl Harbour came up near our anchorage, and the USS *Curtis* threw a smoke bomb to mark where they had last seen the submarine's periscope. I went up on the galley deck house where there were two four-inch guns. I had previously been a gun loader, so I knew a little bit about how they worked. The captain called from the bridge and said, "Is that gun loaded?" I thought he said, "Load it." I grabbed a shell out of the case – all our ammunition was at the ready – and loaded it. Then another man and I trained the gun around to where we would fire if we had to. Low and behold, right as we lined up our sights, we realized the navy hospital was in the background so we couldn't shoot – we couldn't be sure what we were shooting at.

After we'd fired extensively on the planes going for the *Utah* it was pretty quiet. Most of the planes we saw were too high for us to handle. Someone gave me a Browning Automatic Rifle but I didn't know how to work it. That was the problem with our guns – they weren't meant for shooting planes, they were for surface shooting. Shooting at a plane flying by with a machine-gun is kind of difficult. We were just standing by, saying, "Why don't they give us orders?"

We were ready to go.

The attack went on for a little over an hour and then they came with a second wave. The whole thing lasted two hours, which goes in a hurry when you're running around. It was all over by 10 a.m. and the Japanese were on their way back to their carrier groups to the north, but 2,403 Americans had been killed. We were the lucky ones. The other four ships in our division were in the navy yard for an overhaul and they lost men because all that area was bombed.

As the attack quietened down, the executive officer (the second in command) came down the deck and I saluted and said, "Sir, I'm a reserve officer. I volunteered for active duty a little over a year ago. I'm ready to go home now." I was being a wise guy, of course. He put his hand on my shoulder and said, "No, we'd like to have you stick around for a little bit."

Later, we went out on a couple of different missions. One was to steam back and forth with another ship towards the entrance to the harbour, to prevent the Japanese from torpedoing ships entering or leaving the harbour. After that, we went on patrols called "witch hunts": we had a basic sound detection system, a little like radar, and when something came up on the screen we assumed it was a submarine and let go with depth charges (anti-submarine explosives). We didn't come back to Pearl Harbour for three days.

When we did come back the following Wednesday, the devastation was all there for everybody to see. Some of the ships were still burning and the battleships had rolled over. Our flagship, the *Ogallala*, had sunk and she was lying on her side alongside another ship. We were horrified at the destruction. Everybody was very anxious. Not many of us went ashore. We operated in and around Pearl Harbour for several weeks, looking for Japanese submarines – we didn't know how many were loose in there.

The real aftermath story of Pearl Harbour was the salvage work. They did one heck of a job getting those ships together and pumped out. There were a lot of good divers, well-equipped and all ready to go. That is one of the best stories of the Second World War: the rapidity with which the US Navy got things back together. The Japanese really screwed up – there are two tank farms on the edge of Pearl Harbour and an ammunition depot, but they didn't bother attacking them. We'd have found it much harder to recover if they had.

WILLIAM M. BREED

William M. Breed served on the USS Canberra, *which fought in the Pacific War near Japan. The ship caught a torpedo from a Japanese plane and was towed 1,500 miles (2,400 kilometres) to safety and repairs. He told his granddaughter Islay Rose Van Dusen about life in the US Navy.*

In 1943, in my town of Newton, Massachusetts, USA, young men were being drafted into the army day after day. Every boy was assigned a number, and when that number was drawn at a town meeting, he was required to report for duty. As I watched my friends leave for war, I realized I wanted to choose which branch of service to join. There was no way of getting out of being drafted and there was no way of being drafted into the navy, so I decided to volunteer. I tried to sign up for the submarine corps. As part of the registration we walked through a submarine, and I banged my head on the door frame. At six foot two, I was too tall for the submarine corps. I was disappointed, but I could still sign up to the navy.

The navy turned out to be just the right place for me at the age of seventeen. I enjoyed being on the ocean and on the watch for danger, and the uniform suited me well. I joined the USS *Canberra* as one of two yeomen (administrative assistants) to the captain of the ship. We were expected to be available 24 hours a day. Once a month the whole crew was required to attend captain's inspection dressed in their proper seasonal uniform, pressed and spotless. Shoes had to be shined, and hats had to be at the perfect angle. The sailors lined up across the deck and the captain inspected them, pointing out flaws in some of the men's dress. I followed the captain, taking notes. When the captain stopped for a long time in front of a sailor, it was hard not to smirk from behind his back.

As a newbie, you had to go through an initiation (ritual) when crossing the equator to go from being a Pollywog (uninitiated) to a Shellback (one who had completed the humiliation). If you had never crossed the equator as a navy sailor, you were considered a Pollywog. As part of my initiation, I had to kiss King Neptune's toes. To get to King Neptune's toes, I had to wear my worst pair of dungarees and crawl across the deck bare-chested while being pelted with garbage from the galley. As rotten tomatoes and eggs broke on my back and mouth, I looked up to see King

William in his navy uniform

Neptune (a seasoned Shellback) sitting in a chair suspended over a pool of water. The Pollywogs in line before me kissed Neptune's toes and were dropped into the pool of water as Shellbacks. When I looked at the king's hairy toes, I regretted signing up to the navy. Such were the diversions from being alert for the enemy.

GEORGE BRESSLER

George Bressler told Noelle McDonald about his experiences as an officer in the US Navy during the Second World War.

During the Second World War, I acted as the aviation ordnance specialist on Bougainville Island, Papua New Guinea, in the South Pacific. My job involved looking after the weapons and ammunition carried on navy aircraft. I joined the navy straight from college, so it was the first time I had been away from home. I suddenly had a far greater level of responsibility than I had ever had before. It was deadly serious. I was an officer, and even though I'd only had one year of training, I had a crew of soldiers working for me. Being responsible for other people and their work was new to me. As the only aviation ordnance specialist in the unit, there was no one else to look to for help. If I said "Do this", it got done.

It's a bit ironic – although I was in the navy, I never actually served on a ship. My unit was

George in his navy uniform

land based, servicing land-based naval aircraft and marine fighter squadrons. We were moving towards Japan one island at a time, suffering heavy losses during each battle.

There were times when I was very scared. I recall having to run to the dugout (our shelter) during early-morning shelling on Bougainville. We had to stay in the dugout until we could get a plane in the air to bomb the caves on the side of the mountains, where the Japanese cannons were located. They shelled us just before daylight, because they knew we couldn't send up our planes at that time. But although experiences like that were incredibly scary, my greatest fear was that I would mess something up and lose the respect of my crew.

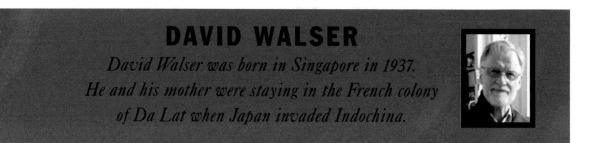

DAVID WALSER

*David Walser was born in Singapore in 1937.
He and his mother were staying in the French colony
of Da Lat when Japan invaded Indochina.*

In the summer of 1940, my mother, my amah (nurse) and I were staying in a French colony, Da Lat, up in the hills of Indochina; Singapore was a British colony and a major military base at the time, and servicemen would send their wives and children into the highlands to get out of the terrible heat. After the fall of France to Germany, the colony was controlled by the Vichy Government, and the French

David as a baby in Singapore

commandant was on the side of the Japanese. When the Japanese started advancing, we were forbidden to leave the town in the hills. Two other English women and their children decided to escape, and they asked my mother if she'd like to share a taxi to Saigon in southern Vietnam. My mother said no, as she thought it was too dangerous, but she managed to get train tickets for the three of us. When the train pulled into the station, it was so covered with people clinging to the outside of the engine that you couldn't see the train at all. It just looked like a mass of people.

By the time we reached Saigon, my mother was running out of money, we were all ill and we were all living on my Cow & Gate baby food – we had no other food. My mother managed to find a ship's captain who agreed to take her to Hong Kong, but a local came up to her and said, "If you get on that boat, you'll never be seen again." So we didn't get on. My mother went on walking the docks for another two weeks, and finally she saw a little white boat coming over the horizon. The captain was English, but he said, "I can't take you – I'm full." She begged and begged, and he said, "Come back tomorrow morning at eight o'clock." But my mother asked around and found out that the boat was leaving at midnight – he was trying to trick us. So we fetched our luggage and came back to the port, and boarded the ship while the ship's crew were all in the pubs. We hid on the boat, and at midnight the captain and crew came back to the ship, drunk, and set sail. The next morning we appeared from behind the funnel and the captain had no choice but to take us on to Hong Kong.

But when we got to Hong Kong, we discovered that my father had been sent back to Singapore. My mother finally secured passage for herself and me to Britain on a Dutch boat, leaving my amah behind. Saying goodbye to my amah and the distress that she was not coming with us is one of my earliest memories. She remained in Hong Kong and we never heard from her again. My parents and I sailed on the *Athlone Castle* from Singapore, arriving in Southampton, England on 24 June 1940.

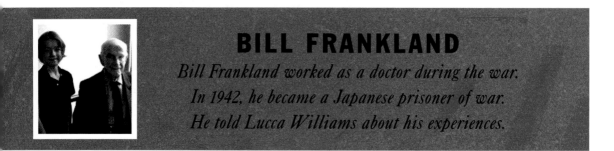

BILL FRANKLAND

Bill Frankland worked as a doctor during the war.
In 1942, he became a Japanese prisoner of war.
He told Lucca Williams about his experiences.

I qualified as a doctor in 1938 and I joined up as a civil medical practitioner three days before the Second World War started. After two years working in hospitals in England, I was sent abroad. We weren't told where we were going – we were just sent to Liverpool to get on a ship. We sailed to Singapore on a convoy, via Africa. The journey took exactly two months to the day. I arrived on 30 November 1941, seven days before Pearl Harbour.

The war didn't last very long there. I was in charge of a hospital, and during the fall of Singapore the hospital came under mortar fire. My colonel was killed. I went down to the far end of the island and I was officially taken prisoner on 15 February 1942.

I still worked as a doctor at the prisoner of war camp I was sent to. There were a lot of people dying of dysentery and diphtheria, so I was very busy. We had such small rations that all we could think about was food, food, food because we were so hungry all the time. The Japanese shot anyone who tried to escape. And where could you escape to? Singapore is an island and there are tigers in the jungle!

You soon learned what you had to do if you saw a Japanese soldier.

You had to bow; if you didn't, you got bashed. When our men misbehaved, we officers were all lined up and bashed by the Japanese. The idea was that we hadn't controlled our men properly. Once I was hit so hard that I didn't feel a thing – I was knocked out straight away. I don't remember this, but apparently I then started to stagger around with my fists up as if I was going to hit the officer who beat me. A Japanese private looked as if he was about to come at me with his bayonet. The Japanese officer stopped him, for some reason. That was a narrow escape. I later said that was the best bashing I ever received because I didn't feel a thing! I did lose a tooth, though.

Another time I was in the hospital when a Japanese private started bashing me around, saying he was going to kill me. He got a chair and tried to bash me around the head, but I put my arm up and he broke my arm instead. I went downstairs and by luck the Japanese doctor was there. I said, "Could you tell this man to stop it, please?" The doctor told him to stop, and that was that.

A week before the end of the war, we woke up to see a machine-gun post at each corner of the camp. We guessed what was going to happen to us – if the Americans had invaded Japan, every prisoner of war would have been shot. But then, on 6 and 9 August 1945, the Americans dropped atomic bombs on Japan, and that finished the war. The Japanese in Singapore decided to go on fighting, though. After five days, we took the great risk of complaining to a Japanese officer. You normally never complained to Japanese officers; they all had swords. We said, "The war is over and we want to be released." The next day, we were released.

It felt simply marvellous to be free. We had thought we were the forgotten army because

Bill during the war

everyone was so happy about the war being over in Europe. When we listened to the radio in the prison camp, most of the information was about Europe, not us.

But I was ill – I had dysentery and all sorts of things. I was flown to Rangoon, the largest city in Burma, and a lady from the Red Cross approached me to ask if I wanted sandwiches. We hadn't had bread for three and a half years. I ate and ate and ate! A doctor then examined me – I was only six stone, like a skeleton. He pressed my spleen and said I must have had a lot of malaria because it was so bloated. I said, "No, that's not due to malaria, that's a loaf of bread!" I was in hospital for three weeks before getting on a troop ship to go home.

We arrived in Liverpool, and we were sent to see a woman who asked us, "Do you want to see a psychiatrist or a doctor?" I said, "I don't want to see either, I want to see my wife!" I don't remember how many men were on those ships, but there were only two telephones and everyone wanted to use them. We heard about a nearby village where they would let you phone home for free. I walked the five miles and phoned my wife. That was marvellous. The next day, I went home. When I got back, I wouldn't talk about what had happened to me. I only admitted I'd been a prisoner of war about four years ago.

All of us doctors were promised that we could get jobs at our old teaching hospitals. We would need to learn medicine again – we knew nothing about modern medicine. I hadn't even heard of penicillin (a natural antibiotic) until a Red Cross lady told me it had been discovered at St Mary's Hospital in London. By 1950 I had worked closely with the man who had discovered it, Alexander Fleming, on the use of penicillin. He was a marvellous teacher and he was mad keen to find this antibacterial substance. He edited a book about penicillin which became every doctor's bible. I got to write the chapter on allergies. He said he wanted it written in a week, so I wrote it, and the following morning he said he had read my chapter and that he wouldn't change anything at all except the last sentence on the last page, which was: "With the increasing use of penicillin, it is to be expected that allergic reactions will become more common." He crossed that out in front of me. He wrote, "With the increasing purity of penicillin, reactions will become less common." I was later proved right, but you can't argue with someone who has won a Nobel Prize!

I've been so close to death so many times, but I've always missed it. I enjoy life and I'm still very busy. I am over a hundred years old, but I haven't retired. What would I do?

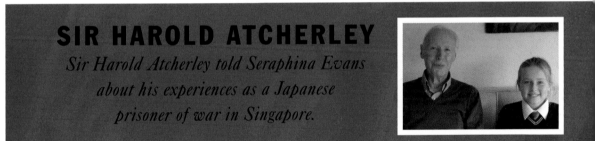

SIR HAROLD ATCHERLEY

Sir Harold Atcherley told Seraphina Evans about his experiences as a Japanese prisoner of war in Singapore.

When war broke out, I joined the Queen's Westminster Rifles as an infantryman (foot soldier) in the army. I was later asked to join the Intelligence Corps, and in June 1940 I was appointed Divisional Intelligence Officer of the 18th Infantry Division.

I went to fight in Singapore, but when Singapore fell to the Japanese in 1942 I became a prisoner of war. The Japanese wouldn't allow any information to get out of Singapore, so my parents simply heard that I was "missing, believed prisoner of war". It was about twenty months before I could send them a 25-word card.

I mentioned that a friend of mine had been killed in the Battle of Singapore, and my parents told that young man's parents – it was the first they had heard of his death.

I was held prisoner in a notorious camp called Changi. For the first few months things weren't too bad. Then we were sent to Thailand. They told us we were being sent to rest camps, where it would be easier to feed us. I think that was the last time we believed a word that the Japanese said to us. We travelled to Thailand by train. There were 600 of us in each train, and there was no space for anyone to lie down.

After four or five days we arrived at Ban Pong, about 50 miles (80 kilometres) from Bangkok, and my group of 7,000 started on a 200 mile (320 kilometre) march towards the Burma frontier to build a railway. When we finally arrived at the camp, we had to clear it of rotting bodies – before us, they had used civilian workers to build the railway, but they had died of cholera, an infection you catch from contaminated water.

Our days were a combination of starvation and overwork. We had to work twelve to eighteen hour days, and we were treated like slaves. For the first few weeks, the huts had no roofs on them. It was the middle of the monsoon season and we had to work, sleep and eat under constant rain. We never got enough to eat because the supplies came up by the River Kwai, which was frequently flooded. We were given a tiny amount of rice, which was usually sour and full of weevils, and when one of us was sick, they cut all of our rations as punishment. We just had to eat whatever vegetation we could find in the jungle. A group of us hunted for snakes – they were very difficult to catch, but we managed to eat a few.

I had malaria and dysentery – practically all of us had it, most of the time we were working there – but if you could stand up, you still had to go out to build the railway. One of the worst illnesses we got was beriberi, which was caused by malnutrition. Beriberi caused semi-paralysis, in my case only from the waist down. Our feet just flopped, so we couldn't walk, but we had to walk anyway, so we used lianas, which are long string-like things that grow on trees in the jungle, to hold our feet up – we wound a big bit around our big toes and attached the other end above our knees. Then we'd go out on parade. The conditions were absolutely appalling.

Out of the 1,700 people who were originally in the camp, only 400 of us were still alive when we finished the railway. That was in October 1943. By the end of the war, I was one of about 200 who were still alive, out of that 1,700. So I'm very lucky to be here.

While I was a prisoner of war, I kept a diary of my experiences. I literally wrote on anything I could find. My diary was eventually published when I was 95 years old. My son, Martin, encouraged me to publish it, because he felt that it was important for younger people to hear about history from somebody who was there.

Harold in November 1945, shortly after arriving home from the Far East

A British soldier with a Japanese sniper he captured near Pegu, Burma

IVOR ROBERT PHILLIPS

Ivor Robert Phillips joined the army aged nineteen.
His daughter Gill Harrison told her grandson,
Joseph Harrison, about his experiences.

I was conscripted into the army – I was made to join by the government. I was sent to Burma with the Welsh Fusiliers. I was a corporal under the command of General Slim and General Wingate, in charge of transporting food and equipment using donkeys.

As soon as we reached Burma, we went to the jungle to fight the Japanese, who were on the other side of the jungle. One of us had to be on patrol at all times in case we were attacked. The conditions were terrible – we couldn't wash, shave or change our clothes, and we had very few supplies. Because it was monsoon season, I suffered from trench foot, which is when your feet spend so much time submerged in water that they turn black. The only way to get rid of that horrid condition was to bathe my rotten foot in wee. When we walked through rivers, leeches would attach themselves to our skin, and we had to burn them off with cigarettes. As we moved further into the jungle, I began suffering from malaria and dysentery.

One night, when I was on patrol, the Japanese attacked. A lot of people died in the battle, but we won in the end. Because of that battle, all of our donkeys ran away, and because I was in charge of the donkeys, I was demoted to private.

I was awarded the Burma Star and the Yankee Star for my service, but all I really want is for the people who fought alongside me to be remembered.

Ivor in his uniform

From the beginning of the war, bombing raids helped Germany to win major victories in countries they hoped to conquer. Cities in Poland, France and the Netherlands were devastated and thousands died. At first, the Allies restricted bombing raids to military targets, oilfields and factories in the Ruhr Valley, an industrial area of Germany, but in 1942 the RAF and the US air force changed their policy: bombers would target whole cities to break the morale of civilians. This was known as "area bombing".

In early 1942, Sir Arthur "Bomber" Harris took control of Bomber Command, the organization that controlled the RAF bomber crews, and on the night of 30–31 May 1942 he launched the first "thousand-bomber raid" on Cologne in Germany. But Harris's tactics were controversial. In July 1943, a raid on Hamburg killed around 40,000 people. In February 1945, up to 25,000 people died in the bombing of Dresden. Many people in Allied countries were horrified at the death toll and Winston Churchill distanced himself from Bomber Command's tactics – even though he had authorised the raids. But the airmen of Bomber Command didn't choose their targets, and 55,573 bomber crew members also died during the war. They were refused a campaign medal at the end of the war, but the surviving members were finally awarded one in 2013, almost 70 years later.

An American B-17 bomber taking part in a raid on a Focke-Wulf plant in Marienburg, Germany, 9 October 1943

THE BOMBING OF GERMANY

HARRY IRONS

Harry Irons joined the RAF in 1940 when he was sixteen, and became a rear gunner. He survived 60 bombing raids. The average lifespan of a rear gunner was just four raids.

I joined up with five or six of my friends because we'd just watched the bombing of London. We were only kids. Little did we know what we were letting ourselves in for.

After six weeks' gunnery training, I was sent on a squadron. When I arrived, an experienced flight lieutenant said to me, "You're going to be my new rear gunner. But on the first trip, you go in the mid-upper turret so that you can see all the way around the plane and you know exactly what's going on." My first trip was in September 1942. I remember it vividly. The bomb aimer saw that we were carrying highly flammable incendiary bombs, and he said to me, "That means we're going to the Happy Valley." I thought, that doesn't sound too bad – I had a picture of German girls blowing me kisses. But that's what they called the Ruhr Valley. It was a terrible, terrible place.

Before you went on ops, the ritual was that everybody got bacon and egg. And the joke was, "If you don't come back, can I have your bacon and egg?" So we had our bacon and egg and went down to the crew room. The commanding officer came in and showed us where we were going: Düsseldorf, which was in the Ruhr Valley. There were about ten or twelve heavily industrialized towns where they produced most of the German weapons, and they were all located in that valley.

We got dressed in silk long johns (long underpants), a silk undershirt, then our uniform, then an electrically heated suit, leather furs – trousers, jacket and helmet – and four pairs of gloves: silk, chamois, thick leather and big gauntlets (strong gloves). The temperature in the mid-upper turret was about -50 degrees Celsius at night. We were all laughing and joking, calling out to each other, ready to go, but when we got to the crew room, no one spoke. I didn't know it then, but everyone was wondering who wasn't going to come back. Most of the crews, before they went on ops, used to write their last letter home, and every time you came back there were two or three crews with those letters left on the pillows. The next day there were all new beds, ready for a new crew.

That first night, we got out to the aircraft and piddled on the rear wheel for luck. Then we waited for take-off. When we got up to about 12,000 feet (4,000 metres), the bomb aimer said, "Dutch coast ahead, skipper. There's flak." This was light flak – small shells that only went up to about 9,000 feet (2,700 metres) and then dropped down. I looked out of the turret – the flak was every wonderful colour you can think of: greens, blues and reds. It was beautiful. Because we were at 12,000 feet, we were above the light flak. I looked down and thought, "If that's flak, we have nothing at all to worry about."

We passed over the Dutch coast, and about three quarters of an hour later the bomb aimer said, "Skipper, target ahead." I swung around to see what this target looked like and I had the fright of my life. In front of us was one huge, massive explosion of shells, and there were about 50 or 60 searchlights waving about. I thought, "Surely we're not going to go through that?" It looked impossible.

When you were flying towards a target you had to fly straight and level. That's because you had to take a photograph of the target to prove you'd hit it. Even if there were great big holes in the aircraft, if you didn't have a photo they'd say, "Sorry, it doesn't count towards your total." We had to do 30 successful bombing trips, which was near enough impossible, just to get our rest.

I saw a Lancaster bomber above us well alight; there was one underneath me alight; and there was another one exploding. I thought to myself, "Dear oh dear." I cannot describe the shelling that went on. We made our bombing run, took our picture, dropped our bombs, slammed our bomb bays shut and did a dive. As we straightened up, going across Holland, the navigator and the wireless operator and the gunner said to the skipper, "We can't breathe. We've got no oxygen." The shells had gone through the aircraft and had cut the oxygen pipes. So the skipper had to dive down below 10,000 feet (3,000 metres) to oxygen level again. As we crossed that Dutch coast where those beautiful lights were glowing, the light flak was whipping past us at an amazing rate. How we got through that I don't know. We got hit a couple of times, but we came back and landed. On the way back, I said to myself, "If that's Happy Valley, I don't want to go somewhere miserable."

When we got back, a briefing officer asked what had happened during the raid. I said I'd seen a few aircraft exploding and on fire, and he said, "No you didn't. You didn't see aircraft exploding. The Germans were firing up shells to mimic aircraft blowing up in the sky to demoralize you." But that was a load of rubbish.

I soon learned that if you saw a German fighter and he wasn't interfering with you, you had to let him go. If you started firing at him, you had no chance. We had four machine-guns with ordinary rifle bullets. The Germans had 20 mm cannons and they used to open fire at a distance of about 400 yards (366 metres). You just had to sit there and watch – there was nothing you could do – your machine-gun used to drop from gravity after about 200 yards (180 metres).

We were losing a lot of aircraft, so two fellows came down from Cambridge and said, "We've got a new device we'll put on the rear turret – a radar. When a German aircraft approaches you from a distance, a red light will come on to tell you there's a fighter near by." We thought it was a great idea.

In October we went over to bomb the city of Munich – Hitler was giving a talk there that night so we thought we'd give him a welcome. All the way over we flew above the clouds so we couldn't be seen, and we dropped our load. On the way back the cloud broke and there, just a few feet behind me, was a JU88 night fighter. We were so close, I could see the crew. He opened fire, but because he was so close to us, his shell flew right over the aircraft. Me and the mid-upper gunner immediately opened fire and shot him down.

Harry (far left) with the rest of his crew
outside their Lancaster bomber

We were very, very lucky. When we told the intelligence officers what had happened, they took the radar out of the turret because they realized the Germans had tuned into our wavelength and followed us all the way through the clouds.

We were veterans by this time – we'd done about ten trips. The men I knew when I first arrived were gradually disappearing. Then one day in October 1942, they said, "There will be another daylight raid on Saturday, to Milan." We were very apprehensive – daylight raids were practically suicide. It was a beautiful day, and as we approached Milan, all the people were out in the streets at restaurants – you could see it as plain as anything, because we were only 200 feet off the ground. We bombed an aircraft factory just outside Milan, but most of the other Lancasters bombed Milan itself. There was a railway station there – there must have been many, many casualties. I think they wanted us to fly in daylight to minimize casualties, because we were more accurate during the day, but just think of all those Lancasters going into a town without warning. It frightened the life out of the Italians, and after that they didn't want to know about the war any more.

Soon afterwards the Germans came up with a really simple solution to air war: they placed two cannons pointing upwards, and they aimed at the belly of the planes, where the petrol tanks were. We used to see bombers blowing up all over the sky. The worst casualties were at Nuremberg. It was bright moonlight, and the Germans had a field day – there were more boys lost on that one raid than in the whole of the Battle of Britain. In 1943 the average lifespan of a bomber crew was four trips. But I survived. I don't know why.

I bombed Dresden. For me, it was no different from bombing any other German town – it's just that everything clicked that night.

We were told to bomb an oil refinery just outside Dresden. The Lancasters went in unopposed, no flak, no searchlights, and dropped their bombs. But the air ministry must have known that the town was made of wood, because most of the bomb load was incendiaries. After we had bombed the oil refinery, we flew back over Dresden and it was well alight. We got all the flak – three or four of our boys were shot down approaching the oil refinery. But we were successful. We pulled the fighters away and allowed the main force to go in. To me, Hamburg was worse. The Germans lost 45,000 people in Hamburg. But we didn't know that would happen. And I tell you what else – every one of the men in the bomber crews knew they would almost certainly get killed, and yet they still went. Bomber crews suffered a lot, too – a lot of them parachuted out and got murdered by civilians. A few of them ended up in Auschwitz-Birkenau. Sometimes their parachutes never opened.

The aerial bombing of Germany had been Churchill's idea, but after the war he just didn't want to know. He wanted to distance himself from what had happened at Dresden.

After Dresden, I had six or seven more trips until I finished my second tour. After you'd done two tours, they wouldn't let you fly any more. One day they said to me, "You've done enough." It was a terrific relief. I'll never forget the war. I've stayed in touch with all the men I met. They are all gentlemen.

GEORGE "JOHNNY" JOHNSON

George Johnson was a bomb aimer in the RAF.
He told his great-granddaughter Ellen Gregory
what it was like to take part in the
Dambusters Raid on 16 May 1943.

In 1943 I was asked to join the elite Squadron X, later known as Squadron 617. Squadron X trained for six weeks for a secret mission. It wasn't until the night of 15 May 1943 that we were told what we were going to do the next day. Our mission was to destroy three dams – the Sorpe, the Eder and the Möhne dams – to choke off the water supply to the Ruhr Valley. We would use a new sort of bomb, the Bouncing Bomb, which skimmed over the water's surface. In order for this bomb to hit its target, we would need to drop it from a much lower height than usual.

I set off that night with 132 of my comrades to destroy the dams. As the bomb aimer, I had to lie face down in the bottom of a plane, with only a glass bubble protecting me from the explosions lighting up the sky. We only had one chance to get it right, but I had complete trust that my pilot and crew would bring me home.

I was in one of the crews sent to breach the Sorpe dam. I put a crack in it, but it would have taken five or six direct hits to bust the dam completely and the other crews didn't make it to the Sorpe. Sadly, 53 men died in the raid. The German guns may well have also shot me down too, but a fault with our plane delayed us in setting out. Lady Luck was flying with us that night.

The other two dams were destroyed that night. We had sent Hitler a message: "You think you're powerful, but we are too, and we won't let you destroy our country."

KEN "PADDY" FRENCH

When war broke out, Ken French volunteered for the RAF. He flew many successful missions as a fighter pilot.

When I joined the RAF, I knew I'd have trouble getting through the medical examination – I had a damaged knee that should have ruled me out of service. I couldn't hide it – the scar from the operation was clearly visible. The senior doctor asked me to sit on a chair and bend both knees as far back as I could. I didn't bend the good one as far as it would go, but I forced the bad one to its limits, more or less lining them up. I find it hard to believe he was fooled, but he accepted me as A1 – fit for service – even though my knee couldn't have survived a parachute jump. It was mad, really.

I was sent to Canada to learn to fly. After completing our training we returned to England, sailing on the *Queen Elizabeth* – the biggest ship in the world at that time. There were 20,000 of us on board, mostly American troops. As we sailed out to sea down the Hudson River in New York, there were two American warships waiting to escort us in case German U-boats tried to sink us, but the *Queen Elizabeth* was so fast that they couldn't keep up with us! One of the things I remember about that journey was the singing on board. The hit tune of the day was "You Are My Sunshine". Someone would start singing it and then the whole ship would join in. It was incredible. If the U-boats had heard us they'd have thought, "These people are mad!"

Once we got back to the UK, we were trained

Ken as a new recruit in 1941

to fly Spitfires. Before flying, we carried out certain checks in the cockpit to make sure our instruments were working properly. One of the checks involved revving your engine, and with a Spitfire the tail tended to lift when you did this, so one of the ground crew would sit on the tail to hold it down. One day a WAAF (a member of the Women's Auxiliary Air Force) was sitting on the tail of a Spitfire, but when the pilot gave the signal that he was about to take off, she stayed on the tail. The pilot didn't realize, so he took off with her sitting there! The controller didn't want to tell the pilot in case he panicked, so he made an excuse and asked him to return, which he did, after completing a full circuit of the airfield at a height of 500–1000 feet (150–300 metres). The poor girl must have been terrified. When the plane landed, she just jumped off and ran away.

Every time I had a medical, they said, "Does your knee hurt?" And I said, "No, I'm fine." But I had a few narrow escapes because of it. One day, we were training for formation flying, and the silly clot behind me came up too close and clipped my tail. If he'd knocked the tail off, I'd have been finished. I reported back to base, and they told me I should bail out, but I couldn't, because of my knee, so I decided I'd just have to land the plane. When I got over the airfield I saw the ambulance and fire engine revving their engines, which wasn't encouraging. When I landed, half the tail fell off. The other pilot had come literally within inches of cutting my control wires.

Shortly after that, I joined 66 Squadron, and I stayed with them right up till the end of the war. The squadron was made up of many different nationalities. It was 1943, and we were escorting our bombers over enemy territory. I never shot anything down, but that didn't matter: on a squadron, there were probably only three or four pilots who ever did. We used to operate in pairs, the idea being that one would defend and the other would attack, because when you were lining up to fire you had to concentrate 100 per cent, and it helped to have someone at your back to look out for you. But in the heat of battle, you often found yourself on your own.

Ken (second from right) with other members of 66 Squadron

I was stationed at various places on the south coast of England. I got used to the job escorting the bombers to and from their targets, but when the Germans brought in their Focke-Wulf 190, a much faster plane than the Spitfire, we started losing pilots. That was an unhappy time.

Then we moved to Cornwall and started escorting bombers to Brest, France, to destroy the submarines that sailed out to attack our ships in the Atlantic. The submarine pens were so deep that they could survive a direct hit, so the bombers would try to smash up the gates going into it and hold them up that way. While we were there, the man I shared a room with got shot down. He was peppered with shrapnel but he survived. He's still alive, and to this day his body is still full of shrapnel. He has adapted to it but he has difficulties with X-rays and he sets off the security at airports.

Then we were sent to Hornchurch where we were given faster planes – the Spitfire Mark IX. We feared nothing in them, not even the Focke-Wulf 190s.

On 4 March 1944, we were sent out as cover for a large force of American Flying Fortresses and Liberators returning from a raid on Berlin. The weather was extremely bad but we managed to fly above the clouds, at over 30,000 feet (9,000 metres). The temperature was about -58 degrees Celsius at 20,000 feet (6,000 metres) – heaven only knows how cold it was up where we were. The only heat we had was generated by our engines. My hands went dead, and I lost all feeling in my feet. I had frost on my eyelids and my windscreen and hood were frosting up, so it was difficult to see out. At one point I blacked out, probably from lack of oxygen combined with the extreme cold. I fell some distance before coming round, but I was able to get the plane under control again. I increased my oxygen and climbed up to rejoin my friends. I don't think they had even missed me! The danger with lack of oxygen is that you get no warning. You think you're functioning normally right up to the point when you black out. When we came back in to land, my hands and feet came back to life, which was very painful, and unfortunately the cold had got to my knee. We all got back to base safely but all in all it was a very unpleasant trip.

Enjoying a cup of tea after a mission, 1943

In the middle of another raid over a German-controlled airfield in France, my engine stopped. I thought I'd been hit by flak, as we were under heavy fire from the ground. Thankfully I got the engine going again, but it was terribly rough, so I called on my radio to say I was in trouble and waggled my wings to identify myself. Once I'd called out, there were voices from all over the place, calling, "Where are you?" They all wanted to come to help. It was like that – we were all friends. One lone Spitfire pilot, an American in the RAF, stayed with me all the way back to our base in France. Sadly he was killed later in the war.

When I landed, the engineers said, "Something's broken in the engine. We can't do anything to fix it here – can you fly it back to England?" They patched it up and said it would be OK, but I wasn't very happy as I'd have to fly a long way over water to get back to my base. When the rest of the lads came back, four of us were told to stand by for a special job. While we were waiting we went down to the village, and an army car with an escort of motorcycles drove past us. The person in the car waved to us – it was Bernard Montgomery, the most famous British general! When we got back, we discovered that Montgomery had just been to meet General Eisenhower, an American general and Commander in Chief of the Allied Forces who later became US President. Our job was to escort Eisenhower to England. We had a little chat with him, but I can't remember what he said – I was too worried about my engine!

On 23 March 1944 we set out on a trip I will always remember, escorting bombers attacking the railway junction of Criel, north of Paris. Over France the sky was clear with just a little morning mist on the ground. Suddenly, sticking out of the mist, we saw the Eiffel Tower. It was a remarkable sight, and quite out of keeping with the bombs raining down on Criel a few minutes later.

Ken, ready for take-off, 1943

At the end of April 1944, the RAF changed our lives by turning us into dive-bombers. I don't think many people realize that the Spitfires were dive-bombing as well. We flew over a target at 10,000 feet (3,000 metres), and when we saw it behind our wing we turned on our backs and went into a steep dive. At 2,000 feet (600 metres) we pulled out of the dive, counted three seconds, released the bomb and pulled back hard on the stick to climb away from any ground fire. You can imagine that if there was a lot of flak, three seconds was very quick – one, two, three! At this point I would always black out because of the g-force (the acceleration due to gravity that produces weight that pushes down on you), but the plane would keep climbing and I'd come round. We later developed a much more effective technique. We would come right down to ground level and fly the plane directly at the target. At the last minute we'd release the bomb, and lift the plane over the top. That way you couldn't really miss, but flying that low was very dangerous.

Later on when we were stationed in the Netherlands, members of the Dutch resistance would come across the River Rhine at night and give us targets to attack. One target was a house in the middle of Amsterdam, which was the Gestapo headquarters. In that house were the details of thousands of Dutch people who were to be rounded up and sent to concentration camps. We sent four aircraft to complete the mission at lunchtime on a Sunday when we hoped there would be fewer people in the streets. The pilots destroyed the building and all of the records, saving many lives. They all got away, and only one person on the street was injured.

Hamburg after an Allied bombing raid, 1943

ANGUS GALLOWAY

*Angus Galloway joined RAF Bomber
Command in 1943. He told his great-nephew
Sacha La Mouche about his experiences.*

I joined RAF Bomber Command in 1943 and flew in one of the famous Lancaster bombers. After our training, we organized ourselves into seven-man crews. Raids in the Lancasters were very intense and could last up to ten hours, so it was important that we were allowed to choose who we wanted to team up with.

Each crew had a pilot, a flight engineer, a navigator, a wireless operator, two gunners and a bomb aimer. I was a bomb aimer and it was my job to line up the bombs so that they would hit their targets, and to help the pilot steer left or right. When the aircraft was above the target I would press a button to release the bomb load. I also doubled as front gunner at times.

Angus during aircrew training

Space in the plane was very limited and the cramped conditions were not at all comfortable. When I was operating the front gun turret I would sit down, but when I was directing the pilot to the target, before we released the bomb load, I would lie down. The poor rear gunner had it even worse than I did. He sat right in the tail of the aircraft – the rear gunner was known as the "tail end Charlie" – and he wouldn't see any other crew members until the aircraft returned to base.

Towards the end of the war we carried out strategic raids on German towns. During these raids, all the bomber planes flew very close together in tight formation. In August 1944, I took part in a daylight raid over the north of Paris. We were flying in one of these tight formations and unfortunately a fellow RAF plane dropped its load onto my plane. Two of our crew were sadly unable to evacuate the aircraft, but I managed to bail out by parachute over Normandy and I was immediately picked up by the Germans and taken prisoner.

I spent six months as a prisoner in the Stalag Luft 7 prisoner-of-war camp in Bankau (now Bąków, Poland). But at the beginning of 1945, the Germans realized the Soviet army was approaching. They made us leave the camp and forced us to march across Germany, so that we wouldn't be liberated by the Russians. One and a half thousand of us set off on the march on 19 January 1945. The walk was hell. We received hardly any food and there was virtually no medical support. Despite it being in the middle of winter and biting cold, we were barely given any clothes or blankets to keep warm. The forced march was so horrendous that it was pure joy when we finally reached our destination on 8 February. We were to continue our imprisonment at Stalag Luft III, another prisoner-of-war camp, south of Berlin. Hundreds of prisoners died on the march. It was a miracle that I survived.

Three years ago the National Lottery gave lottery funds to war veterans to go on a trip down memory lane and return to their Lancaster training camps. I was fortunate enough to be able to fly back to Canada to revisit my old training centres. It was especially emotional for me to visit the Canadian Warplane Heritage Museum and to be back in a Lancaster.

THE FIGHT FOR FRANCE

In June 1944, the Allies were finally ready to invade France and liberate Western Europe from the Nazis in a plan code-named Operation Overlord. The Germans knew the invasion would take place, and they had built a huge line of concrete defences known as the Atlantic Wall along the coast of continental Europe, from Norway to Spain. The Allies fooled the Germans into thinking they would invade at Calais (a port city on the north coast of France) by building fake airfields and landing craft in Kent, just across the English Channel. But American General Dwight D. Eisenhower, who was in charge of the invasion, decided to attack Normandy, further up the coast, which wasn't as well defended.

The invasion began on 6 June 1944, which is known as D-Day. By nightfall, 150,000 British, American and Canadian troops had landed on the beaches of Normandy, taking the Germans by surprise. Hitler still believed the main invasion would happen at Calais, so he held back troops, and by the end of June 850,000 Allied troops had entered France. They pushed on through France to Belgium and the Netherlands and ultimately to Germany, liberating towns and cities as they went. From D-Day onwards, the question was when, not if, the Allies would win the war, but the fighting was not over yet. It would be almost a year before Victory in Europe day.

Allied troops landing on the beaches of Normandy, France, 6 June 1944

HAROLD CHECKETTS

Harold Checketts served as a naval meteorologist during the Second World War, and indirectly helped to decide when D-Day should take place. He told Carys Yates about his experiences.

When I first joined up, I was an able seaman in the navy. I went to Singapore on HMS *Prince of Wales*, but on 10 December 1941, the ship came under attack from Japanese aircraft and it sank.

We lost 327 men, but luckily I was rescued just before the ship went under. They managed to sink another ship, too, HMS *Repulse*. The *Repulse* capsized quickly, and 508 men were drowned. A lot of my friends lost their lives. I'd only got to know them a year earlier, and then they disappeared. That was dreadful.

When I came back to the UK, I trained as a meteorologist (a scientist who studies the weather). My interest in meteorology began when I was a little boy; I grew up on a

Harold in his navy uniform

farm, and we needed to know the weather for the next 24 hours to plan the day ahead. When we received a newspaper, the first thing I always looked at was the weather forecast.

As a naval meteorologist, I worked on HMS *Colossus*. My duties included recording the sea depth and keeping a record of the weather, cloud heights and wind directions so that we could tell the planes the best times to take off and land. This was a vital job during the war. If the wind shifted, it might mean the ship had to move out of the way to avoid a storm or a typhoon.

In Spring 1944, I reported to Southwick House in Portsmouth on the south coast of England. This is where I helped plot the weather charts for the D-Day invasion. The final decision was made by our senior officers, Commander Fleming and Captain Stagg, who were continually reporting to General Eisenhower, Admiral Ramsay and Air Chief Marshal Sir Trafford Leigh-Mallory. Both the admiral and the air chief marshal were killed in action in 1944. I worked alongside another meteorologist, Jean Farren. We got on so well that we got married as soon as the war was over.

We knew how crucial D-Day would be for the rest of the war, and we indirectly helped to decide when the invasion should take place. People would ask us questions about the plans for D-Day in the pub, but we didn't tell them anything, because we had to keep the details a secret and betraying the country at the last minute would have been terrible.

The original plan was to invade at the end of May, but the weather wasn't good enough. On 5 June, the weather settled down sufficiently for us to say, "Tomorrow is the time to go. It won't get any better. In fact, it'll get stormier." That very evening, the planes started going over. They were so loud, you couldn't hear yourself speak!

When we went to war, all the youth of Britain were involved – the ladies as well as the men. Nowadays, you could wage a world war with a very limited number of people, but I hope that won't happen, because of the power of nuclear bombs. Just one bomb could wipe out a city. That's what happened when the Americans bombed Hiroshima and Nagasaki in Japan, and I think that, in some ways, was unforgivable.

Harold's wife Jean

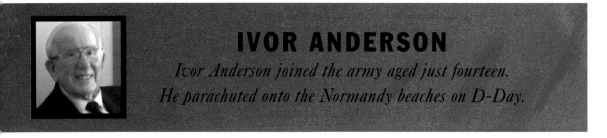
I left school in 1938 when I was fourteen, as you did in those days, and went straight into the army as a boy apprentice in the Royal Engineers. You couldn't do that today. Without my parents' permission, I signed on for four years in boys' service, eight years in men's service and four years in the reserve. Once you had signed this little note, you couldn't get out. At fourteen, I had signed on for sixteen years, but I was invalided out of the army before the war finished, in February 1945.

I lived in Bristol, in the south-west of England, and I had never left the city in my life, except for a day in the seaside resort of Weston-super-Mare. There was another lad who had just joined

up, from the big orphanage in Bristol, and the pair of us were given a railway warrant to get to Gillingham in Kent. We had to travel through London, and I remember playing up and down the escalators on the tube.

In 1943, after my apprenticeship, I joined a Royal Engineer squadron in Suffolk. During our training, we had to practise for the invasion of France by driving these old Churchill tanks up a beach. Once the tank was on the beach I had to get out, run up the beach with an explosive charge under my arm, place it

Ivor, aged eighteen, spring 1943

against a concrete post, put a detonator in it and run back to the tank to blow it up. I thought, "Blimey, I don't like this one bit!" I volunteered to do all sorts of different things instead, and at last an order came around for parachute volunteers, so I thought, "This is my way out!" I joined 591 Parachute Squadron, Royal Engineers.

We trained in Manchester, getting ready for the invasion in 1944. I was nineteen, and we were all young and full of bravado. I was never scared of jumping – during training, I could stand in the door of the Dakota plane and enjoy the scenery, and when the red light went off, out I went.

We were kept in secret compounds for the two weeks leading up to D-Day. We were all excited to go – it was a marvellous feeling! On 4 June, we were transferred to an airbase in Gloucestershire and allocated to planes. Then D-Day was postponed till 6 June. We hung around the airfield all night, sleeping in the open.

Ivor (second from right) entering a Stirling Bomber, 5 June 1944

The next night, 5 June, I took off in a Stirling bomber. There were 21 paratroopers in that plane. We were all singing and happy – we thought we were heroes. We flew low and straight to the French coast, and then, goodness gracious me, all hell broke out – attack fire, machine-gun fire. We had to fly low because we had to jump out of the plane at low altitude, and the plane was shaken about terribly. Inside the aircraft, we were in a complete shambles, being thrown all over the place, because there were no seats – we were sitting on the floor. Even then I wasn't scared of jumping out of the plane – I was glad to get out of the blooming thing. The Germans were trying to shoot us down and it was safer on the ground.

I had to take a spare Bren gun (a light machine-gun) down with me in a big kitbag, which was strapped to my leg. The bag had two pins in it, and once you had left the aircraft you were supposed to pull the pins out and lower the kitbag, because obviously you couldn't land with it strapped to your legs. But it was such a shambles on the plane that I never got the two pins in properly, so as we jumped out of the plane I had to hold the bag in my arms. Then a slipstream (current of air) hit me. I let go of the bag and it fell straight down, with everything in it – my rifle, the spare Bren gun, the explosives, my food, my water, everything. When we got down, machine-guns were firing at us, and I could hear the battle going on, but that didn't bother me. The only thing that bothered me was that I had lost the kitbag with my gun in it. I thought, "I'll get ten years in prison for this!", because the army had told us, "If you ever lose your gear then you'll hear about it!" I laugh about it now – I was worried about that rather than the fact that I was in France and there were Germans all around.

Just after I landed, I met up with my colleague, a chap called Herman. Herman was 23, so he was "my dad" – he was an old man to me, because I was only nineteen. We were on the left flank of the whole invasion. We pretty much stayed in one place, clearing mines and laying mines. But later, because the infantry had lost so many men, we had to mix in with them.

I was in France for about five weeks. We were shelled and mortared constantly. We couldn't sleep at night, because the mortar bombs were coming nearer and nearer, and sometimes a great big shot would come and land quite near you. That was pretty scary. That was the worst part of all of it. The Germans always seemed to know just where we were, and because we were engineers, they wanted us out of the way. The poor engineers always had to go in front, removing mines.

The war ended for me one day when I was dug into a little trench with Herman, being shelled and mortared. The next thing I knew, I was in hospital in Birmingham, England! I only found out what happened about four years ago, when I saw Herman for the first time in a long time. I had been buried in the trench by a shell, and I was wounded in the hip. Herman helped to get me out. I was out cold. I must have had shell-shock – what they now call post-traumatic stress disorder. My mother came to visit me, but apparently I was in a very bad state. I couldn't talk and I was shaking. I was a right old mess. I stayed in hospital for quite a while, and then I was discharged from the army.

Eventually I got myself a nice little job in the Post Office. I was working there on VE day – I was putting a new switchboard in when the news came over the wireless. We had a street party to celebrate.

I gradually came around to living a normal life, but I would jump at the slightest noise – I still do, occasionally. If somebody slams the door, I leap up. But I more or less cured myself.

I didn't do anything that exciting during the war, really. I can't say that I ran around and blew things up or killed 50 Germans, or anything like that. I just lifted up mines – but that was pretty scary. I've gone back to Normandy, where the D-Day landings took place, many times. You know what's marvellous? The children we see when we go back to Normandy. Last time, they all wore these T-shirts that said, "We are the children of freedom. Thank you, liberators!" That was a real tear-jerker.

After the war, I didn't tell anyone I'd been in the army. I didn't

talk about it at all. It wasn't until about 1950 I opened up a little bit. In those days, just after the war, everyone had been in the services. All your workmates and your friends had been in the army or the navy or the air force. The fact that you had been in the army was nothing. But of course we're a novelty now, because there are so few of us left.

ELDON "BOB" ROBERTS

Eldon Roberts joined up in Canada in May 1942, when he was nineteen. He was sent to the UK, where he trained for the Normandy landings. He was the second person to land on the beach on D-Day.

I did front-line service and walked every step of the way from the beaches of Normandy all across France, Belgium, Holland, right to within 100 yards of the border with Germany.

There were thirteen landing craft, bringing people to Normandy. They came one after another, and when each ship was empty, it would go back to England to get more people and supplies until everyone had got ashore. But it took a long time. Most people think the invasion was just one swoop onto the beach, but it wasn't.

The gunboats had been shelling the defences on the beach for about an hour before we landed. The first of us were only one minute from touching down when they stopped shelling. So we hit the beach and had no problems at all. We went straight up the beach and were in the town before the Germans had realized that the shelling had stopped. The town we entered was Saint-Aubin-Sur-Mer. We were two streets into the town by the time the Germans got back into position. They started firing at all of the people coming in behind us.

When we first got into the town, we couldn't see any Germans. We had no idea where they were. I went into a house with my friend La Croix, who could speak French, and we told the owner we were going to search his house for Germans. He led us into his front room and showed us a big trapdoor in the floor.

He said, "They go down here and out through a tunnel, to a position out the front. They're firing from there."

I said to La Croix, "Tell him that we will be back in a few minutes."

We went to find our corporal and I told him what we had discovered. I asked his permission to go through the tunnel and take the Germans out. The corporal disappeared and came back with a flame-thrower (a gun that discharges a stream of burning liquid), which he strapped to La Croix. I had a machine-gun. We climbed through the trapdoor, crawled through the tunnel under the houses, and eventually we saw daylight. There were two men in front of us, standing in front of the cliff, with their gun on top of a four-foot wall. One of the men was manning the gun and the other one was filling magazines to put in it. I let go a burst of machine-gun fire at about knee height, so it wouldn't go out to sea and do any damage. That brought them down. At the same time, La Croix let go a couple of licks of flame. The Germans started floundering about and screaming. Suddenly, two Germans came from the right and four came from the left,

Eldon, 1942

in a semi-circle, firing in all directions. They thought our gunshots had come in from the sea, so they weren't looking in our direction.

I gave another burst of fire, and La Croix gave another burst of flame, and I said, "Come on, we've got to get out of here, quick."

Three days later, a French paper wrote, "The action of these two brave men saved thousands of lives."

The Germans were moving around underground, through tunnels, but we'd had no training for how to deal with that. When we thought it was all clear, the Germans would come up and attack us from behind. But by about 7 p.m. we had got them all out and they surrendered. We lined them up and the French people started coming out and singing their national anthem, giving us vodka and thanking us for liberating them. They were going mad – even though their houses had been blown to pieces, they were really happy. There was one young French girl, about eighteen, who went up to one of our young lads and said, "That's a nice gun. How does it work?" He started showing her how his machine-gun worked – and then her father came up and grabbed the gun and shot her right between the eyes. He shot his own daughter right in the face, and down she went. He said, "She was going to shoot you. She was going to spray bullets all around you. She was a collaborator – she was in with the Germans." And I thought, "We really are at war." That's what hit me straight away– we had to be ready for anything.

Following D-Day we started to move inland and our main target became Carpiquet Airport in Caen. At that point we could only come and go by sea so we desperately needed to secure the airport. The attack involved several regiments. Our target was a hedge running along the back of Carpiquet village. We had to go a long way across an open field, and we could see three German tanks on the hilltop on our left. When we were halfway to the hedge, a barrage of mortar shelling started falling among us and really took its toll – there were lots of casualties and we lost our officers. A private said he would take charge, and we proceeded to our target, but about 300 yards from it, two Germans suddenly jumped out of a trench with their hands up. Our lads killed them, as they were probably the ones who had just attacked us.

We reached the hedge and settled among some nearby trees. All was quiet for a couple of hours, and then snipers started firing from the far end of the hedge, working their way towards us. We didn't respond to their shots – we couldn't see them and we didn't want to waste ammunition. But then I saw one of them. I hid behind a tree and slowly raised my gun and my head, but somehow he spotted me and suddenly I was stabbed in the face by what felt like a red hot needle, and I heard a sharp snap. I dropped my gun and fell to the ground. I put my hand to my face and realized I had been grazed by a bullet. It only just missed my eye but all I had was a blister from the hot metal.

That evening, we organized a guarding rota for the night. The tank crew decided to bed down on their groundsheets beneath the tank rather than in it, and we agreed to wake them if the German tanks facing us moved. Around 3 a.m. we started to hear groaning and shouting from under the tank. We realized that the ground was soft, and the tank was sinking and had trapped the men. We took shovels and tried to dig under the vehicle, but the more we dug the more the tank settled. Then the groans and shouting stopped. The men had been killed.

The next day we got word that the airport had been won. It was the easiest attack we had in the war – we had no casualties to the enemy – but it went down as the worst battle of the war. I feel it's time the truth came to light.

Usually you'd take a town, you'd lose men, and then you'd dig a trench and hang in till you got reinforcements. But the Germans would be shelling us all the time. Once I was in a trench with a man named Kitchener, one of us at each end, when a shell came into our trench. It went right down the back of Kitchener's neck, and blew him to a thousand bits. Oh my God, my head – it felt like a balloon bursting. I could hardly hear anything. Eventually after a couple of weeks my hearing improved, but it's never fully recovered.

As we proceeded, clearing the way along the coast towards Calais, we soon ran into opposition as that was part of the Atlantic Wall – the Nazi system of defences along the coast of Europe. On one occasion we were in an area of undergrowth about 100 yards (90 metres) from the enemy. La Croix and two others were firing at the Germans, sheltering behind a fallen tree. The Germans pinpointed where the firing was coming from and waited until La Croix slowly raised his head above the tree to take aim. Suddenly a bullet hit the front of his helmet. It went right through, and he was killed. I saw it happen and immediately threw my helmet away and put on my beret. I never wore a helmet again.

Another place along that coast was Falaise. We had to surround the Germans so they had no way of getting in or out except by sea, and by then we had control of the sea. After a few days we pulled back from the road leading to Rouen, a city on the River Seine. We called this the Falaise Gap because it was the one way out of the pocket we had created. When the Germans realized the road was open they started coming out with tanks, horses and wagons, everything they could muster, all loaded with troops. We let them go through until the road was completely full, right back to Falaise. Then the Spitfires and Hurricanes started bombing them. What a sight! Dead horses and men scattered everywhere. Tanks knocked out. The few who were left soon gave up. They didn't want any more of that.

On our approach to Rouen there was a river running all along the town with a bridge at the left in front of us. We held up for a day to get organized with reinforcements and eventually decided to make our attack. We had to cross the bridge in single file to leave room for traffic and as usual my section was at the front. So we set off across the bridge. All went well until we were more than halfway across and suddenly we came under fire at a point behind my section. Those behind the line of fire turned and ran back but my section was left with the choice of running back through gunfire or racing forwards and hoping to find shelter on the German-occupied side of the bridge. We knew it would be suicide to try to get back so I dashed forwards. On reaching the town, we rushed down to some houses. One of my lads could speak French so he told the people in the houses what had happened and asked them to hide us until our people made it safely across the bridge and we could rejoin them. Four houses agreed to shelter us, two in each house. They were absolutely over the moon to welcome us. I told our hosts they must not tell anyone we were there; if the Germans had found us we'd have been taken prisoner, or worse.

Late the following afternoon, the French people told us that our regiment had successfully captured the town, so we thanked them and went to join our company. But when we reached them, the commanding officer said, "You and your seven men are charged with treason." They thought we had deserted. But when the commanding officer heard what had actually happened, he praised me for choosing not to take my men back under fire.

The French people rounded up collaborators or "women

associating with the Germans" in every town we took, shaved their hair and marched them through the streets. But in Rouen they went a step further – they took eight women and, as well as shaving their heads, they stripped them naked and marched them around the town. They were in a terrible state, bruised and bleeding, because people were hitting them with sticks and throwing stones at them as they passed. The collaborators didn't dare stop walking, because they'd be kicked to death. It was an awful bit of torture. You had to feel a bit sorry for them.

I'd been on the front line from D-Day (6 June) without a break at all. On 26 August, our commanding officer came along and said, "We're going to go back for four days' rest. Our second division is coming to take over from us." When the second division arrived, the man who walked up and took my position was my brother Ernie. A chance in a million – perhaps the only time that ever happened. I hadn't even known he'd left Canada – I had been in touch with my family, but they didn't tell me he'd joined the army because they knew I was on the front line and they didn't want to worry me. Me and Ernie had a chat for about a quarter of an hour, and then we wished each other all the best. The next morning, he went on the attack and was killed. He saved my life, because I'd have been in that position if it hadn't been for him.

When we reached Calais, the Germans resisted so strongly that we couldn't take them at first. After five days, a big white flag went up to signal that the Germans were surrendering. I was sent down there with seven other men to take the Germans prisoner. We had no idea what we were up against. I lined my men up along the cliff and the Germans started streaming out. There were 250 of them. I thought, "How are we going to manage this?" I shouted out, "Does anyone here speak English?" One officer started to come over towards me, and I said, "Stop there. Put your weapons down in a pile, then come to me so I can check that you don't have any hidden ones, then line up. When we're all clear we'll take you to safety. Now tell the others that in German." He said something to the others in German, and then I said, "You first." He was one of the Hitler Youth, obviously, who had been trained that you don't surrender – you fight to the death. He had his hands up over his head, and as I started patting him down, he suddenly put his right hand into his pocket and pulled out a pistol. I was prepared for that – I had my Sten gun over my shoulder on a strap, cocked and ready, and I just touched the trigger and it hit him in the eye. I was a second from having a bullet in the heart. I shouted, "There are a thousand guns on the top of that cliff. If anyone else makes a false move, you'll all be dead." After that, they started doing what I'd asked them to do.

When I'd searched about half of the prisoners, a mountain of a man appeared. I was on my tiptoes, trying to frisk him, and everyone was giggling, the Germans as well as my lads. It turned out he was Jakob Nacken, who later became famous as the tallest man in the world. He was almost seven foot four (nearly two and a half metres). I'm not a tall man, so we made quite a pair. The Germans had emptied their pockets, so my lads grabbed the cameras they had put on the floor and started taking pictures of us together.

When we had cleared Calais and the remainder of the Atlantic Wall, things got easier. We took Belgium and by Christmas we were in Nijmegen in the Netherlands. On a still, clear, silent evening,

Eldon searching Jakob Nacken, a German soldier who was nearly two and a half metres tall

we were about 300 yards (270 metres) from the German line when a German band started to play "Silent Night". It was really lovely – we all sang along. But then our artillery got the range of it and opened fire. It seemed such a shame.

I always said, "I'll never make it to Germany." It was just a premonition I had. Lots of us had premonitions like that – often in the morning, someone would say, "I've got that feeling. I'm going to get it today." I'd say, "Don't talk silly, it's all in your head." But sure as hell, he'd get wounded or killed or something. That happened so many times. On the morning of our first attack on Germany, it was as quiet as could be. I was sergeant, and I was eating breakfast with the fellow who had taken over from me as corporal. I said to him, "I've got a feeling it's going to be a long time before I get anything else to eat. I've had three large mess tins full of porridge and I'm still starving." He said, "I haven't got any appetite at all."

We went to attack the German border, and we were literally 100 yards (90 metres) away when suddenly all hell broke loose. At the first bit of gunfire, everyone hit the dirt. I noticed my corporal stumble and fall forward. He'd been hit. I was about six feet (1.8 metres) away from him and I could see a big shell-hole a few feet in front of us. I thought I'd drag him into the hole and give him first aid. But when I got over to him I could see he was gone already, so I got in the hole myself. It was about 8.30 a.m. Eventually everything went quiet. No one dared move – anything that moved got shot at. I just stayed in the shell-hole, keeping my head down so any shrapnel would go over my head, until about 2.30 p.m., when three of our tanks came through with flame-throwers. I knew that was our cue to follow, to take the Germans prisoner. I jumped out of the shell-hole, took about three steps forward and turned around to signal to my platoon to follow.

I was completely amazed by how few got up. Three seconds after I'd got out of the shell-hole, a shell landed smack in the middle of it. It would have landed on my head. Instead, it smothered me with mud and water and crushed my leg.

My lads kept following the tanks through. As they passed me, they said, "Best of luck." I lay there thinking, "What a lucky man I am." I could have been gone. I knew it would be a heck of a long time before I got any medical attention, because I was right up the front and the medics were right at the back. I tore my shirt off and tried to stop the bleeding, which seemed to work. I saw a fellow lying there, dead, and I crawled over to him. I took his rifle and used it as a crutch. I wanted to get as close to the medics as I could because I knew I could bleed to death. My knee was smashed to pieces and my leg was twisted backwards, and when I tried to walk my heel dragged through the mud, so I gave that up. Strangely enough I didn't feel any pain – there was so much going on. You were just thankful it wasn't worse, seeing all those dead bodies lying around. Eventually I did get rescued, at about 6 p.m., and I was put in an ambulance and taken on a twelve-hour trip to a hospital in France. I had nothing to eat till I got to the hospital, so I had been right to eat all that porridge.

On VE day I was still recovering in Bruges, Belgium. Soon after, I rejoined my unit in Utrecht in the Netherlands and volunteered to come to England to assist with the repatriation of troops to Canada. I married Vera, my English rose, on 14 December 1945, and we settled in England. I have no regrets. I have four children, ten grandchildren and twelve great-grandchildren. In September 2015 I was awarded the top French military medal, the Légion d'honneur, for the part I played in D-Day and the liberation of France.

ISRAEL VICTOR HYAMS

Israel Victor Hyams told Samuel and Gemma Preston
about life in the 44th Royal Tank Regiment.

I travelled a lot during the war: to Tunisia and Algeria in North Africa, and to Italy, Belgium, Holland and France in Europe. My tank, the Sherman, was my shelter. We stored food in the tank – packs containing chocolate, bacon, bully beef (corned beef) and cigarettes. Sometimes when we took it out to eat, it actually had bullet holes through it!

My most challenging assignment was landing in Algiers, the capital of Algeria, in 1942. The Germans had better equipment, but we had more men. We were there for two years and in the end we beat the Germans. I also took part in the D-Day landings. We were brought back to England from Italy to take part, because we were seasoned veterans. We arrived after the initial landings, on the afternoon of 6 June 1944.

Israel, 1938

I nearly died in the Battle for Hill 112. It was thought that whoever held the hill held Normandy. Sadly, most of my squadron was wiped out there – it was a terrible battle. Our tank came under attack and I had to escape out of a hatch. As I climbed out of the tank and into the cornfield, I was hit by a blast, which left me temporarily blind. I stood up, but a man pulled me back down again and saved my life. I was taken to hospital, but I heard the battle raging all around me all night long.

Israel in his paratrooper uniform

After D-Day, I was sent to train new recruits until the end of the war. I feel lucky, as I have had my children, grandchildren and great-grandchildren, but I also feel guilty about all of those who lost their lives so young.

FRED GLOVER

Fred Glover joined the Parachute Regiment when he was seventeen. He fought at the Normandy landings, the Battle of the Bulge and the crossing of the Rhine. He told the children of Mile Oak Primary School about his experiences.

In preparation for D-Day, we spent two weeks attacking a "dummy" gun battery (a fake fortification). Everything was top secret, so we didn't know where we were going to attack. In the end, my battalion was chosen to carry out a special mission: we crash-landed on top of the Merville Gun Battery, part of the Nazis' Atlantic Wall defences, to stop the gunners shelling the Allied troops landing on Sword Beach. We flew in on three gliders. Up until then we had been playing at soldiers, but this was for real. I was hit by shrapnel from an ack-ack shell (a shell fired by an anti-aircraft gun) in both legs, but I just had to carry on. At the time I didn't feel any pain. I only noticed how serious my injuries were when I couldn't keep up with my unit, and my boots started filling with blood.

I was too badly injured to carry on, so I was captured. I was disgusted to be taken prisoner – I resolved to get away, and I finally managed to escape from a German hospital in Paris. I hid with the French resistance until Paris was liberated. After that, I returned to my battalion, fought in the Ardennes in

Fred during the war

north-east France and was parachuted across the River Rhine.

I can honestly say that during the war I lived with kings. I could totally rely on the men in my regiment and they knew that they could always rely on me.

FRED HEMENWAY

Fred Hemenway volunteered with the Royal Observer Corps during the war. He served during the D-Day landings.

As soon as I was old enough, I tried to join the RAF. I was rejected as a Grade C, which meant I was unfit for military service – they said I had a sticky heart valve, but that wasn't picked up again until two years ago, when I had a stroke.

In 1941, my boss at the farm where I worked, who was chief observer at one of the ports, asked if I'd like to join the Royal Observer Corps, and I said yes. Our job was to identify and track aircraft. We mostly plotted bombers going out and returning. When we spotted something we reported it to our centre, and they put it on a big map and organized a defensive aircraft to go after it.

During the invasion of Sicily, an island off the coast of southern Italy, there was a bad incident when our aircraft went off track, and our gunners shot a lot of our own men down. When it came to Operation Overlord – the Normandy landings – the RAF decided that couldn't happen again. There were going to be a heck of a lot of aircraft in the sky, so they needed to make sure the gunners knew which planes were ours and which were the enemy's. So the Royal Observer Corps asked for volunteers to join the Seaborne Observer Corps. Two observers were assigned to each merchant vessel (ship), and they'd live alongside the gunners, giving them information about the planes straight away. They only selected the best observers – we had to take what they called the Trade Test, to see how quickly and accurately we could identify different aircraft. It was much harder than anything we'd done before.

Before I was accepted into the Seaborne Observers, I was given another medical examination. I got through that all right. I think if you had the required number of body parts and you were still warm, they'd pass you. Some managed to get by with false legs. I was sent to Bournemouth on the south coast of England for specialist training, and I temporarily joined the Royal Navy as a petty officer (aircraft identifier).

During the Normandy landings, I was anchored off Juno Beach. We got to know the gunners really well, and we told them which planes to shoot at and which ones not to shoot at, and we were very successful – the RAF reported that they felt safe.

When we went to sea, we were paid, and we worked in shifts, four hours on and four hours off. It was very hard work. Luckily we had an understanding gunnery officer who said, "There's not much point in you fellows being on after midnight, because it's dark!" So we didn't do the midnight to 4 a.m. shift, which meant we got an eight hour break.

We had a near miss the first afternoon we were there. We were monitoring a German aircraft when it dropped its bomb. It missed us by just 25 feet (eight metres) or so and landed in the water. Luckily it didn't do any damage. We were scared at times – anyone who said they weren't frightened was lying. Two of us were killed during the Normandy landings.

I was at sea for two months. After that I went back to work at the farm, and carried on as a volunteer observer.

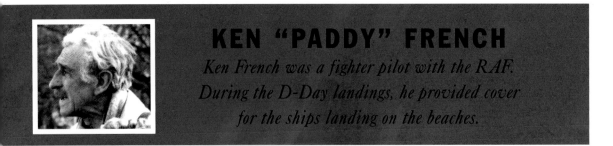

KEN "PADDY" FRENCH

Ken French was a fighter pilot with the R.A.F.
During the D-Day landings, he provided cover
for the ships landing on the beaches.

Leading up to D-Day, we were stationed at Bognor Regis on the south coast of England. We were there to prepare for the invasion, but we didn't know when or where it would take place. Various things were done to make the Germans think that we would invade at the narrowest point of the English Channel. The British built a dummy army, with tanks made of canvas and wood, and assembled it in Kent, across the Channel from the French port of Calais, so the Germans would think that this was where we were preparing to invade. They even dropped a dead body in the sea with fake intelligence about preparations for D-Day in his pockets.

On the afternoon of 5 June, we saw the ground crews painting black-and-white stripes under the wings of our planes. We thought that must mean something. At our briefing that evening they put out a huge map of Normandy. That was our first indication of where we were going. Our brief was to form part of a big umbrella over the beaches to protect the ships and make sure the German air force didn't interfere with them. We were supposed to invade on 5 June, but the weather was too bad. We got a forecast which said that on 6 June there would be a 48 hour lull before the weather got worse again. The powers that be decided to take the risk.

That evening, we couldn't leave camp. I remember it so well – we knew the next day would be the biggest of our lives, but we had no idea what to expect. We thought that the Germans would throw everything at us when they realized that the invasion was on.

From about midnight, a continuous stream of planes started flying overhead. Some were pulling gliders full of paratroopers, others were carrying parachutists and some were bombers whose job was to pound the coastal defences. The Germans thought this was just a diversion at first, but there was still overwhelming firepower to meet the landing Allied troops.

The next morning, when we took off, we could see the ships below us – over 5,000 of them, coming in from both sides. We patrolled the skies over Omaha Beach, where the Americans landed, which was the scene of the heaviest casualties on the day. There was a cliff at the top of the beach – why they chose that spot, I do not know. These poor men would land and the Germans were up on the cliff, dropping hand grenades on them. They had been told that the defences would be wiped out by the heavy bombing, but that didn't happen, and literally thousands of men died. We could see it all happening but felt strangely detached. We could tell there was hell going on down there and see the smoke from the big guns and so on, but we couldn't hear it. It was difficult to take in that so many were dying on the beaches below. I was glad I wasn't on the ground with those brave young lads. They had no protection from the artillery raining down on them, but amazingly enough of them got through to pave the way for more to follow.

We could only stay over the beaches for an hour. Other fighters would come and take over, and

66 Squadron on D-Day

we'd go back to refuel, and then return. I went over three times on D-Day itself, but it was two or three days before I saw a German fighter.

In August 1944, after the Normandy landings, I took part in the Battle of the Falaise Pocket. Just south of Normandy, a whole German army was surrounded, and their only way out was through a narrow passage called the Falaise Gap. Our job was to circle around while wave after wave of our bombers came in to attack the Germans. It must have been absolute hell down there. It was a boiling hot day and you could see the heat and smoke and fire from 10,000 feet (3,000 metres), where we were. The Germans must have had a very hard time. When we were stationed in Normandy we went to the Falaise Gap and saw all the dead people and horses still lying there.

When we landed in Normandy, some of the soldiers said, "Don't go too far from your aircraft – there are snipers around. Some of them are French women, protecting their German boyfriends." It's difficult to blame the women, in a way – the Germans had been there for years, and many of them were very nice lads. Some of them did come back from Germany to marry the girls.

From August onwards we were based in France, and from then on we worked in close co-operation with the army. Every day they'd give us a line on the map and tell us we could attack anything ahead of it. We were sweeping a huge area of the country ahead of the advancing army, keeping the roads clear, seriously restricting the German army's movements. Once, news came through that the Germans had broken cover up in northern France, and every available Spitfire in Normandy made their way up there. It was chaos after the attack. We continued like that all through France.

When the war finished, I was up in Holland. One day a message came through requesting all pilots to assemble on the airfield at 11 a.m. We were told, "There will be no more operations." One of the pilots on our squadron had been killed the day before. That was rotten luck.

On VE day, I sailed up the River Thames to Tilbury in Essex on a convoy of trucks. There were people waving all the way – still waving from the night before, probably. I don't remember much of the night!

After that, they didn't have much for us to do. I was stationed at North Weald in Essex and one lunchtime I went to the canteen and there, standing at the bar, was my old squadron commander. He was then the wing commander in charge of postings at the air ministry. He found me a job near Bath, which is where I met my wife, Joan. The first time she saw me, I was standing in a bucket of sand, telling everyone I was a camel. She probably said to her friends, "Who's that fool?" And of course she was right. But she'd just been to North Africa in the WAAF – perhaps she'd taken a liking to camels!

Ken (centre) and Joan (third from right) on their wedding day in 1947

American infantrymen march near the Arc de Triomphe on the Champs-Elysees, Paris, France, 29 August 1944

THE BABY BLITZ

Towards the end of the war, when the Allies were gaining the upper hand, Germany developed two new kinds of missile to use in attacks on London and the surrounding area: the V-1 and the V-2. The V stood for *Vergeltungswaffen*, which means "revenge weapons". On 13 June 1944, in response to the Allied invasion of France, Germany launched the V-1 flying bomb at Britain. Over the next two weeks, 2,452 bombs were launched at Britain, though a third of them were shot down by fighter pilots or anti-aircraft guns. Around 800 fell in and around London. Then, on 8 September 1944, the first V-2 rocket fell on Chiswick in London, killing thirteen people. V-1s made a loud noise as they were travelling towards their target, but V-2s exploded without warning. The attacks, known as the Baby Blitz, continued until March 1945. They were not as deadly as the raids during the Blitz of 1940–1941, which had claimed the lives of 43,000 people. Nearly 10,000 civilians and 3,000 members of the armed forces were killed by V weapons, and around 20,000 houses were damaged, causing a housing crisis in the South of England after the war.

A nurse (left) and an ambulance driver (right)
at the scene of a V-2 rocket attack on
Farringdon Market in London, 8 March 1945

RUTH BARNETT

Ruth Barnett, who came to England on the Kindertransport, describes the V-1 raids and the impact they had on her brother Martin.

In the autumn of 1944, a little over a year after Martin and I went to live with a new foster family, the Goodrickes, the Nazis started sending V-1s, known as doodlebugs, to London. They were pilotless planes – really bombs on wings. They were catapulted from Peenemünde on the Baltic coast of Germany with just enough fuel to reach London. When they ran out of fuel, they dropped on London. The Goodrickes' cottage in Kent was in the path of the doodlebugs. They came mostly at night, and the warning siren would wake us up. I would sit with my foster siblings Joan and Guy on the bedroom windowsill with our feet dangling down and wait for the fun to begin. It was like bonfire night. First the red flares would go up, to warn the gunners that the radar had sighted a doodlebug and to be ready. Then you would hear the drone of the rocket. You could spot them by the flames coming out of their tails. The guns would begin to fire – *pow, pow, pow*! If they scored a hit, the doodlebug would come down in an arc like a shooting star and explode as it hit the ground. Lastly, the green flares would go up to let the gunners know that no more doodlebugs were coming, and then the All Clear signal would sound. It was all very exciting.

The next morning, if there had been a hit near us, we would go out to see the remains of the burnt-out doodlebug and pick up pieces as souvenirs. Once I found a shiny black nose-tip, and I kept that for many years as a prized possession. If a doodlebug came down in a cherry or apple orchard it would plough through and uproot several trees, which was an awesome sight to see, but nothing like the damage they caused in London.

Occasionally a doodlebug came over in daytime. Once we were walking home from school when the siren went off. Susan, the oldest of my foster siblings, pushed Joan, Guy and me into a ditch under the hedge. She told us to put our heads down and to put our hands over them. A doodlebug came right over us, so low that we could see its markings. I think it had already been hit, as it was flying lopsided.

As a child of nine I had no idea of how dangerous doodlebugs were – it never occurred to me that one could crash down on our house. Mr and Mrs Goodricke must have been very worried about our safety, but they didn't show any signs of it to us children, and that helped us youngest ones get through what could have been a terrifying experience. It was probably quite difficult for the three older children. My brother Martin couldn't be comforted – he was most upset by the doodlebugs. He would go and hide when they came over and he wouldn't talk about it. I feel ashamed now of how we teased him. He would be trembling and shaking and our teasing must have made it much worse.

PATRICIA EDWARDS

Patricia Edwards was born on 16 September 1939, two weeks after war broke out. She lived with her family in London.

My earliest memories of the war are of being frightened during the raids in 1944. We usually had sandwiches and a drink ready to take with us to the Anderson shelter in the garden. Whenever I enter an old damp building now I remember the musty smell of the shelter, mixed with the smell of the paraffin that powered our lanterns. It was terrifying sitting in the shelter, hearing the planes coming our way. The planes would release the V-1 flying bombs, known to us as doodlebugs. When we no longer heard the plane's engine, we would start counting until we heard the bomb drop. It felt like playing a game, but it was frightening at the same time, because we knew the bomb could fall on our house. When we heard the explosion we knew that, sadly, a house or other building had been hit, and we could only thank God that it hadn't been us.

The raids usually took place at night-time, and if we didn't have time to get to the shelter my mother would pull me under the bed or the dining table for protection, in case our windows were blown in or the ceiling came down. Once, a church near our house was hit and the ceilings in our house were damaged. I walked into the hall to find my grandfather covered in white plaster.

Naturally everyone was incredibly happy when the war ended in 1945. I remember being with my mother in Battersea Park, London, watching fireworks over the River Thames. It was a great celebration after all the darkness and worry of the war.

DAME GILLIAN LYNNE

Dame Gillian Lynne is a choreographer, director and former ballerina. She has choreographed and directed over 60 productions in the West End and on Broadway, including Cats, *and worked on eleven feature films and hundreds of television productions as producer, director, choreographer or performer. Her career as a ballerina started during the Second World War.*

I was very happy as a young child. I started dance lessons at an early age; they were recommended to my mother by a doctor because of my constant wriggling. My mother believed I could become a good dancer and she became my tutor and mentor, but she was tragically killed in a horrific car crash on 8 July 1939, just before war broke out. That was the end of my happy childhood. As soon as war was declared, my father was called up to be a major in the army. That saved him, because his heart had been broken by my mother's death.

Because my mother had died and my father was in the army, I was evacuated to the country, like most of the young people in England. It was awful. All the teachers could do daily was cry about the news coming in from the war in France, and there were no dance lessons and precious few other lessons. I hated the waste of time, and so I ran away. I was lucky – I found a couple in a farmhouse who took me in, and they managed to contact my father and tell him where I had disappeared to. He sent an aunt to pick me up. My father wanted me to be happy at a school that suited me, so he found out about the Cone Ripman School (now known as the Arts Educational Schools). I was sent for an audition, and I was awarded a place.

Dame Gillian as the Lilac Fairy in Sleeping Beauty

At first the school was based in the Hallams in Surrey, but when war broke out the army billeted a full company of soldiers to our school, so our wonderful principals had to scour England for another home for us. We were all carted off to a large house called Loddington Hall in Leicestershire.

I became a professional ballet dancer very early on in my life – while I was still at school. Very soon after that, I became a member of the Sadler's Wells Ballet Company after being spotted by Ninette de Valois, who had founded the company. But of course the war was still going on, and one night, while I was dancing *Les Sylphides* at the New Theatre in St Martin's Lane, London (now called the Noël Coward Theatre), we heard a doodlebug approaching. It cut out right overhead in the middle of the ballet. Everything, including the two pianists, the audience and our pink pointe shoes, came to a halt. We waited for the inevitable crash, thinking it would be on us. Actually it landed 100 yards (90 metres) up the street. On our way home that night, a friend and I went to see if we could comfort those who were injured. We were very lucky to have been missed by the doodlebug – in one moment, most of British ballet would have gone up in smoke.

I was sent abroad in khaki to entertain the troops in 1944, when I was seventeen. We were kitted out like proper soldiers, in trousers, skirts, greatcoats and beautiful hats. Dancing all over the continent was very exciting – it was glamorous and dangerous and for those of us that had never been out of England it was an eye-opener.

We felt proud because we believed we were helping the war effort, but it was very hard work. We performed a ballet called *Miracle in the Gorbals*. The men weren't sure about it at first, but once they'd seen us dance, they became fans. I recreated the ballet in 2014, 70 years after we first performed it. I am one of only four people alive who were in the original, but not one of us could remember a step, so I made a new version sticking as close to Robert Helpmann's scenario as I could.

On VE day I was dancing *Coppélia* at the New Theatre with Margot Fonteyn and Robert Helpmann. We were incredibly excited, if not euphoric. There was an electric atmosphere in the theatre, and the minute the curtain fell, we all tore off our costumes, leapt into our clothes and ran as fast as we could to join the crowds in Trafalgar Square. It was very moving and it felt simply quite wonderful to be part of such a celebration.

LIZ DAVIES

Liz Davies was born on 1 September 1944. She lived in West Hampstead, London, with her mother and grandmother.

During the war, my dad was in the army and my mother worked at the Food Office organizing coupons and ration books, so my grandmother looked after me. She was blind, though, so how she was supposed to look after me I do not know. We had family in Wales, and there was talk of us going there to be out of harm's way, but my grandmother was very frightened of losing the

Liz with her dad Norman, in his army uniform

house in London, because it was her one possession in the world. When people in London were bombed out, they went looking for somewhere to live, and if a house was empty they would go in and take it over. So we stayed in London, and slept under the stairs, because my mother thought that was the safest place to be.

At 4 p.m. on 8 January 1945, I was in my cot in the bay window of my parents' bedroom when I started crying. My grandmother picked me up and sat in a chair to cradle me, and the next minute the window blew out and soot fell down the chimney, completely covering the room. A V-2 rocket had been dropped on the railway embankment a few streets away. My grandmother must have been terrified. I was screaming, and she didn't dare move, because she was blind – she just sat there in the chair. My cot was filled with smashed glass – it was a lucky escape.

My mother worked in Finchley Road, which wasn't that far away, and everyone in her office heard the V-2 fall. They said, "Anyone who lives down that way better go home," as they realized everyone would be bombed out. So she ran home, and the nearer she got, the worse the destruction was. She ran into the house and found us still sitting in the chair, covered in soot and broken glass.

That blast destroyed fourteen houses, badly damaged 152 and caused minor damage to about 1,600. Luckily only two people died, though hundreds more were injured.

Liz's mum Peggy after the V-2 fell. The windows in the house have been covered with cardboard.

KEN "PADDY" FRENCH

Ken French was a fighter pilot with the RAF.
Towards the end of the war he bombed the V-1
launch sites in northern France.

Shortly after D-Day, we had our first taste of Hitler's secret weapon – the V-1 flying bomb, commonly known as the doodlebug. A very nasty thing it was. It was a comparatively simple device – a bomb with wings and an engine. Once launched they flew until they ran out of fuel, and then they came down as a bomb. Launched against large targets such as London, they were deadly. Their sound was very distinctive; while you could hear them, you didn't have to worry, but when the engine stopped, it was time to duck. They travelled at about 400 miles per hour (650 kilometres per hour) but they could be shot down. Some were shot down by Typhoons and Tempests (fighter planes), and others by anti-aircraft guns, but sadly too many reached their targets.

For some months we escorted bombers to attack woods in various parts of northern France which turned out to be the launching sites for these flying bombs. Sometimes we carried out dive-bombing missions on the woods ourselves. When we arrived in Normandy after the liberation of Paris, we walked into the surrounding woods and found a number of launching ramps. These were the targets we'd been dive-bombing for so long, and we found many bomb craters around them. We also found a number of wrecked doodlebugs at the sites. The local people told us that some of the bombs exploded on the launching ramps. Launching a doodlebug was so dangerous that the Germans would offer Frenchmen 1,000 francs to sit in the dugout and press the launching button, but not many people took them up on it.

Red Army soldiers raising the Soviet flag over the Reichstag in Berlin, Germany, 30 April 1945

THE FALL OF
GERMANY

As Allied forces advanced towards Germany from Normandy, the Soviet Union's Red Army invaded Poland and approached Germany from the east. Allied bombing raids were still devastating German cities, too, but the Nazis were determined to fight on at any cost. Hitler was directing what was left of his armed forces from a bunker beneath the Reich Chancellery (his official residence and office) in Berlin. He ordered his troops to destroy everything in the Allies' path, no matter the cost to the German people. He told his minister Albert Speer, "If the war is lost, the nation will also perish. Besides, those that remain after the battle will be the inferior ones, for the good will have fallen."

On 25 April 1945, American troops met the Soviets on the River Elbe in Germany. The Americans held back while the Soviets approached Berlin. As they advanced, the Red Army raped thousands of women and killed boys and men, just as German soldiers had starved, raped and tortured Soviet citizens during the Nazi occupation of the Soviet Union. On 30 April 1945, Hitler committed suicide rather than surrender to Allied troops. A week later, on 8 May 1945, the war in Europe was over.

BARBARA CROSSLEY (NÉE LIPKE)

Barbara Crossley was born in Germany in 1935.
When the Russians invaded Germany at the end
of the war, she and her family fled to safety.

I was born two years after Hitler came to power. My father had been in line to inherit a lovely house with a large estate in Mecklenburg, Prussia, but the year before I was born, on 20 May 1933, my grandfather was executed by the Nazis for anti-Party behaviour. The Nazis had intercepted a letter he had written to the Polish workers who came every year to harvest the crops, inviting them that year as usual. But this was treason – under the Nazis, German jobs had to be given to German workers only. The official line was that my grandfather was executed because he was in a position of responsibility and was setting a bad example. But I don't know why they were watching him in the first place – this could have been an excuse. Either way, the ripple effect for my family was massive. Apart from the emotional shock, my parents were left with no home to inherit. This had a major impact on what happened to us in later years.

In 1939, when I was four years old, my mother took me and my younger brother, Hans-Jürgen, to visit her sister Inge in Leipzig, Germany. At the time Inge ran a kindergarten, and she suggested that I stay with her for a couple of weeks while my mother sorted a few things out. But during those two weeks, war was declared and everything changed. One of the first things that happened was that all the train lines were commandeered for war use only and petrol was rationed, so it became almost impossible to travel around. My mother couldn't get back to Leipzig to collect me as originally planned, and for lots of complicated reasons I ended up spending the entire war with Inge.

One of my strongest memories is of a time when my mother did manage to visit me in Leipzig. We went out for a walk, and I asked her, "When can we go home?" She said, "But there isn't a home any more." At the time, my mother was working as a photographer with the German army in Russia, and my brother was living with our grandparents in Hamburg, although he was later sent to my other aunt in East Prussia. We lived hundreds of miles away from each other. I don't think anyone realized how badly I missed my mother, because I am naturally quite a happy person.

When I was five, I was very ill with mumps. My father managed to visit me, but I was too ill to talk much. I just remember him sitting in the chair by my bed. I fell asleep and when I woke up, I was heartbroken to discover that he had gone. So it was just as well that I didn't know that I would never see him again. At some point he was called up and he spent the last stage of the war as a prisoner of war in England.

Inge was wonderful to me. Even when she and Hans, her future husband, were courting, they took me with them. I was a bridesmaid at their wedding, and I was considered one of the family. Their household was strongly Christian, and I loved the way they structured their daily lives, with Bible study before breakfast and family music-making.

Leipzig was heavily bombed during the war, but as a child this seemed exciting to me. I particularly loved watching the flares which the planes dropped to light up their targets. As far as I was concerned, it was magical to see the night sky lit up in this way. Our house wasn't bombed, but bombs fell near by and blew our windows out.

I remember one night when wave after wave after wave of planes flew overhead. The adults were talking and whispering and wondering what was happening. We found out the next day that the planes had been on their way to Dresden.

During the final years of the war, there were bombing raids virtually every night. We slept in a shelter, and I always took a rucksack packed with my two most precious possessions: a photo album and a book which my great-aunt, Tante Elsa, had made for me. She had written out all of the German folk songs we sang at kindergarten, the music as well as the words, and illustrated it.

One of the ways the Nazis knew who was for and against them was through teachers, who reported back anything suspicious they heard children say. So obviously in that climate it was important to make sure your children didn't know your political views. I was ten years old before I discovered that my family did not consider it a good thing to be a Nazi. When you were ten you joined the Hitler Youth, and I had been looking forward to it – all the older children were members, and you got an iron badge when you joined, and a much prettier enamel one later. I swapped my prized collection of shrapnel for one of these enamelled badges. The first time I wore it, Inge saw it and ripped it off my coat. She threw it over the fence and into the bushes. The other women who were there quickly gathered around Inge, telling her what a dangerous thing she'd just done – and in public, too – but Inge just said, "Surely this will all be over soon." I never saw my badge again.

After that, a few other things began to make sense. Why the portrait of Hitler which Inge was obliged to have on the wall at the kindergarten lived permanently behind the piano, for instance – Inge always said it had "just fallen down". Whenever there was an inspection, somebody had to run ahead, dust down the portrait and hang it back up before the inspectors reached that room!

Shortly after the episode with the badge, the Americans rolled into Leipzig like triumphant Roman conquerors. They sat on their tanks, throwing sweets and bananas to us children. There was an air of excitement; we had spent the previous three days and nights cooped up in the unbearable heat and cramped conditions of a shelter, wondering what was happening outside. When word reached us that the Americans had come, everyone was relieved. However, in February 1945, Allied leaders met at Yalta on the Black Sea for a conference and decided how Europe would be structured after the war. They agreed to divide Germany into four zones, each controlled by an Allied power: the Soviet Union, Britain, France and the US. Leipzig was in the Russian zone. The Americans pulled out of the city, and once again I witnessed incoming conquerors. But this time the atmosphere was totally different.

The Russians arrived at dusk, on carts pulled by ponies. We could hear their wonderful, deep, haunting voices singing Russian folk songs long before we could see them. It was wonderfully romantic – but this didn't tally with the atmosphere of fear among the people around me. Everyone dreaded the Russian occupation – and with real terror. My mother managed to fetch me and my brother, and we set off on a long trek to Hamburg.

It was impossible to get on the train – the station was packed and the train was bursting. People were handing their children to strangers on the train but my mother wasn't prepared to do that so we set off on foot. That turned out to be the last train out of Leipzig: after that, the Russians put mines on the tracks. We walked for days, sleeping wherever we could. We stayed in a barn on a straw-covered floor for two weeks while we waited for a guide to take us to a crossing point into one of the western zones. We were stopped a couple of times; I particularly remember one Russian guard who wanted to know if we had watches – he had watches that he'd taken from people all the way up both of his arms. But we were let through and eventually we reached the border of the British-occupied zone. The British soldiers insisted that my mother leave my brother with them while she queued for food. This made her panic, but she didn't have a choice. Once she had collected the food, they handed him back to her. We stayed in a refugee camp for a while, sleeping in bunk beds, until we managed to catch a freight train to Hamburg. It was a real adventure for my brother and me – we sat right on top of the cargo, which was coal, and because the train wasn't moving too quickly we could climb around and enjoy the scenery. From Hamburg it was only a day's walk to my grandparents' house.

I think I must be one of the few people who experienced the German, American, Russian and British occupations first-hand. I remember the very different atmospheres under each regime. Life under the German army was normal for me, of course. Then the Americans came with the confidence of victors and were full of high-octane energy. The Russians, on the other hand, were cruel and merciless and I remember the desperate urgency with which people were fleeing from them. And when we reached the British-occupied North, our home was one of those taken over by the British army. This was grim, but the soldiers were kind to us children – they teased us and joked with us and we loved to copy the soldiers as they did their drill every day, marching up and down the road behind them. The soldiers didn't like this and they always shooed us away, but it would have been unimaginable to even try this with the Russian soldiers.

Inge and Hans decided to stay where they were in the East,

because they felt that God had put them there and that this was where they were needed. They lived long lives and were a thorn in the side of the communist regime – they raised money to fix their church bell so that they could make a big noise every Sunday and show them that the Christians were still there! After the Berlin Wall came down, Hans was tickled pink to look at the records kept by the Stasi (German secret police) and discover how often he'd come close to being arrested. They couldn't afford to arrest him, because he was virtually the only orthopaedic surgeon in the area!

My father came back to Germany after the war was over but he was one of the many men who was rounded up by the Russians and marched off to a camp. Sometimes people came back and sometimes they didn't – and unfortunately my father was one of those who disappeared. Some years later, a man visited us out of the blue. He told us that he had been released from the camp where my father had been held, and that my father, who was very ill, had asked him to find us and tell us where he was. In 1948 we heard that my father had died. Since the fall of the Berlin Wall in November 1989, we have been able to find out more about what happened to him. We learned that he was arrested for treason on 17 July 1946 and sentenced to ten years in the Bautzen Camp – the Soviet secret police's "Camp No. 4" – where 2,714 people died between 1945 and 1950. There was one final note in his file – in Russian with a German translation – which said that he had been "officially rehabilitated" (pardoned).

Barbara, aged seven, briefly reunited with her brother in 1942

Destroyed military vehicles and rubble piled
outside the remains of German Minister of Propaganda
Joseph Goebbels' house after the fall of Berlin to Allied troops

GERDA DREWS

Gerda Drews was a teenager living in Berlin during the Second World War. She told her daughter-in-law Elinor Florence about her family's experiences when the city fell to the Soviet army in 1945.

Gerda before the war

When the Battle for Berlin started in April 1945, I was staying with relatives on a farm south of the city. There was little hope that we could hold out against the Russians, but I wanted to be with my family when the worst happened, so I returned to Berlin. As I walked home, I was passed by German soldiers trying to break through to the north of Berlin to escape the Russians and surrender to the Americans instead. We had heard some terrible stories about what was happening to the German people as the Russians advanced.

I made it to the train station, but it had been bombed to pieces. Instead I caught a ride into Berlin with a truck full of soldiers. Artillery shells were landing on both sides of us, and I could see the vapour of the Russian rockets flying over my head. When I left the soldiers and entered my neighbourhood, there were shells landing all around, but I made it to our cottage in Wittenau on the north-west edge of the city. I let myself in with my key and went into the cellar we used as an air raid shelter and locked myself in.

Suddenly the trapdoor opened, and my father appeared! My parents and sister had moved into a nearby bunker to shelter from the bombs. They were convinced I had been killed. My father had come to see if the house was still standing. At first we couldn't make it back to the bunker because the shelling was too heavy.

241

Finally there was a break, and we ran to the bunker. We stayed there for days while the fighting raged. We didn't know what would happen to us, and we were worried about my brother Heinz, who was fighting with the German army on the eastern front.

Finally, on 5 May, the shooting outside stopped. Russian soldiers battered down the door and entered the bunker. They said two words in German: "Women, come!" Then our neighbour's mother was raped. It was horrible. They kept several women inside the bunker, but some of us, including my family, managed to escape.

We thought we would be shot the minute we went through the door. We ran back to our house and hid in the cellar, and my father covered the trapdoor with rugs and blankets, but there was no escape from the Russians. I prefer not to talk about what happened when they found us, because it is too painful.

As a woman, you didn't have to be afraid of the front-line Russian troops. They shot every man they saw, but they left the women alone. It was the Russians who came afterwards who were the worst. They did all the raping and looting. They went through all of the houses and took whatever they wanted, stripping homes of every single possession, right down to the toilets.

The Russians forced everyone to work. Berlin had practically been demolished by the Allied bombers, and the roads were blocked with rubble. We had to clear them by hand, which was a difficult job. The women did most of the work. There is a German name for the women who cleaned up after the bombing: *Trümmerfrauen*, which means "rubble women". Gradually the city began to emerge from the wreckage. After just one month, the first trams started to run again, and some streets were cleared for traffic.

After two months of Russian occupation, Berlin was

partitioned into four zones: one controlled by the British, one by the Americans, one by the French and one by the Russians. My neighbourhood ended up in the French zone, but while the transfer of power was taking place there was a two day period when no one was in charge. During those two days, the Russians seized the opportunity to round up 50,000 people and send them to prison camps. My father had been too old to join the armed forces – he was 48 years old, and a naval veteran from the first war. But because he had served as an air raid warden for our neighbourhood, the Russians considered him a Nazi official. On 10 August, my father was ordered to report to the local police station. Then two men came to the door and told my mother and me to take a suitcase full of his clothing to the police station, as he was being taken into the country to help with the harvest. We packed the suitcase hastily and took it to the station. We could see men being loaded into trucks and driven away. People were crying and calling to each other. I jumped on my bicycle and followed the trucks, along with hundreds of others who were frantically trying to see where the trucks were going. Eventually the Russians drove us back with gunfire. I never saw my dear father again.

In the months that followed, my mother, my little sister and I had a bad time. We were alone, unprotected and very hungry. People from the city began going from farm to farm, trying to barter for food. The 1944 potato harvest was still stacked in large heaps and farmers would allow people to root around in the leftover piles of potatoes, most of which were rotten. You had to plunge your arms into a slimy mass of rotten potatoes, and if you were lucky you would find a few good ones. The best things to trade for food were flints for lighters, salt, paper and school books. After a few months, the farmers began to demand silver, linens and anything else of value. Eventually there was a saying: "The farmer has everything but a Persian carpet for his pig!" We had to go further and further afield to find food. This desperate search was called *hamstern*, which is to behave like a hamster.

The winter of 1945–1946 was very difficult. My mother's family had been forcibly ejected from their home in eastern Germany because that part of the country now belonged to Poland. At one point there were thirteen people living in our two bedroom house, all of whom were hungry. Ration cards were issued by the Allies. They were numbered between one and six. Level six was the highest, which allowed 2,000 calories a day for a working man. Level one provided next to nothing. The occupying forces took turns issuing food. We were happy when it was the Americans' turn, because they had the most food to give.

In June 1946 my cousin and I went to a farm in the country to help with the harvest. One day I was mucking out the pigsty in my apron and rubber boots when a handsome young man appeared, looking for food. His name was Kurt Drews, and he had recently been released from a Russian prison camp. His accent told me he was from Berlin, and it turned out he didn't live far from my home.

Kurt began to visit me, and soon we were in love. I was eighteen years old, and I had led a very sheltered life; my mother thought it would be inappropriate for me to go to social events while my father was in prison.

My mother wouldn't give me permission to marry Kurt while my father was away, but on 1 December 1947, my twentieth birthday – the day I reached the age of legal majority and didn't need my father's

Gerda and Kurt on their wedding day

permission – we were married. We traded some things for flour, and I had saved some poppy-seed oil and sugar from my time working at the farm, so we were able to bake a wedding cake. Nothing ever tasted as good as that cake!

In 1953, I finally learned what had happened to my father. A man had come home after spending years in Sachsenhausen, the prison camp located north of Berlin in Soviet-occupied Germany. I went to his house and showed him a photograph of my father. He told me that my father had worked in the camp kitchen, but that he had caught dysentery and died in 1947. The man wrote down the details and signed a document so that my mother could collect a small widow's pension. We also found out what had happened to my brother Heinz that year. He had disappeared after the war without a trace, and we had assumed he was dead, but he had changed his identity and had been hiding out with a farmer's family in East Prussia, now part of Poland. He returned to Berlin with the farmer's daughter, who he had married. It was a very happy reunion!

On 13 August 1961, the Soviets built the Berlin Wall and divided our city in half. The wall went up at the end of our street, just a few blocks away. Fortunately for us, our home was on the western side, in the zone controlled by the British, Americans and French. We lost contact with our friends and relatives on the other side in East Germany, and the wall was a constant reminder of the Soviet presence. Kurt and I had two sons, and I was always worried about them getting shot – they used to throw rocks against the tripwires along the wall, just to see the floodlights come on and the guards run along the top of the wall with their machine-guns. The wall came down in 1989 and Berlin was unified once again. The Americans, British and French finally withdrew from Berlin in 1994.

Elinor Florence's novel Bird's Eye View, *set during the Second World War, is available from Amazon.*

DAVID WALSER

*David Walser visited his father in Germany shortly
after the war. He recalls the scenes of devastation.*

After the war, my father became the British commandant in charge of Cologne, in Germany. I went to see him during the school holidays and he took me up to the top of the cathedral, which was still intact. I looked out over this extraordinary ruined city. It obviously

Carl, the Walsers' driver, with the Opel

shocked me because I can still see it, as clear as a photograph in my mind, but I don't think I connected what I saw with the misery and the terrible events that had destroyed the city.

The German roads were cobbled, on the whole. We had a car that I thought was terribly grand – an Opel Admiral. They tried to persuade my dad to take a really grand car called a Horch, but he turned it down because he didn't want to appear to be flaunting the fact that we'd won the war. Once, we were driving along at night when the driver stopped suddenly. He got out of the car, and there was no bridge – the road just ended. There were no signs – if he hadn't been paying attention we'd have just driven off a cliff.

We moved around every year. For a while, we lived in what had been a shooting lodge in the Ardennes, where the Germans

A damaged bridge across the Rhine

fought back and regained some of the land they'd lost just before the end of the war. The woods around our house were full of tanks, guns and ammunition. I used to play in the tanks. I remember the gardener showing me a pile of unexploded shells in the wood. It's rather amazing that I survived, but it was very exciting.

The house had belonged to a Nazi general and it was full of the most wonderful things that I wanted to have, including a collection of daggers and pistols. My father wouldn't let me have any of it, and he wouldn't let my mother keep any of the china. He said, "This all belongs to the German people." He was a completely honest man. There were people who took advantage and who sent shiploads of things like cars back to England, but my father was never like that.

In Belgium my father was awarded the Belgian Military Cross, First Class, for his work. He had already been awarded the British Military Cross in the First World War. He managed to arrange the disarmament of the resistance groups (he got them to give up their weapons). In countries that had been occupied by the Germans, there were terrible tensions between those who had resisted and those who had collaborated. That is the key difference between Britain's experience of the war and the experience of occupied countries: we never had to face the terrible dilemma of whether to collaborate or to resist. I have a lot of sympathy for people in continental Europe.

David's father and mother

A group of school children in German-occupied Amsterdam. They each have a yellow Star of David sewn onto their clothes to show that they are Jewish.

THE HOLOCAUST

By 1942, the Nazis had arrived at the "Final Solution" to the "problem" of what to do with Jewish people: they would murder every single Jew in Europe. By the end of the war, six million Jewish people – two thirds of all the Jews in Europe – had died in what became known as the Holocaust. Jews in Nazi territories were transported to death camps such as Auschwitz-Birkenau, where they were executed in gas chambers. When they arrived at the camps, the Jews were split into two groups: those who were worked and starved to death, and those who were sent to the gas chambers straight away. During the Holocaust, the Nazis persecuted other groups of people they considered inferior, too, including Roma people (Gypsies), disabled people, homosexuals, Jehovah's Witnesses and communists.

The extent of the atrocities only became clear to the rest of the world after Germany fell and the concentration camps were liberated.

Hungarian Jews arrive at the Auschwitz-Birkenau concentration camp in German-occupied Poland, June 1944. They have just disembarked from cattle trucks and are being "selected" by German officers. The fittest were sent to work, and the sick, the elderly and women with children were sent to be killed in gas chambers immediately.

JUDITH KERR

Judith Kerr is an illustrator and author of children's books. She was born in Berlin, but she and her family fled Germany when the Nazis came to power. Her experiences inspired her children's novel, When Hitler Stole Pink Rabbit.

My father Alfred Kerr was a distinguished writer and drama critic in Berlin before the Nazis came to power in March 1933. He was a fierce critic of Hitler and the Nazis and he often made fun of them in his writing and radio broadcasts, which they hated. I wasn't really aware of it at the time, but he was in great danger. Later, my mother told me that during the last winter before Hitler became chancellor, the Nazis had a list of people they would shoot when they came to power. My father's name was second on the list. He used to broadcast live on the radio, so people knew that on a certain day at, say, 11.30, he would be travelling across Berlin. The broadcasting company thought it was so dangerous that they sent him a car with an armed bodyguard. My brother and I just thought it was very splendid to be picked up in a car because we didn't have one. My mother told me long afterwards that my father once wrote her a farewell note in case he didn't come home.

Then one day, someone phoned him to say that there was a plan to take away his passport and that he should leave Germany immediately. The person who phoned wasn't anyone we knew – just someone who knew and liked my father's writing. My father was ill in bed with flu at the time but my mother packed him a small bag and he took the first train out of Germany.

My mother, my brother Michael and I followed after a tense

delay during which we had to keep my father's absence and our own imminent departure a secret. We packed just what we could take in a few bags. That was when I decided to leave my "Pink Rabbit" behind and take a new soft-toy dog instead. We took a roundabout route to cross the border, travelling on small "milk" trains to Switzerland, as my parents feared that the authorities might be looking out for us on the big express trains. My father's fear was that, if our plans were known, the Nazis might keep us as hostages to get him back.

We reached Zurich, Switzerland, where my father was anxiously waiting for us at the station, on the day before the elections that gave Hitler complete power. Afterwards we heard that early on the morning following the elections the Nazis came to our house to demand all our passports.

The day before my mother, Michael and I left Berlin was a Friday. Children in Germany used to go to school on Saturdays, so on the Friday I did what my mother had told me and told my teacher, "I won't be at school tomorrow as we're going to Switzerland for my father's health." My mother actually wrote a letter to Michael's headmaster; the letter was preserved in an old book that I was presented with in 2013, when I went back to Berlin to make a film for the BBC. The next day, Saturday, we caught a train to Zurich. My mother said to us, "When we get to the border, don't say a word!" I kept totally silent while the man checked our passports, but as he was walking out of the carriage, I started to say, "There, you see, nothing happened!" My mother gave me a terrible look. I nearly gave us all away. It's awful to think what might have happened.

I didn't really miss my life in Berlin too much because my parents made it all feel like an adventure. I missed my friends, of course. Our best friends in Germany were a brother and sister, Peter and Madi, who lived down the road from our house in Berlin. Madi loved drawing, so we had that in common, and I remember she was very good at it. Peter and Madi didn't leave Germany. They were Jewish too, or at least their father was. We didn't write to each other as it would have been too dangerous, because the Nazis watched everything. But later we found out that their father was sent to a concentration camp. Their mother got the children out of the country after about a year. Peter was sent to a boarding school in England and Madi to a boarding school in Switzerland. Eventually their father got out as well, but he was never quite the same again. We kept in touch for a long time. One thing that struck me was this: Madi told me that one week after Hitler came to power, she was no longer allowed to go to assembly at school because she was a Jew. That was within a week!

We stayed in Switzerland for six months. I got terribly ill with strep throat and nearly died, as there weren't any antibiotics. We were very poor because as soon as Hitler came to power, the paper my father worked for stopped all payments to him and weren't allowed to publish his writing. It must have been really hard for my parents with no money and no work. My father found it difficult to be published in Switzerland because the Swiss didn't want to offend Hitler, so we moved to Paris. My father could speak perfect French, so he could work there. I loved Paris and the school I went to, and both my brother and I learned the language quickly. I remember once looking out at Paris from the window of our tiny flat and saying to my father, "Isn't it wonderful to be a refugee?" For me it was an adventure, but for my parents it must have been very hard.

We came to London by boat in the spring of 1936 after the film director Alexander Korda bought a film script from my father.

The film never got made but the money certainly helped us to settle in London. People were very kind to us here. When I first came to England, I had lessons with two American girls who were being educated at home. We became tremendous friends. I learned English in a very relaxed way with an American accent. Then some very kind people clubbed together to send me to an English boarding school. I didn't enjoy it at all and wasn't very good at sport. I particularly hated the game lacrosse. I remember when I left my report said, "Judith has learnt how to cradle her crosse at last." It wasn't a very good school and it closed down when the war started.

I was sixteen when war broke out. I was evacuated to some friends in the country, but when nothing happened I soon came back to London. I went to the London Polytechnic. I was supposed to divide my time between art and learning shorthand so I could get a job, but I was incapable of learning shorthand so after a week I just did a foundation course in art, which I liked very much. But then we ran out of money again, and the war got serious. I got a job with the Honorable Mrs Gamage, who ran a project called Comforts for the Forces. They sent wool to women all over the country who knitted it up into sweaters etc. for the armed forces. She also ran another project called Officers' Kit Replacement. Officers had to pay for their own uniform, and when they were killed, very often their family didn't know what to do with their stuff. They'd send it to us, and we would have it cleaned and then hand it on to other officers who had lost everything when they had been shot down or shipwrecked. I would have loved to "do" something more exciting, like working in the war office, but I couldn't, because I wasn't born in Britain. They had various categories for foreigners during the war. There were "friendly aliens", who were the French and the Polish, and then there were "enemy aliens", who were Italians, Germans and Japanese. But we were different – we were Germans, but we were known to be anti-Hitler, so we had a special category: "friendly enemy aliens".

When I think about it now, it hits me how quickly we got used to the war. I remember buying a cup of tea at Lyons Corner House – you got the tea, and then they poured in the milk, and then they asked if you wanted sugar, and they put exactly a teaspoon full of sugar in your cup. I remember drinking this tea and marvelling at the fact that, before the war, there used to be a bowl of sugar on the table. I thought, "How could that have been? Everyone would have just taken it." I couldn't believe there used to be so much sugar that everyone could just help themselves. And that was within a year. Extraordinary.

My family stayed in London for the rest of the war. At first we lived in a hotel near Russell Square, but we were bombed out, so we moved to Putney. I remember the Blitz very clearly; one day there was a dogfight in the sky. My father and I were watching from a window and someone shouted to us to get inside. Like all Londoners, we spent very frightening nights in the cellar and saw the damage from the bombs each morning. I was lucky. I never saw anyone wounded or hurt. I think that if I had I would have been even more frightened. But of course, all this was nothing compared with what happened to the Jews who had not been able to escape Germany.

LADY ZAHAVA KOHN

Lady Zahava Kohn's family were living in Amsterdam when Germany invaded Holland in 1940. She and her parents were sent to two concentration camps: Westerbork and Bergen-Belsen. Her book, Fragments of a Lost Childhood, *tells her story with the help of the treasure trove of documents her mother kept throughout the war.*

I was born in Palestine in 1935. My parents had left Europe to escape the Nazis, but my mother suffered with the climate in Palestine – it was too hot and humid, and she became very ill. The doctor advised my father to take her back to Europe. In an ill-fated move, we returned to Holland in April 1937.

In 1941, soon after my brother Jehudi was born, my parents applied to become citizens of Honduras in Central America so that we could move there and escape the mounting threats in Europe. They were thinking of escaping under the cover of night, but the risk of my newborn baby brother making a noise and giving us away was too great – and would have put many other people's lives at risk – so my parents decided the safest option for everyone was to give Jehudi to the Dutch resistance. Handing over my brother was unbearable for my mother. I remember the awful sight of her sobbing inconsolably.

Unfortunately, our papers for Honduras arrived too late. On 26 May 1943, the SS came for my family. They took us to Westerbork in Holland, which was a transit camp: a place where Jews were imprisoned before being taken to concentration camps such as

Zahava's mother and baby brother

This photograph of Zahava's brother and his foster sisters was smuggled to their mother in a bag of beans

Auschwitz-Birkenau. Life at Westerbork was surreal: it was completely abnormal, of course, but there were elements of normality too. For example, some of our fellow prisoners were former teachers who organized lessons for us, and we put on performances for our parents. We were also still allowed to receive food packages at that time and once my mother received a bag of raw beans. She thought, "Why would I be sent raw beans? We have no cooking facilities. There must be a reason." That night, she sifted through the entire bag and eventually found a tiny photograph of my brother. The woman from the Dutch resistance who was caring for him had taken an enormous risk to let my mother know he was still safe. That discovery kept my mother strong. I still have the photo today.

There were various rituals and routines at Westerbork, too. Every Monday night they read out the names of the people who were going to be taken to Auschwitz. The SS had told my parents we would not be sent there; because I had been born in Palestine, which was under British mandate (controlled from Britain), we could be exchanged for German prisoners. But one Monday, our names were indeed read out. My parents couldn't believe it.

The next morning, when everyone was filing onto the cattle truck to go to Auschwitz, my parents made their way slowly towards the train: they suspected this would be their last journey and they wanted to be with their friends. There was no rush. Just one moment before we got on the train, a Dutch officer ran up to us. He said, "I wish I had this message for more people: you're being taken off the transport." Had he come a minute later, we would have been on that train and there is no way he could have found us. This amazing stroke of luck – or fate, if you will – saved us.

We stayed at Westerbork for several more months and then we were sent to Bergen-Belsen. Bergen-Belsen wasn't as dreaded as Auschwitz – it wasn't an extermination camp. The SS did start building gas chambers towards the end of the war, but thankfully the camp was liberated before they were completed.

I don't remember very much about Bergen-Belsen, but one thing I do clearly recall is standing outside for roll-call. The SS would read through everyone's names to make sure we were all accounted for – but it wasn't really that straightforward. The soldiers played cruel games with us: they kept us outside for hours on end in extreme weather, and would regularly pretend to have lost count, meaning that they would have to start again. Meanwhile we burned in the sun, or froze, barefoot in the snow. As far as food was concerned, in the morning we would get a crust of bread, and in the evening there would be soup which was mostly water. Nothing we ate had any nutritional value whatsoever, so people just starved to death.

Men and women were separated in Belsen, so we didn't see my father often: he was sent to a different section of the camp. My mother and I shared a bare top bunk, one of three bunks between the floor and ceiling. It was basically a plank of wood. My mother had to work for the SS, cleaning their offices, so very often I was left lying there, too weak to get up because I was starving. I think I had tuberculosis at one time, too. There was just one beam separating our bunk from the next one, which was occupied by a woman who was very seriously ill with typhus (a potentially fatal disease transmitted by fleas and lice). We had no toilet facilities, so she kept a tin pot on top of the beam for when she needed to use it. One night, she accidentally knocked the pot over and the contents went all over me. We had no washing facilities, so I couldn't get clean. My mother was so worried that I might catch typhus as a result that she queued up the following morning at 5 a.m. to get a bit more of the water they called coffee to wash my hair. That was the only way to avoid having to shave it off. I had lovely long, thick plaits, which to my mother represented so much: humanity, beauty, growth, normality. She was desperate for me to keep my hair. When I cut my hair short years later, I kept those plaits. I still have them because I know how much they meant to my mother.

We were at Bergen-Belsen for over a year. Then in January 1945, when I was nine, we were released in exchange for German prisoners. The rest of the camp was liberated by the British in April, but I would not have survived the final four months. Before we left, my mother, who was unbelievably selfless, took our crusts of bread and gave them to my father's uncle who had to stay in the camp. She thought we wouldn't need the crusts if we were being freed – and if we were being taken to our deaths, we wouldn't need them either. Unfortunately, our relative didn't survive.

When the time came for us to leave, I was seriously ill. My parents told the barracks' leader how weak I was and said they doubted I would be able to make the journey out. Her response was, "Just push her through the control. You need to get out and you won't get another chance." So my parents held my hands and pulled me onto the train. We were extremely weak and desperately wanted to sit down. However, there were Polish prisoners in the carriage already. Each of them was lying on a row of seats, and they refused to sit and make room for us. We could barely stand and they were lying down on several seats each. I've never been able to forget that.

After that we spent several months in army barracks at Bibberach in the south of Germany, and then in the summer of 1945 we went to Switzerland where my mother's parents lived. We spent over a year there receiving treatment after the mental and physical ordeal

Zahava's brother, Jehudi

we had all been through. After a while I went to school in Zurich and made friends.

When the war ended, my father went to Holland to find a job and establish a home for us, and, most importantly, to try to find my brother. He was briefly reunited with Jehudi in Holland, but it was then decided that it would be better for Jehudi to go to live with my mother's cousin in Stockholm, the capital of Sweden, until my mother and I were able to return to Holland. As soon as my mother and I were sufficiently well, we travelled to Stockholm to collect him. This was in late 1946. It must have been extremely difficult for my brother: he was just five years old and had been separated from us since he was a baby. He spoke Dutch and Swedish, not German, and he had "siblings" in Holland. Then, out of the blue, a strange woman arrived and said she was his mother and I was his sister. Unsurprisingly, he didn't want to come to Amsterdam with us – he wanted to stay where he was, where he felt settled with the only family he knew. My mother was upset but then she had an idea: she bought him a big balloon, which he found very exciting. When it deflated, he became very unhappy, so my mother told him, "Daddy is in Amsterdam, and he will be able to make the balloon bigger again." After that, my brother couldn't wait to get there!

When we were settled in Amsterdam, my parents never spoke to Jehudi and me about what had happened to us. Some of my friends were traumatized by what they had been through and my mother didn't want that to happen to us. She wanted us to be able to embrace life and live it to the full. My parents did talk to friends, many of whom had also experienced difficult things. They would play cards and talk about what happened, but as soon as I entered the room they would change the subject.

Many years later, when my mother died, I was clearing out her room and at the back of a cupboard I found a small, very old suitcase full of letters, cards and photographs from before and during the war – the useless papers for Honduras, the photo of my brother she had found in the bag of beans, everything. I just couldn't get over it. I have no idea how she kept them all – we had no cupboard, no space, no proper mattress on the bunk we shared in Bergen-Belsen. If anyone had found them she would have been killed immediately, but she kept them anyway. They have helped me build up a picture of what happened to us and have given me an even greater love and respect for my incredible mother.

FREDDIE KNOLLER

Freddie Knoller was a teenager living in Vienna when the Germans annexed Austria. You can read more about his story in his book, Desperate Journey, *written with John Landaw.*

From my early childhood, my family and I were subjected to anti-Semitism; Austrians were well known for being anti-Semitic. I was set upon every so often by Christian children on my way to school. After the Anschluss, when the Nazis invaded Austria and made it part of Germany, these attacks became even more extreme. After Kristallnacht, when the Nazis burned down all the synagogues, my parents insisted that we children should leave the country. I was the first to leave, going illegally to Belgium. My brother Eric was next – he left for Florida, USA. Then Otto went to England. My parents didn't want to leave; they thought they were too old for anything to happen to them.

Freddie aged seventeen, Vienna, 1938

I was just seventeen when I moved to Antwerp, Belgium. At first I lived with two other refugees about the same age as me, and then I joined a camp for Jewish refugees, where I played in the camp orchestra. When the Germans invaded Belgium in May 1940, everyone in the camp fled on foot to France. At the border, I was arrested by the French as an "enemy alien" and taken to Saint-Cyprien Interment Camp. All Germans were taken there, regardless of whether they were Jewish or Nazi. The living conditions were disastrous, and soon typhus broke out. I escaped one night and walked ten kilometres to the next town. From there, I went to Gaillac, where my aunt, uncle and cousins lived.

In the meantime, the Germans had occupied Paris and the North of France, but Gaillac was still in the unoccupied zone, ruled by the German-controlled Vichy government. I grew bored of living there, and I craved a new adventure, so I decided to visit Paris. My relatives tried to stop me, but I was determined.

I was fascinated by the Paris nightlife and I earned my living by taking German soldiers to nightclubs, brothels and cabarets. I earned a percentage of whatever the soldiers consumed. I managed to get hold of false identification papers and took on a new identity as Robert Metzner, born in Metz, Alsace-Lorraine. I met all kinds of people: decent German soldiers, abusive Nazis, French collaborators and a wonderful Frenchman who worked in the resistance.

Once I was arrested by a Gestapo officer who claimed that he could tell the difference between the head of a Jew and that of a true Aryan. He took my head between his hands and felt my skull. He then said that I was telling the truth when I said I had been born in Alsace-Lorraine and said I had come from a good German background. But he didn't want me to keep working in nightclubs – he wanted me to work for the German Reich. I didn't want to do this, so I had to go underground.

In May 1943 I joined the Maquis, a band of resistance fighters in south-west France. Other members of the group included Jews, French communists and young people who didn't want to work in Germany under the new compulsory labour law. Apart from one attempt to blow up a German troop train and lots of political arguments, we didn't do much resisting. We did, however, work for the local peasants and farmers, and they paid us in food.

I had a relationship with a young girl from the next village, who I thought I was in love with. Like a fool, I told her I had false papers. One day we had an argument, and I told her that I did not want to see her again. A few days later, I was arrested by the French police, and when I showed them my papers, they just laughed. They tortured me and asked me for names of people in my resistance unit and wanted to know where I came from. I told them I didn't know anything about a resistance unit but that I was a Jew from Vienna hiding up in the hills. I was taken to Drancy, where Jews were sent before being deported to death camps.

At the beginning of October 1943, my name came up for deportation to the east. I was taken to the railway station and 100 of us were squeezed into each cattle wagon. There was not enough room for everyone to sit on the floor, and there was only one bucket filled with drinking water and one empty bucket to use as a toilet. We youngsters made room for old people, sick people and women with babies. I will never forget the stench, the arguments, the screaming of the babies and the moans of those who were dying. I was squeezed against a middle-aged Frenchman called Robert, a gentle person who looked very much like my father. I made him as cosy as I could and we became good friends. He told me that he was a doctor. I didn't realize it at the time, but he would save my life.

After three days and nights, the train stopped at a station. We saw a sign reading *Oświęcim* on the platform, and we guessed that we were somewhere in Poland. We were right. We were going to Auschwitz. The platform was full of SS with dogs, and we saw some young people in striped prisoners' clothes. The SS told younger people to walk to the camp, but older men and women with their children were taken away by trucks. We heard some alarming rumours about what was going to happen to them but most people didn't believe them. Some of those who did believe the rumours killed themselves by walking straight into the electric fences.

When we got to Auschwitz, I realized I had two choices: I could either give up and be dead within three days, or I could fight to survive. I chose the latter. I didn't listen to the people who moaned about hunger, or look at those who neglected their personal hygiene – a sign that they had given up. I had to take care of myself. I had to get out alive, so I could tell the world about this barbarism.

On a visit to the camp hospital, I saw my doctor friend from the train, Robert. He had been put in charge of the hospital, and he said he would help me with extra food whenever he could. He told me to go to the hospital every evening when I returned from work.

At work, I had to carry 25-kilogram cement bags on my back, day in, day out. It wasn't possible to do this and survive on the tiny amount of food we were given. People dropped like flies. I am sure I only survived because of the extra food I received from Robert.

On 18 January 1945, when the Russians were approaching Auschwitz, the camp was evacuated. We went west, walking on icy, snow-covered roads, still wearing our striped, thin clothes. Many people collapsed and were shot. We had to throw the corpses into the ditch next to the road. Eventually we reached a brick factory and were allowed to rest. Only half of us were still alive when we

got there, and the next morning some people didn't get up.

Then we were taken to a railway station and squeezed into a cattle wagon. We travelled through Austria and Germany for seven days and seven nights until we reached our new camp, Nordhausen-Dora. Nine people in our wagon died during the journey.

Nordhausen-Dora was the place where the V-1 and V-2 rockets were manufactured. We worked in the tunnels beneath the Harz Mountains, pushing wagons on rails and carrying heavy metal objects. One night, Allied planes bombed the entrance to the tunnels, and many of our comrades died.

When American troops began approaching Nordhausen-Dora, we were evacuated to Bergen-Belsen. The German SS disappeared, and we were now guarded by Croatian and Hungarian SS units, who didn't beat us. But there was no food at all. We tried to find edible roots in the ground, but many people collapsed and died from hunger and dysentery. On 15 April 1945, British troops entered Bergen-Belsen. We were given hot milk with rice to eat, which we devoured like wild animals. Many inmates stuffed themselves with food which their stomachs could not digest, and they died. A British officer asked for volunteers to go to nearby farms and bring back any food we could find. I joined this group, with a soldier carrying a gun. We loaded food onto a trolley in front of the protesting farmer and his wife. When I found a large photo of Hitler hidden behind a wardrobe, I took a knife and cut the photo to pieces. The old farmer went red in the face and shouted at me, "Du sau Jud!" ("You filthy Jew!") After everything that had happened to me as a Jew, my emotions overtook me and I sank the knife into his belly. I just couldn't stop myself. We left the farm soon after that.

I returned to France and my brother Eric tracked me down

to the little village where I had been sent to recuperate by the French Government. Our reunion was very emotional. Eric told me that our parents had perished at Auschwitz in 1944.

When my brother Eric died in 1996, his widow found a bundle of over 100 letters from my mother and father, dated 1938–1941. I was stunned when I saw my father's unmistakable, elegant handwriting. Why had Eric never told me about the letters? Did he have the guilt that all Holocaust survivors have? Why did it take me over 30 years to tell my family and the world what I had been through? Was it the same feeling of guilt?

BETTINE LE BEAU

During the war, Bettine Le Beau and her family were held in concentration camps. She moved to England in 1945 and became a successful actress.

I was born in 1932 in Antwerp, Belgium, to Polish-Jewish parents. When Germany invaded Belgium in May 1940, my father, who was a fur trader, was away at a convention in London. He advised my mother to head to Paris and to apply for a visa at the British consulate. My mother cashed in all of her money at the bank and travelled with my older brother and me to Paris. Every day, she tried to secure a visa from the British Embassy, but Germany invaded France before she could do so.

My mother didn't want to inconvenience the friends we were staying with, so she took us out every day to see Paris. I enjoyed it, though I was looking forward to seeing my daddy again. After the Germans

Bettine with her mother and brother in Paris, 1940

invaded, we had to go to the mairie (town hall) every week to sign in, but we thought, "This will be OK until the end of the war." But then we were sent to our first internment camp – a castle in the south-west, near Audaux, surrounded by barbed wire.

We never had enough food at the camp, but there were lots of other children and I was allowed to stay with my mother and brother, so it wasn't too unbearable. For the first time in my life, I saw grown men crying. I didn't understand what was going on, but I felt anguish for the adults. The men began to collapse, falling ill or losing their memories. The women were the strongest.

After a while we were transferred to a camp at Gurs along with other people the German government perceived to be dangerous. My brother and I were separated from our mother. I only saw her through the wire fence between the children's and the women's barracks. I could speak to her, but I couldn't touch her.

We lived in a draughty, wet wooden hut with an earth floor, and slept on straw. The camp was overcrowded, and conditions got worse as winter approached. There were enormous rats, lice and fleas. Disease was everywhere. People were starving to death.

We came up with a system for sharing food fairly: we cut the morning loaf into 30 pieces and took turns choosing a portion. That way we each had a chance of getting the biggest piece. When it was my turn to pick, my brother would say, "Pick that one! It's bigger. Wait! That one is better." The person who picked last and got the worst portion was entitled to the crumbs. We would lick our fingers and pick each one up. I used my imagination to pretend I wasn't hungry. We came up with games – playing Jacks with stones, things like that – and we made up stories. But when the winter came, a lot of the children got dysentery and typhus. They gave up hope and lay on their straw beds, crying. A lot of them died.

But then, in 1940, Oeuvre de Secours aux Enfants (OSE), a Jewish humanitarian organization for children, offered to smuggle children out of the camps. A lot of women said, "No. My children are staying with me." But my mum said, "Please take them to safety, but keep a record of where they go. If God helps me and I make it out of here, I will need to know where they are." When she said goodbye to me, she said, "You've got your brother. Your father is safe. I will join you one day." She did not cry, so I believed her.

The OSE took my brother and me to a home for rescued children. I was lonely, I was lice-ridden from the camp and I wet the bed as I was frightened. I longed to go back to Gurs where I had friends and was near my mother, despite the awful conditions there.

In 1942, the Nazis resolved to kill every Jewish person in Nazi-occupied countries. The French Government agreed to co-operate. The OSE shut down the home before it could be raided by the SS, and started sending children to live with families in remote areas. The OSE saved my life – the following year, French officials turned over 3,900 Jewish prisoners from Gurs to the Germans. Most of them were transported to extermination camps.

The OSE started smuggling children across the border from France to Switzerland, over the Alps, under a barbed wire fence. My brother and I were chosen to go behind the other children; we had French accents, so we could be more easily assimilated into a French family if we needed to be. Just before we were due to go, the guide responsible for smuggling the children was arrested and murdered by the SS. So we had to stay in France.

My brother was already fourteen, so the OSE found him a job as a shepherd high up in the mountains. I was given a new name, Betty Frickier, and a new back story: my father was a prisoner of

Bettine's brother Harry working as a shepherd in the mountains, 1942

war and my mother was dead. I was given strict instructions not to reveal my Jewish identity – that however lovely people were to me, I should never tell the truth.

On Christmas Eve 1942, a truck dropped me off at the side of a road with another girl, Henny. We followed the directions we had been given until we reached a farm. We were both frightened – we held hands – and then the door of the farm opened and light flooded out. It reminded me of the Christmas story. We stayed on the farm for the rest of the war and attended the tiny village school. No one ever challenged my identity. I never really felt at home; the couple I lived with were so kind, but completely different from my family.

When the war ended, my brother Harry arrived at the farm to take me home. He didn't even say thank you to the family for looking after me – he had been treated very badly by the family he stayed with, and the war had taken away all of his charm.

I was reunited with my parents, but the war had destroyed my family. We came to England, and my father tried to be nice to my mother, but in the five years they had been separated he'd had a child with another woman. I never met my half-sister. I like people – what if I liked her? It would have been disloyal to my mother.

After I moved to England, I had a successful acting career. I appeared in *The Benny Hill Show*, *The Prisoner* and the first James Bond film, *Dr. No.* My mother wasn't interested in my career, but my father wrote to the producers to thank them for casting me.

I laid my parents next to each other when they died. The war pulled them apart, but they are together in death.

ANITA LASKER-WALLFISCH

Anita Lasker-Wallfisch was a child in Germany when Hitler came to power. Her story is told in her book, Inherit the Truth, 1939–1945, *published by Giles de la Mare.*

I was born in the town of Breslau, which was then in Germany, and is now in Poland. My father was a lawyer and my mother was a very fine violinist. I had two sisters and we all learnt to play an instrument – I played the cello. There was no particular emphasis on being Jewish; we were a typical completely assimilated Jewish liberal family. We had a very happy home.

I first encountered anti-Semitism at school, when I was eight. I was about to wipe the blackboard when one of the children said, "Don't give the Jew the sponge." Soon afterwards, some children spat at me in the street and called me a "dirty Jew". I did not really understand what was going on. You just had to accept that you were different – you did not belong to the master race.

When I was twelve, my cello lessons stopped. There were no Jewish cello teachers left in Breslau, and it had become too dangerous for an Aryan cellist to teach a Jewish child. My parents got permission for me to leave school and go to Berlin, where I had lessons with the only Jewish cello teacher still living there. But life as we knew it came to an abrupt end on 9 November 1938, Kristallnacht. Ernst vom Rath, a minor official at the German Embassy in Paris, was shot by a young Jewish man by the name of Herschel Grynszpan. This incident "spontaneously enraged the German people", as the press put it at the time, and the first major pogrom (massacre) of the Nazi era took place. Synagogues were burned down, Jewish shops were smashed up and looted, and Jewish homes were invaded and demolished. Most men were arrested and the expression "concentration camp" became part of the vocabulary.

Kristallnacht was a kind of dress rehearsal for things to come. The willingness of the mob to attack undefended targets was a green light for the Nazis – there were no limits to what they could do. After Kristallnacht, we were not allowed to own radios; we had to hand in our bicycles; we had to add the name Sara (for women) or Israel (for men) to our names; we had to wear a yellow star on our clothes, and so on. It became clear that we could no longer remain in Germany, but many people did not get away, my family included, and I assure you that it was not for lack of trying.

After I returned home from Berlin, I tried to go back to school – a Jewish one, this time. But eventually Jewish schools were shut down. Then, on 20 January 1942, senior Nazi officials met in a suburb of Berlin, called Wannsee. At the Wannsee Conference, they discussed – and it took just an hour and a half – how to exterminate all of the Jews in Europe. We are talking about eleven million people.

On 9 April 1942, the Nazis sent my parents to a place called Isbiza near Lublin in Poland. My sister Renate and I wanted to go with them, but our father wouldn't hear of it. "Everyone gets to where we're going soon enough," he said. Needless to say, I never saw them again. After the war I learned that, where my parents went, the victims had to dig their own graves, undress, and be shot into their graves. It was a messy way of getting rid of human beings. A more efficient way had to be found, and it was – gas chambers.

My sisters and I were now completely alone. We were conscripted to work in a paper factory with other Jews, Poles and French prisoners of war. I wasn't prepared to be killed just because I'd been born a Jew, and I wanted to give the Germans a better reason for killing me, so I involved myself in illegal activities. I forged papers for French prisoners of war to escape with. We were forbidden to talk to the French prisoners, but we found a way – there was a hole in the wall of the toilet used by Jews, and on the other side of this wall was the French prisoners' cafeteria. A prisoner and I would go to opposite sides of the wall and whisper or push messages through the hole. One day, I found that the hole had been blocked up – we had been seen. That was when we decided to make a run for it. The idea was to get into the unoccupied zone of France, somehow. It was not exactly the most thought-out escape plan, but you didn't think too far ahead in those days. There was only one thought in our minds: to get out of Germany.

We only got as far as the railway station before we were arrested. I appeared in court, charged with forgery, helping the enemy and attempted escape. The absurd thing was that committing a criminal offence actually helped me – it meant I stayed in prison for over a year, postponing my arrival at a concentration camp. When I was eventually sent to Auschwitz-Birkenau, I did not have to go through the usual selection on arrival at the notorious unloading ramp, where the SS chose who should live and who should die in the gas chamber. I had a criminal record, and criminals did not get gassed automatically.

I was at Auschwitz for nearly a year, and I have no doubt that I survived because I became a member of the camp orchestra. As long as the Germans wanted an orchestra, they would keep us alive. We played marches every morning and evening at the gate of the camp so that the work commandos could march neatly in step. We also played for individual members of the SS who wanted to hear some music after sending thousands of people to their deaths.

Although I was privileged, I knew I would end up in the gas

chamber eventually. It didn't seem possible that anyone would come out of Auschwitz-Birkenau alive. But a miracle happened. The Russians advanced and we were taken west to Bergen-Belsen.

Bergen-Belsen was very different from Auschwitz-Birkenau. In Auschwitz, people were murdered in the most sophisticated manner; in Belsen, they simply perished. There was no orchestra there. We sat about and watched each other deteriorate. Belsen was ill-equipped to deal with the thousands of miserable skeletons who arrived there because of the ever-advancing Allied troops. In the final weeks, death marches from all over Germany arrived and half-dead people dragged themselves into the compound.

There are no words to describe this inferno. The dead bodies started piling up; there was no food, no water – nothing. It was clear that we had come to the end of the line. It was very hot that April and the effect of the temperature on the mountains of bodies was horrendous. Feeble attempts were made to move the corpses; those of us who could still walk were given some string, and we were told to tie the arms of the dead together and drag them along the road to a big ditch. But this operation was soon abandoned. We were too weak, and the bodies remained in the camp. The corpses were so much a part of the landscape that we barely noticed them.

We heard a lot of shooting and rumbling noises in the distance, and it was rumoured that tanks were approaching. I was furious when someone said tanks might be British. I felt more "at home", so to speak, with the thought of impending death than the thought of being liberated by the British army.

It was about 5 p.m. on 15 April 1945 when the first British tank arrived. We were liberated. No one who was in Belsen will ever forget that day. We did not greet our liberators with shouts of joy. We were silent with disbelief. We thought we might be dreaming.

DAME ESTHER RANTZEN

Writer, broadcaster and campaigner Dame Esther Rantzen is the founder of ChildLine, the helpline for young people, and The Silver Line, the support line for older people. During the war, her family sponsored a Jewish mother and child who were forced to flee Nazi Germany.

I was born in June 1940, so I was only five when the war ended. You may imagine, then, that I really don't have many memories of the war, and you would be right. My family had moved out of London before the war started because they realized that the city would be a target for Nazi attacks, so I was born in a little town in Hertfordshire called Berkhamsted. We would hear planes flying overhead and sirens that warned us that bombers were heading towards us. I watched my grandmother putting blackout material over the windows, and we practised sitting under the dining-room table wearing gas masks that made us look like elephants with strange rubber trunks. But no bombs fell anywhere near us, and our life was quite tranquil and happy.

My father went to work in London during the week, because he was Head of Engineering Lines and Designs for the BBC, so he was in a "reserved occupation" – in other words, he was necessary

Esther and her mother during the war

to the war effort. He had to sort out the music that was played on the radio, to make sure that they didn't accidentally include any songs that had a particular message for resistance workers in France. Some songs had secret meanings. For instance, one song told French resistance workers that a plane was about to arrive with British agents on board.

My father didn't entirely miss the bombs, either. One fell on the house next door to the one he was sleeping in. As he rushed to the window to see what had happened, the window blew in, and he just escaped having his head cut off by flying glass. My mother was very cross when he told her about that. He was also around when a bomb fell on the BBC's Broadcasting House. A policeman walking by tragically died because, against instructions, he was wearing his helmet with the strap under his chin, and the blast blew the hat backwards.

But the most poignant memory I have is of a little boy called Charlie.

Charlie, aged five, and Esther, aged one, with Esther's mother, 1941

In the late 1930s, as the Nazi Party's persecution of the Jews became more and more violent, many Jews tried to flee to save their lives, and the lives of their children. It wasn't easy (just as it isn't for refugees today) – to get into Britain, Jews needed sponsors who would guarantee that they would be provided with homes by the Jewish community and that they would never become a drain on the state. My grandparents agreed to sponsor a charming little red-haired boy, Charlie, who was about six or seven years old, and his mother Ursula. When Ursula managed to find a job as a housekeeper, Charlie came to live with my parents. They loved him, and he loved them. My grandmother paid for his schooling.

Meanwhile, my aunt Jane had joined the Quaker Relief (a voluntary organization that provided help to civilians), and she drove an ambulance into the Bergen-Belsen concentration camp with the first civilian party after it was liberated. She worked hard to try to help the survivors, and wrote an amazing report about the terrible way the inmates of the camp had been treated. Then she went to Poland to do what she could to help there. While she was abroad, she sent a postcard to Charlie. My mother told me, "The morning it arrived Charlie was late for school, so I called upstairs to him, 'Hurry up Charlie, there's a postcard for you.' He came tumbling down the stairs, shouting, 'It's from my daddy, my daddy!' I had to explain to him that it was from Aunty Jane. But I knew then that he had to be told the truth about his daddy."

The terrible truth that Charlie's mother had never been able to bring herself to tell him was that his father had not been able to escape from Nazi Germany. Charlie would never get a postcard from him; he would never see his daddy again. Charlie's daddy had been rounded up with the rest of the Jews and taken to a concentration camp and killed. My mother told me that he had been a tall, good-looking, red-haired physical training instructor. I never knew him, of course, but Charlie himself grew up to be tall, red-haired and very good-looking. (As a teenager I had a crush on him. I don't think he ever knew that.)

After the war, Charlie left school and went to work in Europe – he was excellent at languages. I met him while he was living in Holland, and he later moved to Spain. But to celebrate his 60th birthday, he returned to England and gave a wonderful party, where my mother was the guest of honour. I sat next to his daughter, who was a little mystified by my family's relationship with Charlie. I told her his story: the tragic murder of his father in a concentration camp; the way his mother had to struggle to find work as a housekeeper; that my grandparents had sponsored him, and my mother and father had fostered him, and how much they loved him. She was astonished – he had never told her any of this. He had clearly kept the pain he suffered as a child hidden in his heart. Perhaps it hurt too much to talk about it, even to his own children.

There were many people, like Charlie, for whom the events of the war were so agonizing that they never talked about

their experiences. I believe it is important that we hear these stories now. Perhaps one day we may learn from them.

Esther with Charlie, 2015

RONALD BAILEY

Ronald Bailey served in the British army during the war. He was in Germany during the liberation of the Bergen-Belsen concentration camp.

I was near Bergen-Belsen when it was liberated but none of us would have dreamed of going there – no way. I knew of it and saw photographs of it, though. The 11th Armoured Division liberated the camp. What they saw was too terrible to talk about. Some of them took lots of photographs of the camp and pasted them all over the inside of a lorry. Then they took the local German people and made them walk through the lorry and look at the photographs, so that they could see just what their people had done to other human beings. When the locals saw the photographs, they said they'd known nothing about what was happening, but they were really frightened. They really thought that the British were going to send them somewhere like that.

A lot of Germans surrendered to us because they were so scared of the Russians. They had done terrible things to the Russians so they knew they would be better off with us and the Americans. Some of the Germans we took prisoner were just schoolboys, fourteen, fifteen, sixteen years old. It was a terrible thing.

Ronald during the war

As soon as Germany surrendered on 7 May 1945, people around the world celebrated the end of the war in Europe. The official day of celebration, Victory in Europe day or VE day, took place on 8 May (9 May in Commonwealth countries). In London, crowds gathered in Trafalgar Square and around Buckingham Palace. The Prime Minister, Winston Churchill, appeared on the balcony of the palace along with the Royal Family, giving his "V for Victory" sign to the crowds. The king and queen allowed their daughters Margaret and Elizabeth (the future Queen Elizabeth II) to slip out of the palace incognito and join in the celebrations.

In the United States, VE day fell on the same day as President Harry S. Truman's birthday. He dedicated the victory to his predecessor Franklin D. Roosevelt, who had been president throughout the war but died on 12 April 1945, just days before Germany's surrender.

However, the war wasn't over – the war with Japan had yet to be won. And for many, the celebrations were tinged with sadness. Some still had relatives fighting in the war in the Pacific, loved ones in prisoner of war camps or friends and family who had died during the war.

Winston Churchill, the British Prime Minister, celebrating the end of the war with Germany on VE day, 8 May 1945

PHYLLIS ROWNEY

Phyllis Rowney worked as a land-girl during the war.
She remembers the VE day celebrations in
the village where she lived.

On VE day I went to a party in the little village hall just up the road. I ended up having stitches in my head – the windows in the village hall used to open inwards and there were sharp catches on the end of them. I had been sitting underneath one of them and everyone had been dancing around, and somehow the window swung open and cut my head open.

We dressed up to celebrate the end of the war, and we dressed the dogs up too. As soon as we heard that the war was over on the radio, I put a big red bow on Punch's lead. He was a big Labrador. The farmer's wife had gone out shopping on the bus, so I took the dog and went down to meet the bus to tell her the news. The farmer's wife was delighted – she was very patriotic.

MONICA MILLER

Monica Miller served in the army during
the war. She told her great-grandsons
Jonathan and Jamie Brooks about the scene
outside Buckingham Palace on VE day.

On VE day, I was in London. What a treat! We were told that if we were going to a celebration we should leave our hats behind as they would be stolen, but going out in the streets in uniform without a hat was unheard of. A friend and I went to Buckingham Palace. The king, the queen, the two princesses and Winston Churchill came out onto the balcony and waved at the crowds. Afterwards, the princesses came down to mingle with the public, though I didn't see them. Winston Churchill did his "V for Victory" sign to everyone. We were all singing and dancing and having a lovely time. We didn't want to go home – it was great to see everyone so happy.

OLIVE WHITEFORD (NÉE VEEVERS)

Not everyone celebrated on VE day – Olive Whiteford was waiting for her father to come home from a prisoner of war camp. This is her story.

I was born on 7 June 1933 in Clitheroe, Lancashire, so I was six when the war started. I had three older sisters – Elsie, nine, Nancy, thirteen, and Mary, fifteen. My dad joined the Territorial Army in 1938, so of course he was sent out as soon as the war started.

I remember listening to Prime Minister Neville Chamberlain saying we were now at war. My father went down to the mill in Clitheroe that very day to report. My mother said, "He's gone without his pyjamas!" She wrapped them up in a brown paper parcel and took them down there. The captain came to meet her – he was only in his early twenties – and he promised he'd get them to him. Soon after that, the men were sent to France, as the British Expeditionary Force.

On 24 February 1940, Dad came home on leave from France. He was billeted with a family in Belgium at the time. He said they were very poor and that they had two little girls who didn't have much of anything, and he asked if we had anything he could take back with him. My mother had made us silk dresses the previous year, so Elsie and I sent those. Then we had to decide whether to send our dolls or our teddy bears. We decided on the teddy bears. It was very hard for us. We often wondered what happened to those little girls, and whether they lived to enjoy our bears.

Then came the evacuation of Dunkirk. We weren't warned that Dad would be arriving home, but I remember it was lunchtime, and I was eating baked beans on toast off a willow-patterned plate when we heard footsteps coming around the side of the house. My mother said, "Who on earth's that coming at this time?" And I said, "Daddy's coming." And sure enough, it was him.

Then, in July 1940, he came on a 48-hour embarkation leave. I remember walking down the road with him with my feet splayed, and my dad said, "Olive, walk with your feet straight." That stuck with me all through the war. I remember thinking, "I must be walking with my feet straight when Dad comes home."

One day, in May 1941, my mother suddenly said to my sister, "I just heard your father say, 'I'm all right, Clara.'" We later heard that my father had been taken prisoner during the fall of the Greek island of Crete on that very day – 31 May. I remember the telegram coming, which said, "Missing, presumed killed." But my mother was convinced he was still all right, because he had told her he was. Some people think that sort of thing is nonsense, but I don't think it was in their case. They were very close.

It wasn't until four months later that we heard he was a prisoner of war. I remember running up my friends' garden path to tell them. Their mum said, "Olive, what's wrong?" I said, "Daddy's a prisoner of war!" She said, "Oh, Olive." I said, "But he's alive!"

At church, the minister used to pray for all the servicemen, and he always ended with, "Ralph Veevers, prisoner of war". That kept us going.

My father was kept on Crete for about six months. Eventually he was taken by cattle truck up to Stalag VIII-B, which wasn't very far from Auschwitz-Birkenau on the German-Polish border. I still have the

Elsie, Mary, Nancy and Olive with their mother in 1942. They sent this photograph to their father at the prisoner of war camp.

letters he sent me from Stalag VIII-B. He sent me a postcard on my birthday. I have the letter I wrote back to him, too. He kept it all the way through the war. How he managed to keep it I do not know.

During the holidays, I used to go and stay on a farm where an Italian prisoner of war worked. He had nice meals, so I thought, "Dad's all right, it'll be like this for him too." Of course it was nothing like that for prisoners of the Nazis.

Towards the end of 1944, we had our last letter from Dad. After that we heard absolutely nothing. At school, my teacher Miss Race always asked me, "Have you heard anything from your father?" I said, "No, Miss Race." She said, "You know those maps in the paper, showing the Russian advance, with the big black arrows? Your father is marching ahead of the Russian advance, on his way home." And she was dead right.

On VE day, when everyone was putting the bunting and flags out, Elsie and I said, "Can we put our flag out, Mum?" And Mum very gently said, "Well, no, love. The war's not over for us yet."

I remember very, very well – it's one of my most treasured memories – the day that the telegram arrived. Again, it was lunchtime. Mary was working in the bank, Nancy was at college at Salisbury in south-west England and Elsie had gone back to school to have her form photograph taken. I was the last to go back for afternoon school. Mother went down to the butchers, and she said, "You don't need to lock the door when you go, because I'll soon be back." So I went down the road on my bike – but when I got as far as the butchers, I saw my mother standing there with a yellow envelope. And as calmly as anything, Mother said, "Olive, it's from your daddy. He's arrived in England, and he's coming home tomorrow." Just like that. "You'll go and tell Mary at the bank on your way back to school, and you'll tell Elsie at school." And I said, "Yes, I will." Mother managed to get in touch with Nancy at college, too. I went to school, and I thought, "I'm not going to tell anyone else about this. I'm going to keep this big secret all to myself." It was too joyous – I wanted to enjoy it by myself. But at the end of the afternoon, Miss Race said, "Have you heard anything from your father yet?" And I said, "Yes Miss Race, he's arrived in England, and he's coming home tomorrow."

He came home on 16 May 1945. It was so strange. My uncle took my mother to meet him off the train. Elsie and I waited at home, and Nancy got home from Salisbury in time – her friends clubbed together to give her enough money for the journey. Mary couldn't get off work, but she came home soon afterwards. We were in the sitting room when my dad came home. He was wearing a new uniform, and they'd given him a beret hat. He was only a little man, and the hat was resting on his ears. He just looked amazed. We hadn't seen each other for five years, and I often think what a shock it must have been for him, coming home to see us grown up instead of little girls – I was almost twelve when he came home. It was a big, big experience, really.

I often think of how hard it must have been for my poor mother while my dad was a prisoner. I said to her once, "You were so wonderful to us during the war," and she said, "Oh Olive, but nobody knows how many tears I shed at night, after you'd gone to bed. If it hadn't been for you girls, I wouldn't have survived."

My dad never ever complained about what had happened to him, but I used to hear him crying out at night. He had seen some terrible things. There were Russian shells falling on the camp as they left, and they marched from December 1944 till April 1945, through the snow, with very little to eat. He said Russian prisoners were shot for picking turnips out of the fields. But he didn't actually talk about what had happened for about ten years. Then one Saturday lunchtime he just sat down and started talking and he was still talking well after teatime.

I came across the diary he kept when he was a prisoner of war one day, in a drawer where we kept gloves and stuff. I said, "What's this, Dad?" And he said, "It's just something I wrote, love, you take it."

A telegram Olive's father sent to let his family know what time he was coming home

THE FALL OF
JAPAN

As the war in Europe was ending, the United States was preparing to invade Japan, but they knew that this would involve an immense loss of life on both sides. They decided to try to end the war without invading by using a new kind of weapon: the atomic bomb. An international team of scientists led by American physicist Robert Oppenheimer had begun developing atomic bombs in 1942, in a programme code-named the Manhattan Project. By the summer of 1945, the team had developed two different atomic bombs, using the energy inside atoms of uranium and plutonium to create devastating explosions.

On 6 August 1945, a US bomber crew flew over the Japanese city of Hiroshima in a plane named the *Enola Gay* and dropped the uranium bomb, code-named Little Boy. Two-thirds of Hiroshima was destroyed in the blast. Around 80,000 people were killed instantly, but about 55,000 died later from the effects of radiation from the bomb. On 9 August, another US bomber crew dropped the plutonium bomb, code-named Fat Man, on the city of Nagasaki. Around 40,000 people died instantly, and 10,000 more died later from the effects of the bomb. Japan could not go on fighting. A surrender was signed on 2 September 1945, six years and one day after war broke out. This is now remembered as Victory over Japan day, or VJ day, in the US. In Europe, it is celebrated on 15 August, when Japan first agreed to surrender.

A column of smoke rises more than 18,000 metres into the air over Nagasaki after an atomic bomb was dropped on the city from a US B-29 bomber, 9 August 1945

THEODORE "DUTCH" VAN KIRK

Dutch Van Kirk had just left high school when the US entered the war. He joined the United States Air Force, and on 6 August 1945 he was navigator of the Enola Gay during the bombing of Hiroshima.

I never expected to live through the war. If you had told me I was going to live to my present age, I'd have said, "No way." But here I am, 93 years old. I should have been dead years ago. That's just luck.

I joined the air force and became a navigator with the 97th Bomb Group. We went to England to fly missions in Flying Fortress bombers. Our commanding officer was a young captain named Paul Tibbets. He was an outstanding pilot. He could do things with a plane that I swear nobody else could do. And when you were in a plane with him, he wouldn't suffer any mistakes. You had to be picture perfect.

Tibbets and I flew a lot of missions in England and Africa together. I remember the day we flew American General Dwight D. Eisenhower to Gibraltar, a British territory on the south coast of Spain. The weather was so bad on the airfield before we took off, you couldn't see the wings of the plane. Eisenhower was pacing up and down, impatient to leave. He called us all together and said, "You're younger than I am. If it were you, would you fly in this weather?" We said, "Oh, we'd have left already." He said, "Well hell then, let's go." I said, "There's a big old steeple out there on the left, general. I don't want to be blamed for smearing a two-star general around a big steeple." But he said, "I'll take that chance, let's go." We got away with it that time.

After I'd flown 58 missions, they wouldn't let me fly any more – you were only supposed to fly 50, but somehow I ended up flying eight more. I came back to the United States and taught other navigators at the navigator school. One night when I was on leave in New Orleans, I got a call from Tibbets. He said, "This is Paul," and I said, "Hell, I know who it is, you're the only guy who would call me at 5 a.m." He said, "I'm getting a new group together and we're going overseas. I can't tell you what we're going to be doing, but if it works, we're either going to end or shorten the war. And I want you for my group navigator." I said OK, and I got orders to report to Project Silverplate in Wendover, Utah.

Project Silverplate was the secret programme that was trying to work out how to drop the atomic bomb. I knew very little about atomic energy, and we were told very little about our mission. One guy told us, "You'll be okay if you're eleven miles away when the bomb explodes." I looked at him and I said, "You've got to have holes in your head. We can't get eleven miles away from the bomb that quickly." And he said, "Well then you'd better work on getting away faster." It became evident that our problem would be getting enough distance between us and where the bomb exploded.

The first step was gaining altitude more quickly. We measured everything. How long did it take us to turn away? How could we do it more quickly? Paul Tibbets went to Los Alamos in New Mexico and spoke to Robert Oppenheimer several times to discuss our mission. Oppenheimer was often called the "father of the atomic bomb" – he was the leader of the Los Alamos Laboratory, where they designed the bombs.

Dutch in front of a B-29 bomber

Paul and I flew out to Tinian Island, off the coast of the Philippines, the launching point for the atomic bombs. It was about 1,500 kilometres (932 miles) from Tokyo. Practically everything the Japanese built there had been destroyed, and we rebuilt the airfield so the layout was an exact copy of Manhattan Island. If you knew Manhattan, you could find your way around Tinian. Even the streets were named after Manhattan. While we were there, we tested the planes and the bombs. We'd send a guy to Japan with a pumpkin bomb – a bomb the same size and weight as the atomic bomb, but armed with conventional explosives – and tell him to hit a certain factory. Not a city – anybody can hit a city. What we learned was that we'd have to fly higher, because those guys got shot at.

In the days running up to the Hiroshima mission, we used pumpkin bombs to test both the Hiroshima bomb and the plutonium bomb that was used on Nagasaki. Neither of them exploded. We got back to Tinian and one of the scientists said, "For Christ's sake, we're going to drop one of these in two days, and we still can't get an explosion!" We were taking bets on whether the bomb would work. I bet that it wouldn't work. I lost a lot of money.

On 5 August, the day before the mission, Tibbets said, "I want a name for the plane. I've been thinking about putting my mother's name on the side." I knew his mother, and so did Tom Ferebee, the bombardier (who was in charge of aiming and dropping the bomb). She was a marvellous lady, so we said, "Why don't you send the painter down to do it?" So he did. Her name was Enola Gay.

That night, the scientists told us everything they could about what would happen when we dropped the bomb. They said that the bomb would destroy everything within a certain distance. One of them said, "It'll give off enough power to send a steamship across the ocean." Another said, "It'll give off enough energy to power the city of Los Angeles for an entire week." I never believed them. They told us that the bomb would detonate 1,800 feet (550 metres) above the ground, so that a shock wave would sweep down and out – they wanted it to detonate at that height so there would be a bigger shock wave when the bomb exploded. But the scientists themselves weren't sure what the bomb would do. One said that the effects of the radiation would cover the same distance as the effects of the shock wave, so we wouldn't have to worry about radiation. That was wrong. Some of them thought the bomb might set light to the atmosphere. That was wrong too. So when we set off, we had no real sense of what would happen, or even whether the bomb would take the plane with it.

After our briefing, they told us to get some sleep. Now, how the devil they expected us to sleep after we'd been briefed that we were going to drop an atomic weapon, that was absolutely beyond me. Tibbets didn't sleep, Tom Ferebee didn't sleep, I didn't sleep.

We were taken down to the plane in trucks, and when we got down there, there were more people than you could count. Everyone wanted to shake hands with us and wish us well, from the reporters to the scientists. They were taking bets, too, by the way, about whether or not we'd come back. Made us feel real good.

We weren't certain that we were going to bomb Hiroshima until just before we took off. There were four proposed targets: Hiroshima, Nagasaki, Kyoto and Kokura. Hiroshima was the top target – that's where the defence of Japan was going to be organized, that's where the infrastructure and weapons and materials were. But the final choice of target depended on the weather – the sky had to be clear for us to drop the bomb. So they sent three weather planes to Nagasaki, Kokura and Hiroshima.

The sky was clear over Hiroshima, so off we went.

We crashed a lot of planes on take-off while we were in Tinian, because the runways weren't long enough. If we had crashed with an atomic bomb on board, that would have been a disaster. So Captain Parsons, one of the designers of the bomb, said that he would arm the bomb (turn it into a working atomic bomb) in flight – he practised and practised beforehand. During that flight, he and Jeppson, who was the assistant weaponeer, were hanging over the bomb bay-doors for about 45 minutes. Jeppson was handing tools to Parsons, who was doing the work, taking out the plug of explosives and replacing it with a plug of uranium. Tibbets was flying at low altitude all that time, and I was saying, "Christ, can't we get some more altitude? This thing is bouncing around like a yo-yo." Paul said, "Be patient, Dutch, wait till they get the bomb armed." His watchword was "patience" all the way through. Eventually, when Parsons came out from arming the bomb, his hands were raw from the threads on the bomb (the ridges that the uranium plug screwed into), which were extremely fine.

I thought, "That's an atomic bomb back there. Christ, there's an atomic bomb back there." Did that worry me? Hell no. The only way we were going to get rid of it was to take it up and drop it.

After the bomb was armed we gained another 7,000 feet (2,100 metres), up to about 10,000 feet (3,000 metres). It was a lot smoother up there. I navigated using the stars till we got to Iwo Jima, an island off the coast of Japan. If you get lost from Iwo Jima to Japan, you are the lousiest navigator in the world. There's a bunch of volcanic places that have thrust up through the water, and once you'd flown over those as many times as I had you could name every one of them. Once we'd passed Iwo Jima, we went up to about 30,000 feet (9,100 metres),

Colonel Paul Tibbets in the Enola Gay, just before taking off on the mission to Hiroshima

where the Japanese fighter planes couldn't get us.

We were at 33,000 feet (10,000 metres) as we approached the target. That's as high as we could get our B-29. I was six seconds late getting us there. We turned, heading into the wind. Tom Ferebee said, "I've got the target," which was a T-shaped bridge called the Aloi Bridge. I went up and looked over his shoulder, and I said, "That is the target." Paul Tibbets said, "That is the target." Dick Parsons said, "That is the target." We agreed it was the target. So we went in and we dropped the bomb. The bomb was on automatic pilot when it left the plane. Ferebee called, "Bombs away!"

Then Tibbets took the plane into a 150-degree turn. You'd better be sitting down when you go into a turn as steep as that. I had my place all picked out beforehand. If you were standing up, your legs got weak and you just gradually sank to the floor.

Ferebee was looking out to make sure the bomb was clear of us, and we were running to beat the devil, to get away from it. We all had welder's goggles on and we couldn't see a damned thing. The next thing I knew, *zing*, a pair of goggles went right by my head. Tibbets said, "Hell, I couldn't see to fly the damned plane, get rid of those things."

It took 43 seconds from the time the bomb left the plane until it reached 1,800 feet. So we were all counting, but the time had gone by and the bomb had not gone off. We concluded that the bomb was a dud. Suddenly there was a bright flash in the plane. That was the only indication we had that the bomb had gone off.

We were about twenty miles (thirty-two kilometres) away from the centre of the blast when the bomb exploded. We got all kinds of turbulence from it. I think we were flying upside down at one point, but Tibbets said we were never on our back.

He said he wouldn't have been able to fly the plane upside down. But the turbulence was very wicked.

We flew on until we got the second round of turbulence, which was the reflection from the ground. After that, Tibbets said, "I think it's settled down. Is the plane OK?" I said, "We're still flying, Paul." He said, "Well, that's good. I'll turn around and go back to Hiroshima so we can see what's happened."

So he made a 180-degree turn to go back to Hiroshima, and as we made the turn, those of us who had windows looked out and saw that mushroom cloud. It was above our altitude already, so we stayed out of the cloud. That was the number one rule.

As we approached Hiroshima, we couldn't make any definite relationship between what had been there and what was no longer there. All we saw was black dust, black dirt, everything below us was destroyed. All we could see was some fires burning, down in the south where the docks had been. Obviously the devastation had been complete. I looked at Parsons and Parsons looked at me. He said, "That's better than before." And I said, "Yes it is, captain, that's your baby, you put the bomb together." Seeing as we couldn't make any visual observations whatsoever, I said, "We may as well go home." So Tibbets turned to the south, and we did. When I looked down on Hiroshima, I thought, "This war is over. The Japanese cannot continue to fight this war." We instructed our radio operator to listen to the Japanese broadcasts to see if there was any announcement that the war was over.

We later found out that only about 1.4 per cent of the bomb actually detonated. The devastation would have been much worse if it had all gone off. The bomb was a semi-dud, but look what it did.

It was a long flight back. As soon as we landed, Tibbets was given the Distinguished Service Cross, which is the second highest military honour that can be given to a member of the United States military. Everybody wanted to greet us, and the guys wanted to pay off their bets. All we wanted to do was drink some Jack Daniels and hit our beds. We discovered that the war wasn't over yet but we figured it soon would be. All we needed were a few more bombs, and we knew we had more than enough.

I definitely felt that the mission had been an extraordinary event, but I don't think I let that affect me much. I went back to college. I got three degrees in chemical engineering. I ended up a vice president with DuPont, an American chemical company. I think I lived pretty much the same life I would have done if it hadn't been for the war.

Under the same circumstances, I would do it again. You have to understand that we were about to invade Japan. Our losses would have been horrendous – over 500,000 people, in my estimation. That's about equal to our losses in the entire war up until that time. I didn't see how we could have taken losses like that. If you look at it from that perspective, dropping the atomic bomb saved lives. No question about it. Mostly Japanese lives. Nobody on the crew had any second thoughts about doing it. Dropping the bomb demonstrated what nuclear war was like, and nobody wanted to see that again. Weirdly, maybe we prevented the world going to war again.

I think that since the bomb was dropped, everyone is more aware of life. We're all aware that if an atomic bomb is aimed at you, you're dead, no question about it. America has lived with the atomic bomb for quite some time. Now other countries have it, and are learning to live with it. Whether we can learn to live with it well is still to be seen, I think.

TAKASHI TANEMORI

*Takashi Tanemori was eight years old when Little Boy,
the first atomic bomb, was dropped on Hiroshima.
He describes what happened when the bomb fell and
the impact it has had on the rest of his life.*

*Takashi (bottom row, centre)
with his family*

In 1945, I was a second grade student living with my father, my mother and three of my five siblings in downtown Hiroshima (two of my sisters had been evacuated because of the war). My grandparents lived four blocks from us. At that time, Hiroshima was a major industrial, cultural and social centre. The army, navy, air force and military shipyards were all located there. About 430,000 people lived in the city. I thought that as long as Japanese soldiers marched through the streets, Hiroshima was invincible. But I think, by the spring of 1945, people knew that it was a case of when, not if, the Americans would attack Hiroshima. I remember sensing an urgency in my father, in the way he went over and over and over the things he wanted me to know, particularly the code of the samurai. For as long as I could remember, my daddy had taught me to live for the benefit of others. A samurai is not a warrior; the real meaning of "samurai" is "servant". My daddy always said, "If you live for the benefit of others then everyone will benefit. That is the simplest way to make the world a safer, more peaceful place."

On 5 August 1945, the US launched six or seven air raids on Hiroshima. The next morning, as I was leaving for school, I saw my mother crying. She said, "Son, do you remember what your father taught you? Don't you ever, ever forget." So I said, "Mum, why are you crying?" She was holding my fourteen-month-old baby sister. "Just remember what your father taught you," she said again. That was the first time I had ever seen my mother cry. My father was at home that morning too. Japanese men don't usually hug, but my father hugged me that morning. He didn't say anything – he just looked me in the eye and I knew exactly what he wanted me to know, that I needed to be true to myself, regardless of the consequences. That was my daddy's mantra.

My friend and I ran all the way to school, and when we got there we began to play hide-and-seek. I happened to be "It", and I was counting, "One, two, three" in Japanese: "Ichi, ni, san." I was standing at the window, looking at the yard, where several hundred Japanese soldiers were doing a drill. When I had counted to seven or eight, there was a flash in the sky. Pure white. I had never seen such a pure white. I couldn't see anything except white. I had been counting the numbers on my fingers, and when the flash came I saw all of the bones in my fingers, just as if I was looking at an X-ray. After the flash was a silence, a deafening silence. Then, 43 seconds later, the explosion took place. It was like the entire universe had exploded. The sound almost split my skull. That's the last thing I remember for quite some time.

I don't know how long it was before I woke up, but it was pitch black. I couldn't even see my own hand. I tried to move, but I couldn't. Then I heard my classmate Taro, my best friend who lived three houses down from us, cry out, "Takashi, Takashi, it's hot! Come and help me, rescue me!" I said, "Taro, I can't move." Then my friend Sumiko began to scream, and then my other classmates began to call out, saying that they were hot, calling for their mothers and fathers to rescue them. Then in the pitch darkness I saw fires, leaping out like serpents' tongues. The fires were getting closer, closer, and Taro was engulfed, then Sumiko, then another classmate. I was gasping for air and I screamed my heart out too, saying, "Daddy, Daddy, come and help me."

The soldiers who had been doing the drill in the yard heard me. They moved all the debris and one soldier pulled me out and clutched me in his arm. He weaved in and out of the fires heading towards the river behind our school. On the way I saw something charred, burned, on the floor, and then it called out, "Water, water, please," and I knew it was a man.

But a miracle happened for me. The soldier and I went to the river and hundreds, maybe thousands of people were there on the beach and on the riverbank, trying to escape the fires, pushing and shoving. Then I heard a voice calling my name: "Takashi! Takashi!" That was the sweetest sound I have ever heard: my daddy calling my name. "Takashi! Takashi!"

I said to the soldier, "That's my daddy's voice." The soldier handed me to my daddy who clutched me to him with the greatest energy I've ever felt, and in that moment I knew I was safe. That's why I like to hug people. Just to give them that energy.

The soldier saluted my daddy and said, "I have a duty to perform, I must return to my base." He wished my daddy and his family longevity and disappeared into the crowd. My daddy stood there among all the screaming, the pushing and shoving, looking in the direction the soldier had disappeared, bowing over and over again, saying, "Arigato, arigato, arigato" – "Thank you for saving my son."

Around 10 a.m., when the tide was coming in, I saw a dark cloud in the south-west. And then it was as if someone had opened an oil drum: blackness poured out, covering the sky in darkness. Then, suddenly, the rain. Each raindrop was black, the size of a marble. The rain filled the rivers so quickly that many people were swept away, dead and alive. My daddy took us onto an embankment, about eight metres wide, full of people pushing and shoving. Many people fell into the river on one side, or into the fires on the other side.

But the rain. Black, soot-like rain. All of the debris that had gone in the explosion came down again in the rain. I can still remember how painful it was when the raindrops hit my body. It felt like someone throwing marbles at me.

Later, we managed to find my paternal grandparents, my older sister Masuyo and my four-year-old brother, but my mother and my baby sister were taken. Their bodies were never found.

Two days after the explosion, my daddy said, "We have to escape the burning city." He decided that we should go to my maternal grandparents' house across the river, but all of the bridges over the river had been burned. There was no way of getting to the other side. However, all of the bodies that had been washed away by the rain had piled up against the pylons in the river, making a dam. Many people tried to walk over it, but they slipped and didn't have the energy to get up and no one dared to help them, so the human bridge became stronger and stronger every minute. My daddy took us across the human bridge. As we walked across it, my daddy was saying, "Gomen nasai, gomen nasai", which means, "Excuse me, I'm sorry", apologizing to the people we were walking across.

Once we were on the other side, my grandfather stood in front of my father and put his hands on his shoulders, looked squarely in his eyes and said, "Suman, suman", which means, "Thank you for the trouble you've taken for me." That image of my father and my grandfather is burned into my heart. Two men, standing in the middle of all that, expressing gratitude towards each other. As my daddy always said, "Takashi, learn to say thank you. That will make your life easy." I am so grateful for that image.

Because I had been standing at the window that morning when the blast hit, the glass cut me all down my left side. I have scars on my neck, shoulder blades and knees, and a burn on my left arm. The retina on my left eye was burned, so when I accidentally look at the sun it's like an arrow going through my brain. It took me a year before I was able to walk normally again. My injuries were so bad that everyone thought I would die. But I was the one who survived, in the end. I lost both my parents, my paternal grandparents and two of my sisters to the effects of the atomic bomb.

In the spring of 1946, almost a year after the bombing, I decided to go back to Hiroshima. My father, who had searched day after day in Hiroshima for my mother and youngest sibling, had died by that time from radiation exposure, as had my oldest sister Masuyo. I wanted to continue the search for my mother and my baby sister. I was only nine years old, and I didn't have the money to buy a ticket, but somehow I managed to get on the train. As soon as I stepped out of the station in Hiroshima, everything came back to me – the flash in the sky, the black rain, the fires. I couldn't bear to go back to the place where we'd lived, not that I'd have been able to find it – there was nothing left in the city except a shack made of brick and tin, and the people there were like ghosts, looking for food, trying to make something they could sell. There was still a stench in the air.

So instead of going home, I went to the river. The embankment was black, burned, scarred. I sat there on the sand and cried. I was transported back to the morning of 6 August 1945. I could hear the crying children, I could see the man begging the soldier for water. I cried until I had no more tears. Then suddenly I turned to my left, and three metres away, behind a burned rock, I saw something sticking out of the ground. I scooted over and I saw it was a blade of grass. I scooped this blade of grass into the palm of my hand, and I said to myself, "If this frail blade of grass can emerge from the ruins of Hiroshima, then I'd better do it too. I can do it." I put the blade of grass back and covered it. I have made a lot of artwork and written poems about that. Some are entitled "A Blade of Grass ... in a Dreamless Field". That blade of grass and I became one. Talk about an image of strength. No matter what comes my way, I never feel I'm defeated. Yes, I may fall down, but I'm never going to stay down. I don't know how to tell you how grateful I am for the gift of life that blade of grass gave me.

I was so angry for so many years about what happened to the city of Hiroshima. But in 1985, I had an epiphany. Since then, I've tried to make peace with the people involved in dropping the bomb. I tried to meet Dr Glenn T. Seaborg, the scientist who discovered the plutonium used in the Nagasaki bombing. He and I lived in the same city, Lafayette, California, and I tried to extend my hand for reconciliation. Sadly, he refused. But in 1995, I met Dr Robert Christie, a wonderful scientist who had worked on the bomb, and I was able to reconcile with him. Then, and this is the big one, in the spring of 2000 I went down to Albuquerque, New Mexico, because I heard that General Paul Tibbets, the captain of the *Enola Gay* – the plane that dropped the atomic bomb – was going to speak at one of the convention halls. I managed to meet him. I said, "Sir, have you ever felt remorse or guilt for what you did, now that you see how the atomic bomb impacted people?" He said, "Heck, no." Those were his exact words – "Heck, no." He said, "That was the best thing we ever did. All the Japanese thank me for it." I said, "Really? Every Japanese person? Have you ever been back to Japan? Have you been back to Hiroshima?" He said, "No, I didn't have to." Then I asked one more question. I asked, "Sir, knowing what we know now, about what happened at Hiroshima and all of the consequences, would you get back in the cockpit and drop the bomb once again?" He turned to his bodyguard and said, "Let's go." I was standing right smack in his way, and he gently pushed me so I had to move. Then they left. I called after him and said, "General Tibbets, I will pray for you until you find the peace in your heart."

I went through 40 long years before I came to a place where I could reconcile with my history. My personal epiphany took place on 15 August 1985. My father appeared to me in spirit, in his regal kimono, and stood in front of me with his hands on my shoulders, just as my grandfather and my father did after we had crossed the river. My father looked me squarely in the eye, and said, "My son, you have found the greatest way to avenge your enemy: by learning to forgive." I'd come to America for revenge, and most days I felt full of rage, like I was banging my head against the wall, but ever since my father appeared to me, I've been at peace.

Forgiveness is the first step towards peace. Without forgiveness, the human heart will wither. Now my life's mission is promoting peace through forgiveness. I am so grateful for the gift of life that forgiveness has given me.

American planes fly over USS Missouri and Tokyo Bay to celebrate the signing of the Japanese surrender, 2 September 1945

RON BULLOCK

Ron Bullock volunteered for the navy in 1941. He spent four years as an electrician with the Fleet Air Arm. After the war he went to Hong Kong to liberate prisoners of war being held by the Japanese.

When we arrived in Hong Kong, we went to an airfield and got lots of Japanese clothes – we thought it would be better to wear their things out than of our own. An army major turned up and was horrified at us for wearing Japanese clothes. He said, "You've got to change." We said, "We don't work for you, we're in the navy."

Our job was to go to a prisoner of war camp at a place called Sham Shui Po, take out the Commonwealth prisoners and put the Japanese in. When the Japanese surrendered you couldn't get them to hold a rifle. They were like us, they just wanted to get home. I used to sign out 150 prisoners every day and get them to clear up the mess. One day I took some Japanese bank clerks to HSBC and got them to destroy their own currency. The Chinese people wanted to cut their throats because they had been at war with Japan since 1937 and millions of Chinese had been massacred by the Japanese.

We took prisoners from all over the world back to Singapore. One day we smelled smoke on the ship. An Indian prisoner had lit a fire to cook his dinner. We had 500,000 gallons of petrol on the ship. He nearly got thrown overboard! There was one very nice Australian guy. On the way to Singapore, I touched his arm. The flesh sank in and didn't come out. He said, "There's no cure, they've told me I haven't got too long." I said, "You'll be all right," but he wasn't. He was dead before we got to Singapore.

Ron in his navy uniform, 1942

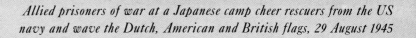

Allied prisoners of war at a Japanese camp cheer rescuers from the US navy and wave the Dutch, American and British flags, 29 August 1945

SUBJECT INDEX

INDEX OF CONTRIBUTORS

GLOSSARY

This glossary explains some of the words in this book. If a word in a definition has a separate definition of its own, it appears in *italic* type.

|A|

air raid
An attack by enemy aircraft.

air raid shelter
A place people go to keep safe during a bombing raid.

air raid siren
A warning noise to let people know that a bombing raid is about to take place.

All Clear signal
A siren that lets people know that an *air raid* is over.

Allies
The countries that fought against the *Axis* during the Second World War. The main Allied nations were Great Britain, the United States of America, the *Soviet Union* and France (until its fall in June 1940 and then again after the liberation of Paris, 25 August 1944).

Anderson shelter
A small pre-made *air raid shelter* consisting of an arch of corrugated metal, designed to be partly buried in people's gardens.

anti-aircraft guns
A gun or *missile* designed to destroy enemy aircraft.

anti-Semitism
Prejudice against Jewish people.

armistice
A peace agreement.

artillery
Large guns for use on land and sea.

Aryan
A northern European person of non-Jewish descent, supposedly with blonde hair and blue eyes, believed by the *Nazis* to be racially superior to members of all other races.

atomic bomb
An explosive weapon developed during the Second World War that releases a huge amount of energy by splitting elements such as uranium or plutonium.

Auschwitz-Birkenau
A notorious *Nazi concentration camp* in Poland where more than 1.1 million people were killed during the *Holocaust*.

Axis
The nations that fought the *Allies* during the Second World War. The main Axis countries were Germany, Italy and Japan. They were later joined by Rumania, Hungary and Bulgaria.

|B|

barrage
A long burst of gunfire which holds the enemy back while soldiers move forward.

barrage balloons
A large balloon attached to the ground by metal cables that acts as an obstacle to low-flying aircraft.

battalion
An army unit made up of several companies (groups of 120 soldiers).

bayonet
A knife that attaches to the front of a rifle.

billet
A place where soldiers are given temporary accommodation.

the Blitz
German *air raids* on Britain that took place from 7 September 1940 to 21 May 1941.

blitzkrieg
A sudden and intense military attack intended to overwhelm the enemy.

|C|

citizenship
The status of being a legally recognized national of a state or country.

civilian
A person who is not a member of the armed forces.

colony
An area under the control of another country.

commando
A soldier trained to carry out particularly dangerous or difficult attacks.

communism
A political system which promotes the idea of a classless society in which money, property and industry are supposedly controlled by the state on behalf of the people. People who follow this system are known as communists.

concentration camp
A camp where prisoners are held during wartime.

conscription
Compulsory recruitment into the armed forces.

|D|

democracy
A political system in which people are able to freely elect people to represent them in government.

deport
To expel someone from a country.

dispatch rider
Someone who delivers messages by motorcycle.

dive bomber
An aircraft that releases bombs during a steep dive towards a target.

doodlebug
Another name for a *V-1*.

|E|

empire
A group of territories controlled by another country.

enlist
To sign up for the army.

evacuate
To send people out of a dangerous area for safety. Someone who has been evacuated is known as an evacuee.

|F|

fascism
A political system usually run by a dictator, characterized by the belief that one national group is superior to all others and usually involving the state control of all areas of society. People who follow this system are known as fascists.

front line
The boundary along which opposing armed forces fight each other.

|G|

garrison
A group of soldiers stationed in a town or building to defend it.

gas chamber
A sealed room that can be filled with poisonous gas, used for killing people.

genocide
The deliberate killing of a whole nation or people.

glider
An aircraft with no independent power source and which is usually towed by another aircraft.

|H|

hangar
A large building in which aircraft are kept.

Holocaust
The mass murder of Jews and other minority groups by *Nazis* during the Second World War.

Home Guard
A volunteer army formed to defend Britain against invasion during the Second World War.

|I|

incendiary bomb
A bomb designed to burst into flames when it hits its target.

infantry
Foot soldiers.

Iron Curtain
The imaginary divide between countries in Western Europe and the *communist* countries

of Eastern Europe from 1945 to 1989.

|J, K|

Kindertransport
A humanitarian mission to help children escape German-occupied territories by train.

|L|

Liberation Day
A day when people celebrate the liberation of a country from an occupying force.

Luftwaffe
The German air force.

|M|

missile
A weapon that is fired or thrown towards a target.

morale
The collective spirit of a group of people.

Morse code
A code used for sending messages in which each letter of a word is represented as a series of short or long radio signals or flashes of light.

Munich Agreement
The settlement between Britain, France, Germany and Italy

agreed on 30 September 1938 that allowed Germany to take over the *Sudetenland*.

munitions
Ammunition.

|N|

nationalism
Extreme pride in your country and the belief that nations do better when they act independently rather than co-operating with other countries.

naturalized
A person who has become a citizen of a country they were not born in.

Nazi
A member of the German National Socialist Party, the extreme right-wing party that came to power in Germany in 1933 under Adolf Hitler.

|O|

occupy
To seize and take over an area.

Operation Dynamo
The codename for the evacuation of *Allied* soldiers from the beaches and harbour

of Dunkirk, France,
between 27 May and
4 June 1940.

|P|

pacifist
A person who believes
violence cannot be
justified and who
refuses to take part in
a war.

partisan
A member of an armed
resistance group.

patriotism
Loyalty and pride
in your country.

Phoney War
The eight months at
the beginning of the
Second World War
after war had been
declared but before
fighting had begun
in earnest for Britain.

prisoner of war
A person who is taken
prisoner during a war.

propaganda
Information that is
spread to persuade
people of something or
to promote or damage a
political cause.

Prussia
A former German
kingdom.

puppet government
A supposedly independent
government that is
actually controlled by
an *occupying* force.

|Q|

Quaker
A member of the
Religious Society of
Friends, a *pacifist*
Christian movement.

|R|

radar
A system for detecting
the presence of objects
and working out how
far away they are by
letting off radio waves
and detecting the signals
reflected back from the
objects in their path.

radiation
Energy given off by
atoms, which can be
harmful.

ration
A fixed allowance of
food, fuel or clothing
during a time of war or
shortage.

Red Army
The army of the *Soviet
Union*.

Red Cross
A humanitarian
organization established
to help people who are
wounded or captured
during a war.

refugee
Somebody forced to
leave their home and
seek refuge in another
country because of
religious or political
persecution, or during
a war.

Reich
The name the *Nazis* gave
to their government.
Reich means empire
in German.

repatriation
To send a *prisoner of
war* or a *refugee* back to
their country of origin.

resistance
The movement and
secret organizations
that fought to
overthrow *occupying*
forces during the Second
World War.

Rhineland
An area of Germany
along the banks of the
Rhine river.

Royal Air Force
(RAF)
The air force of the
United Kingdom.

|S|

sabotage
To damage or destroy property to hinder the enemy.

secret service
A branch of government engaged in spying and intelligence gathering.

semaphore
A signalling system in which flags or a person's arms are held in positions that represent letters and numbers.

shell
A hollow *missile* containing explosives.

shrapnel
Flying fragments from the casing of an explosive or *shell*.

Soviet Union (USSR)
A former federation of republics which, since its dissolution in 1991, have all become independent states, including Russia, Ukraine and the Baltic states.

squadron
A military unit.

SS (Schutzstaffel)
An elite organization of the *Nazi* Party that originally served as Hitler's personal security force.

stretcher-bearer
Someone who carries a stretcher.

Sudetenland
The German name for the area of Czechoslovakia mainly inhabited by German-speaking people which Germany occupied in 1938.

swastika
The adopted symbol of the *Nazi* party.

synagogue
A Jewish place of worship.

|T|

Territorial Army
The volunteer reserve army.

Tommy
Slang word for a British soldier.

torpedo
An explosive device that travels through water.

|U, V|

V-1s and V-2s
Flying *missiles* used against Britain and *Allied-occupied* territories towards the end of the Second World War.

veteran
An experienced member of the armed forces, or a former member of the armed forces.

Vichy France
The part of France under the control of a government that co-operated with Germany during the war.

Victory in Europe day (VE day)
The public holiday on 8 May 1945 to mark the official end of the war in Europe.

Victory over Japan day (VJ day)
The day Japan surrendered, ending the Second World War. The day is celebrated as 15 August 1945 in Europe and 2 September 1945 (the day the peace agreement was signed) in the US.

visa
A permit allowing the holder to enter or leave the country which issues it.

|W, X, Y, Z|

ACKNOWLEDGEMENTS

Photo credits: p1 © 2016 Universal History Archive/UIG via Getty Images; p4–5 courtesy of National Archives and Records Administration; p6 © 2016 Keystone-France/Gamma-Keystone via Getty Images; p8–9 (b, l–r) three pilots © 2016 Franciszek Kornicki; children with car © 2016 Michèle Ozanne; George Bressler in uniform © 2016 George Bressler; Falaise Gap © 2016 Ken French; wedding portrait © 2016 Arthur Taylor; pilots © 2016 Ken French; p9 (tr) © 2016 Eddie Mulholland - WPA Pool/Getty Images; p10 (tr) © 2016 Amélie Mitchell and Kristina Ferris; (bl) © 2016 Jeremy Vine; p11 (tr) © 2016 Anna Williams; (tl) © 2016 David Boardman; (m) © 2016 Clayton McDonald; (br) © 2016 Alexandra Ghose; (bl) © 2016 Hilary Van Dusen; p12 (tl) © 2016 Pippa Gregory; (tr) © 2016 Nina Devereaux; (m) © 2016 Polly Faber; (br) © 2016 Nicola Brooks; (bl) © 2016 Eric Poirrier; p13 (tl) © 2016 Ibtisam-Nabil Abdo; (tr) © 2016 Jacinta Yates; (bl) © 2016 Russ Clapham; (br) © 2016 Gillian Maclean Arnold; p14 (tl) © 2016 Nicola Brooks; (tr) © 2016 Mandy Birchley; (bl) © 2016 Fiona Paris; (br) © 2016 Jessica Davies; p15 (tr) © 2016 Mark Harrison; (tl) © 2016 Camilla Devereux; (br) © 2016 Gabrielle Preston; (bl) © 2016 Alexandra Evans; p16–17 courtesy of National Archives and Records Administration; p19 courtesy of National Archives and Records Administration; p20–21 © 2016 Douglas Poole; p22 © 2016 Veronika Syrovatkova; p24–28 © 2016 Franciszek Kornicki; p29–30 © 2016 Ken French; p31 © 2016 Jasmine Blakeway; p32–33 © 2016 Imagno/Getty Images; p34 © 2016 Nick Winton; p35 © 2016 Russ Clapham; p36–37 © 2016 Margaret Clapham; p38 © 2016 Mary Black; p41 © 2016 Bernd Koschland; p43–48 © 2016 Ruth Barnett; p51 courtesy of National Archives and Records Administration; p52–53 © 2016 Marguerite Colombe; p55–56 © 2016 Dr Francois Conil-Lacoste; p58 © 2016 Michèle Ozanne; p59 © 2016 Micheline Mura; p60–61 © 2016 Arthur Taylor; p63 courtesy of National Archives and Records Administration; p65 © 2016 Bert Hardy/Getty Images; p66 (tr) © 2016 Sharon Barnes–Rider; (ml) © 2016 Peter Barnes; p67 (tr) © 2016 Karen Edwards; (bl) © 2016 Ken Edwards; p68 © 2016 Jimmy Sime/Central Press/Getty Images; p70 courtesy of National Archives and Records Administration; p72 © 2016 Margaret Connor; p73–74 © 2016 Arthur Taylor; p77 © 2016 Wolfgang Suschitzky; p78–79 © 2016 Sally Burr; p80 (tl) © 2016 Jeremy Vine; (bl) © 2016 Barbara Burgess; p81 (tl) © 2016 Barbara Burgess; (mr) © 2016 Barry Brooks; p82 (tl) © 2016 Joanne Beauchamp; (br) © 2016 Joan Whitaker; p83–84 © 2016 Ken Swain; p85 © 2016 Nick Ferrari; p86–87 courtesy of National Archives and Records Administration; p88 © 2016 Phyllis Rowney; p89 © 2016 Walker Books Ltd; p90 © 2016 Shirley Hughes; p91–92 © 2016 Sylvia Simmons; p93 © 2016 David Boardman; p94 © 2016 Mary Boardman; p95 © 2016 John Simmons; p96 © 2016 Karenza Thomas; p97 © 2016 Fred Hemenway; p99 © 2016 Paola Del Din; p100 (tl) © 2016 David Mackintosh; (mr, bl) © 2016 Jan Pieńkowski; p102 © 2016 Jan Pieńkowski; p104–111 © 2016 Per Lindeblad; p112 © 2016 Hulton Archive/Getty Images; p113 © 2016 Nina Devereaux; p114–122 © 2016 Paola Del Din; p123–129 © 2016 Francesco Gnecchi-Ruscone; p130 © 2016 Central Press/Hulton Archive/Getty Images; p132 © 2016 Jean Barker; p134 (tl) © 2016 Charlotte Le Butt; p134 (bl) © 2016 Eve Branson; p135 (tr) © 2016 Eve Branson; (bl) © 2016 Jack Brockway; p136–137 © 2016 Molly Rose; p138–139 © 2016 Gladys Lambert; p140–141 © 2016 Phyl Pipe; p142 (tl) © 2016 Camilla Devereux; (br) © 2016 Margaret Neat; p143–145 © 2016 Mildred Schutz; p146–147 © 2016 Joy Hunter; p148 © 2016 Phyllis Rowney; p150 (tl) © 2016 Nicola Brooks; p150–151 © 2016 Liza Miller; p152 courtesy of National Archives and Records Administration; p154–157 © 2016 Len Burritt; p158 © 2016 Peter Western Dolphin; p160 © 2016 Rear Admiral Oakley E. Osborn, USN (Retired); p162 © 2016 NHHC (NH 101654); p163–164 © 2016 William M. Breed; p165 (tr) © 2016 Clayton McDonald; (br) © 2016 George Bressler; p166 (tr) © 2016 George Bressler; (ml, bl) © 2016 David Walser; p168 © 2016 Anna Williams; p169 © 2016 Bill Frankland; p171 © 2016 Alexandra Evans; p173 © 2016 Harold Atcherley; p174 © 2016 Keystone/Getty Images; p175 © 2016 Mark Harrison; p177 courtesy of National Archives and Records Administration; p181 © 2016 Harry Irons; p184 © 2016 Pippa Gregory; p185–189 © 2016 Ken French; p191 © 2016 Keystone/Getty Images; p192 © 2016 Jill Galloway; p195 © 2016 Photo12/UIG via Getty Images; p196 (tl) © 2016 Jacinta Yates; (mr) © 2016 Harold Checketts; p197 © 2016 Harold Checketts; p198–199 © 2016 Ivor Anderson; p202 (tr) © 2016 Ivor Anderson; (ml) © 2016 Eldon Roberts; p203–209 © 2016 Eldon Roberts; p212 © 2016 Israel Victor Hyams; p213 © 2016 Fred Glover; p214 © 2016 Fred Hemenway; p216–219 © 2016 Ken French; p220–221 © 2016 Neurdein/Roger Viollet/Getty Images; p222 © 2016 Picture Post/Getty Images; p224 © 2016 Ruth Barnett; p226 © 2016 Patricia Edwards; p227 © 2016 Andy Ross; p228 © 2016 Gillian Lynne; p229 (mr) © 2016 Daniel Kordik & James Ferris; (bl) © 2016 Liz Davies; p230 © 2016 Liz Davies; p231 © 2016 Ken French; p232 © 2016 Sovfoto/UIG via Getty Images; p234–239 © 2016 Barbara Crossley; p240 © 2016 William Vandivert/The LIFE Picture

Collection/Getty Images; p241–244 © 2016 Gerda Drews; p246–247 © 2016 David Walser; p248 © 2016 Zahava Kohn; p250–251 © 2016 Galerie Bilderwelt/Getty Images; p252 © 2016 Judith Kerr; p257–261 © 2016 Zahava Kohn; p262–266 © 2016 Freddie Knoller; p267–271 © 2016 Lucy Lebow; p275–278 © 2016 Esther Rantzen; p279 © 2016 Ronald Bailey; p280–281 © 2016 Popperfoto/Getty Images; p282 (tl) © 2016 Phyllis Rowney; (br) © 2016 Nicola Brooks; p283–287 © 2016 Olive Whiteford; p288 courtesy of National Archives and Records Administration; p290 © 2016 Leslie Woodhead; p291 © 2016 Vicki Triplett; p294 courtesy of National Archives and Records Administration; p299 (tr) © 2016 Ed Smith/Guide Dogs for the Blind; (tl) © 2016 Takashi Tanemori; p300 © 2016 Takashi Tanemori; p306 courtesy of National Archives and Records Administration; p307 © 2016 Ron Bullock; p308–309 courtesy of National Archives and Records Administration.

The testimony of Bernd Koschland and Bettine Le Beau is reproduced courtesy of the Holocaust Memorial Day Trust:
www.hmd.org.uk
The testimony of Douglas Phillips is reproduced courtesy of the Naval Historical Foundation:
www.navyhistory.org
The testimony of Freddie Knoller and Anita Lasker-Wallfisch is reproduced courtesy of Quill Press in association with the National Holocaust Museum and Centre:
www.nationalholocaustcentre.net
The testimony of Theodore "Dutch" Van Kirk is reproduced courtesy of Finestripe Productions
The testimony of Takashi Tanemori is reproduced courtesy of Finestripe Productions and the Silkworm Peace-Kaiko Heiwa Institute: www.hiroshima-forgiveness-tanemori.com

Special thanks to Dr Howard Bailes and Isabel Sutton

Thanks also to:
Phil Dawe, Christopher John Ford, Jane French, Sue Jones, Troels Lindeblad, Jo Samuel, Paul Tacon, Bruce Taylor, Mark Wheeler and Malcom White
The Bomber Command Association and the Royal Air Force Museum: www.rafmuseum.co.uk
Blind Veterans UK: www.blindveterans.org.uk

Every effort has been made to trace and acknowledge ownership of copyright. If any rights have been omitted, the publishers offer to rectify this in any future editions following notification.